Who's Talking? The Effect of Personalised Voice on Speech Generating Devices for the Child with Autism

Who's Talking? The Effect of Personalised Voice on Speech Generating Devices for the Child with Autism

By

Susan Ní Chuileann

Cambridge
Scholars
Publishing

Who's Talking? The Effect of Personalised Voice on Speech Generating Devices for the Child with Autism

By Susan Ní Chuileann

This book first published 2016

Cambridge Scholars Publishing

Lady Stephenson Library, Newcastle upon Tyne, NE6 2PA, UK

British Library Cataloguing in Publication Data
A catalogue record for this book is available from the British Library

ISBN (10): 1-4438-9448-6
ISBN (13): 978-1-4438-9448-7

This book is dedicated to my parents, Aidan and Evelyn Cullen.

TABLE OF CONTENTS

LIST OF ILLUSTRATIONS

LIST OF TABLES

PREFACE

This book is a focus on the importance of voice for a child with autistic disorder. It is in part an exercise in education, and, in part, a story of my life. In relation to the latter, my youngest son, Evan, was diagnosed with autistic disorder in 1999 when he was almost three years of age. He has never functionally used speech over the past twenty years of his life, but he has used a number of devices and strategies to communicate his needs to others during those two decades. One of the most popular communication tools available for him was the speech generating device (SGD), which is an electronic aid used to produce digitised or synthesised speech upon activation by an individual with little or no speech.

The SGD was special because, for the first time, Evan had a voice! I recall him sitting on a swing-bench in the garden and typing his thoughts into the SGD before squealing with delight when they emerged vocally from the device seconds later. At last, he could express his needs vocally to anyone in earshot. He was so very empowered by this small, inexpensive gadget, which produced vocal sounds.

However, the voice on the device did not resemble his own in any way at all. It sounded electronic, with a slight American accent that was devoid of much inflection or emotion. It also struggled to pronounce certain words, which caused some hilarity for Evan's brothers and sisters, but at times, great frustration for Evan himself. It struck me that perhaps Evan was not using the device to communicate as often as he could because he could not truly identify with the voice of that particular system. In addition, there was a distinct possibility that as family members, we did not engage as much as we should have done with Evan because of a subconscious lack of acceptance for the electronic voice on his SGD.

Fortuitously, research was coalescing to develop technology that performs a voice transplant of the child's natural voice onto the augmentative and alternative communication (AAC) device, so that the device's voice would sound like the child's own (www.nlmfoundation.org). This is where my book becomes somewhat educational.

Researchers were beginning to hypothesise that an AAC device with a personalised voice that mimics the child's voice, could only serve to psychologically reinforce powerful motivational factors and a sense of 'owness' for communication so that the frequency and richness of AAC use, and its acceptance by family members and friends, would be enhanced. In addition - as a tool for improving a child's speech capabilities - a system that could speak with a voice similar to the child's own voice would likely be more effective than a system that could speak with a default synthetic voice. The computer could provide a model that is closer to the child's speech and hence would be easier to emulate by the child.

To understand all this a little better, I did some research of my own and soon I was enthralled by the study of voice. It was fascinating to discover that voice is much older than speech for instance. It became apparent that speech appeared only relatively recently in evolution as a particularly complex and abstract use of voice by the human species (see Fitch, 2000; Hauser, 1996). Indeed, it was vocalisations that were most prominent in the auditory environments of vertebrates for, 'millions of years before speech emerged' (Fitch, 2000: 258). Furthermore, the ability to accurately decode the information contained in these vocalisations (e.g., are you a friend or foe, male or female, child or adult) had great importance for survival (Fitch, 2000).

I quickly learned that voice is the result of a source in the larynx filtered by the supra-laryngeal vocal tract (Belin et al., 2004; Fitch, 2000). The chest, throat, tongue, lips, and weight all affect the sound quality of a person's voice (Cavarero, 2005). Minute inter-and-intra-individual variations around those structures mean that each voice is as different as each being that sends their vocalisations into the air. It is directly influenced by our age, gender, culture and vocal habits (Spence, Rollins, & Jerger, 2002). This explained why no two people ever sound the same, and no two utterances by the same person are ever identical (Ambridge & Lieven, 2011), and led me to understand that voice manifests the unique *being* of each human being. As a result, I began to realise how important a natural voice on a SGD would be for me, my family, and in particular, my son.

However, would he want this? Would he like the sound of his own voice on this communication device? Moreover (possibly more to the point), given his diagnosis, would he *recognise* the sound of that voice on the device as being that of his own? How easy is it for a typically-developing (TD) child to recognise self-voice? How important is it, for the child with autistic disorder, to listen to any voice? These questions formed the basis of much study for the next four years. I immersed myself into the recruitment of participants, the procurement of SGDs as test material, and the analysis of numerous studies. This book is the outcome of those four years.

In writing this book, the main aim is to provide the reader with an exciting yet accessible introduction to the role of voice as a marker of identity. The book provides a broad overview of this phenomenon, and, at the end of the book, a list of further reading for each chapter is provided.

This is my first venture in writing a book. The research and writing often took place well into the small hours after a long day lecturing psychology in a small College in Ireland, and then involving myself in being a mother to four young adults. After each draft chapter was completed, I had often forgotten birthdays, school collections, and the paying of important bills. Therefore, it is with special gratitude that I extend thanks to all of my family, and to my partner, Anthony. I also need to express sincere gratitude to: The staff and students of Carlow College, Co Carlow, Ireland, for their patience and for listening to the woes of book-writing over the past year or so; to Sam Baker and the team at Cambridge Scholars Publishing for their encouragement, support and advice; and last but never least, thank you to my son, Evan, whose diagnosis of autism taught me more about myself than I care to mention.

ACKNOWLEDGEMENTS

This book would not have been possible without the children who participated in my research. I wish to extend special thanks to each and every one of those children, all of whom showed huge patience with me over the course of their school days. Thank you to the parents, guardians, and teacher's, special needs assistants and all other adults and children who gave of their time and expertise during this time.

It is important to thank several people who supported me academically, emotionally and practically throughout this process also, and they are Dr Jean Quigley of Trinity College Dublin, Conn Prenderville, Helen Whelan, and Anthony Byrne.

A special mention of gratitude to Management and Staff at Carlow College, most especially Dr Thomas McGrath for his support and constant encouragement.

A very special mention goes to my Grandmother and my wonderful Uncle Richard Whitty. You gave me a love of reading as a child and filled my world with hopes and dreams. I love you both more than words can say.

To all the team at Cambridge Scholars Publishing (CSP), please accept my sincere gratitude for your professionalism, patience, encouragement and support. I look forward to working with you again in the future.

Finally, I wish to extend special thanks and gratitude to my four beautiful children; Shane, my eldest son and my rock, Rebecca, my beautiful and witty daughter, Rachel, a little jewel and a gorgeous daughter, and of course, Evan, my youngest son and my very precious snowflake. Thank you one and all.

INTRODUCTION

Autism Spectrum Disorder (ASD) is characterised by impairments of social interaction and communication, accompanied by rigid interests and repetitive behaviours (Eigsti, et al., 2011; Lord & Paul, 1997; Rogers & DiLalla, 1990). Some of the specific communication difficulties associated with autism include the following: Delayed language acquisition (Dahlgren & Gillberg, 1989; De Giacomo & Fombonne, 1998; Eigsti et al., 2011); deficits in pragmatics and discourse processes (i.e., how language is used) for those with a diagnosis of Asperger Syndrome (Rutter, Mawhood, & Howlin, 1992); and echolalia, or the immediate or delayed imitation or echoing of language the child has heard from other speakers or from media, such as TV shows or cartoons (Tager-Flusberg & Calkins, 1990).

While language and communication impairments are present across essentially all individuals with autism (Eigsti, et al., 2011; Lord & Paul, 1997; Rogers & DiLalla, 1990), the child with autistic disorder is distinguished by an even more severe, towards profound, set of language and learning difficulties (Boucher, Mayes, & Bigham, 2012; Eigsti et al., 2011). For instance, there are suggestions that up to 25% of these children never acquire functional speech across their lifespan (Eigsti, et al., 2011; Lord & Paul, 1997; Rogers & DiLalla, 1990).

One method of enhancing the communicative abilities of individuals with autistic disorder has been the development of augmentative and alternative communication (AAC) devices (Boesch, Wendt, Subramanian, & Hsu, 2013; Koul, 2003). Defined as the supplementation, or replacement, of natural speech through alternative means of communication (Sigafoos & Drasgow, 2001), two of the most common forms of AAC for the child with autistic disorder currently comprise sign language and the Picture Exchange Communication System (PECS) (Bondy & Frost, 1994).

One of the most basic and popular forms of AAC for the non-verbal, or minimally verbal, child with autism is the use of manual signs (http://www.lamh.ie). Manual signs have been successfully used as a mode of communication for children with autism who do not speak (Paul, 2008; Tager-Flusberg, 1999). Children with autism have been known to adapt reasonably well to this form of communication (Goldstein, 2002), but Seal & Bonvillian (1997) have suggested that, as the acquisition of signs is related to fine motor skills, some children with autism - with low levels of fine motor abilities - are less likely to benefit from this form of AAC.

Another very popular form of AAC for the child with autism is that of picture exchange communication systems (PECS; Bondy & Frost, 1994). PECS involves the, 'systematic instruction of self-initiated communication skills using six phases' (Boesch et al., 2013: 481). It begins with teaching a single word request, by means of exchanging a picture for an object, with learned behaviour systematically built on in order to achieve more communicative independence (Boesch et al., 2013). In the final phases, it is anticipated that PECS users will be able to make more detailed requests (e.g., *'I want to go for a drive with Dad'*) and make comments (e.g., *'It is a very sunny day today*'). While PECS is readily adapted for children with autism (Goldstein, 2002; Paul, 2008), probably based on the observation that children with autism prefer visual stimuli over auditory stimuli (Mirenda & Schuler, 1988; Schuler & Baldwin, 1981), very few achieve level six communicative ability (Boesch et al., 2013).

One of the most significant advances in AAC has been the development of voice operated communication aids (VOCAs) or speech generating devices (SGDs) (see Boesch et al., 2013; Koul, 2003; Sigafoos & Drasgow, 2001; van der Meer & Rispoli, 2010). The SGD can be defined as, 'an electronic communication aide that produces digitised or synthesised speech upon activation by individuals with little or no functional speech' (Boesch et al., 2013: 481). Unlike sign or PECS, the SGD is designed to emit a 'voice,' providing the child with the ability to express verbally their needs (Shane, Laubscher, Schlosser, Flynn, Sorce, & Abramson, 2011). These devices allow the child to communicate verbally with anyone within earshot (see Sigafoos & Drasgow, 2001; van der Meer & Rispoli, 2010).

The typical SGD varies widely in terms of cost, appearance, functions, and features (Boesch et al., 2013). Many use a text-to-speech synthesis design, in which, 'alphabets, digits, words, and graphic symbols are entered from an input such as a keyboard/switch/touch screen, and are converted into a speech waveform using a set of algorithmic rules' (Koul, 2003: 49). Others are very low-tech in their design and comprise no more than 24 pictures, which emit speech sounds when touched by the child (http://www.assistireland.ie).

Specifically, the SGD addresses a general problem with AAC tools (such as manual sign and PECS) insofar as the speech output function on the SGD facilitates a more independent mode of communication for the child with autism (Mirenda, 2001). For instance, much like natural conversation, the voice from one of these systems is immediately available to anyone within hearing distance and, unlike sign language or PECS, there is *no expertise* required on behalf of the listener to understand the child's message (Boesch et al., 2013). In addition, children with autism adapt well to SGDs as it is well established that these children are naturally drawn to technology and digital media (Dautenhahn, 1999; Kee, 2012). This positive adaptation of the SGD by the child with ASD is likely because these electronic devices provide a safe, reliable, and predictable outcome - an effect typically preferred by children with autism (Billard, Robins, Nadel, & Dautenhahn, 2006).

Moreover, these devices fit in with a contemporary *zeitgeist* where technology is pervasive and tightly meshed into a host of speech generating platforms commonly used for work, life, and leisure (Kee, 2012). Overall, for the linguistically challenged child with autism, of all AAC currently available, the ability of the SGD to project a voice provides the child with low-functioning autism (LFA) a potential means of overcoming several barriers to inclusion, participation, and social interaction (Beukelman & Mirenda, 2012). This AAC, and this AAC alone, gives the child with autism a voice.

However, the voice is either digitised, or synthesised, in its composition (Lloyd, Fuller, & Arvidson, 1997). As an example, consider the speech output produced by the SGD of the British physicist, Stephen Hawking (http://www.hawking.org). While digitised voice utilises recorded human speech, synthesised speech devices use computer-generated speech. The voice output on Professor Hawking's device is synthesised in its nature. There are pros and cons to both types of voices. Digitised SGDs, although more 'normal' sounding, are limiting because they can only say the words or phrases programmed on the device. They do not allow for free-thinking. Synthesised SGDs allow the user to have pre-programmed phrases or words, but also have the ability to spell out novel thoughts (Lloyd, Fuller, & Arvidson, 1997). In either instance, the voice of a SGD does not resemble in any way the voice of the child with autism using the device (see van Santen & Black, 2009).

It is exciting, and of interest therefore, that researchers began to consider finding a way for the voice of a minimally verbal child to be transplanted onto SGDs (Klabbers, Kain, & van Santen, 2010; van Santen & Black, 2009). This simple and yet stunningly creative innovation would appear to make maximum sense given the role of voice as a marker of self, and a signal for identification to others (see Belin et al., 2004). However, while those listening might better recognise this voice rich in accent, dialect, age, gender and ethnicity, it seemed important to me to ascertain whether, or not, the child using the device could also.

In relation to listening, there is evidence that adults, 'encode and maintain information about characteristics of voices and that this speaker-specific knowledge facilitates their processing of linguistic information' (Spence, Rollins, & Jerger, 2002: 215). For instance, a study assessing adult listener's abilities to identify words and sentences by Nygaard and Pisoni (1998) found that performance was more accurate when the voices heard were of people that were familiar to them as opposed to voices of unfamiliar people. There is also evidence to suggest that adult listener's judge a heard word as 'old' more accurately if the same speaker, at familiarisation and test, speaks the word, as opposed to when different speakers are used (Palmeri, Goldinger, & Pisoni, 1993).

This raises questions about what types of attributes are encoded and essential for recognising a speaker and whether these attributes are linked/related to semantic knowledge (e.g., name, age, gender, and role) about the identity of the speaker. Studies conducted with adults, using no more than eleven speakers uttering sentence-length voice samples, demonstrated speaker-recognition rates above 97% (Abberton & Fourcin, 1978; Bricker & Pruzansky, 1976; Hollien, Majewski, & Doherty, 1982). It is now accepted that an adult's voice-recognition accuracy is directly influenced by the stimulus set size, the duration of the voice sample, and the listener's familiarity with the speaker's voice (Spence et al., 2002).

Research on the ways voice is recognised by the typically-developing (TD) child has begun to accumulate only in the last few decades. In a seminal study by Bartholomeus (1973), children's voice recognition, via both the auditory and visual modalities, was assessed on tests of tape-recorded speech samples obtained from their classmates, and teachers, five months after the start of the school year. In this study, the, 'absolute identification of normally recorded voices by naming was compared with identification of the same stimuli by matching voices to pictures of faces' (Bartholomeus, 1973: 465). The results of this study suggests that by the age of four years, the ability of the child to recognise the voices of familiar people is at a near-adult level, but it is not as accurate as their ability to recognise familiar faces (Bartholomeus, 1973).

A similar study (Mann, Diamond, & Carey, 1979) found age-related improvements between the ages of 6 and 10 years for children's recognition of recently encountered voices (Mann et al., 1979). Similarly, Strömbergsson (2009) tested 4-8 year old children's recognition of voices, and these children performed at near-adult level accuracy - but again showed wide variation in their scores (Shuster, 1998; Strömbergsson, 2009). Combined, the findings of these studies suggest that faces are easier to recognise than voices, and that the ability of children to recognise unfamiliar but recently encountered voices and faces develops more slowly than recognition of familiar voices and faces, which may not reach adult-level-performance until about the age of 14 (Mann et al., 1979).

What might this mean for the child with autism therefore? Certainly, studies of voice recognition in children diagnosed with autism spectrum disorder are less common. One study however - which assessed recognition via both auditory and visual modalities – tasked the relatively able schoolchildren with autism to match vocal recordings of staff members from their schools to photographs of the same people at test (Boucher, Lewis, & Collis, 1998). The findings of this study showed that the children with autism were impaired on this task compared to language-matched typically-developing children. Significantly, the researchers noted that the children with autism had had, 'rather more opportunities than controls for exposure to the adults whose voices and faces were used as stimuli given that they had been in school for longer than the controls' (Boucher et al., 1998: 180). This led the researchers to conclude that 7 to 9 year old children with autism, 'either did not, or could not, utilise these opportunities to achieve normal familiarity' (Boucher et al., 1998: 180).

A second recognition study, tapping both auditory (voice recordings) and visual modalities (photographs), was conducted with slightly older children with autism (Boucher, Lewis, & Collis, 2000). This time, no impairment was found in this group relative to language-matched children with specific-language impairment (Boucher et al., 2000). As such, the findings from studies of voice recognition in the child with autism are scarce, and provide mixed results.

Accordingly, I reached the conclusion that, while all over the world children learn to recognise the sound of their mother's voice - and then, slowly, but surely, the voices of people in their ever-widening social circles - the child with autism may find this function of development and experience somewhat more tasking. Why is this? Is it a lack of social motivation? Is it possibly a lack of interest in faces and voices? Alternatively, could it be a deficit of memory?

Memory is vital to development and to the acquisition of language in particular. The elaborate trajectory that children take in learning the diverse aspects of language is one of the most fascinating areas of human psychology—and one that is underpinned by memory—and is a journey you are now invited to follow with me.

CHAPTER ONE

MEMORY AND AUTISM

Arguably, all communication is supported by memory function. For instance, a typical conversation requires that the individual attends to, stores, and retrieves linguistic and contextual information almost instantaneously, while also producing, comprehending, and monitoring the production of words and sentences (Atkinson, 2002). We also rely on aspects of memory for communications that occur via digital media - such as Skype or video-links - with the most common device used to communicate across time and space being that of the mobile phone. Different facets of memory may be called upon when communicating via such mediums as the listener is tasked with recognising *what* is being said (e.g., perceiving the language, the words, and the content of the message), while also recognising *who* is speaking (analysing the age, the gender, the accent and identity of the speaker) (Kuhl, 2011).

Our focus is on the linguistically challenged child who communicates via voice-enabled augmentative and alternative communication (AAC) devices, or speech generating devices (SGDs). The aspect of memory we propose as the most relevant is that of recognition memory. Technology has developed so much that even small segments of the child's actual voice can be transformed via speech mimicry technology to create a SGD that sounds just like the voice of the child using it (Klabbers, Kain, & van Santen, 2010; van Santen & Black, 2009). Our focus is not primarily on the child's ability to recognise *what* is being said, but is on their ability to recognise *who* is speaking on the personalised SGD. If they can recognise the voice as that of their own, and come to prefer the voice-type - over and above any alternative available on the device - there is every possibility that the frequency and richness of AAC use, and its acceptance by family members and peers, will be enhanced (van Santen & Black, 2009). If not - if self-voice is neither familiar nor recognisable to the child - there is every chance that the device will be subject to complete or partial abandonment by the child (Van-Biervliet & Parette, 1999).

Memory in high-functioning autism (HFA) has been extensively researched in the past forty years (for reviews see Boucher & Bowler, 2008, 2010) and - while the behavioural findings generated have been variously interpreted - most commonly, a memory systems classification has been used as the basis of interpretation (Tulving, 1985). This means that when recognition performance fails or succeeds in autism, it is conceptualised as the consequence of impaired, or spared, systems of the memory. Significantly, this approach assumes memory can best be understood as a series of several functionally distinct systems (Nyberg, Cabeza, & Tulving, 1996; Tulving, 1982, 1985; Tulving & Markowitsch, 1998; Tulving & Schacter, 1990; Wheeler, Stuss, & Tulving, 1997). Within this, each system can be defined by a given criteria, such as the *type* of information it holds, and *for how long*, and the *levels of awareness* the systems give rise to in the individual (Gardiner, 2008).

Recently however, it has been suggested that we begin to discuss the findings on memory in autism, in terms of a dual-process model that cuts across pure systems-based distinctions (see Joseph, Steele, Meyer, & Tager-Flusberg, 2005). According to this approach, recognition is either accomplished, or not, on the basis of two distinct but mutually interactive processes - namely 'recollection' and 'familiarity' (Aggleton & Brown, 2006; Jacoby, 1991, 1998; Mayes, Montaldi, & Migo, 2007; Yonelinas, 2002).

This chapter is a journey with a set goal. We want to examine in minute detail the assumptions of these competing approaches to understanding memory, and the methods that have developed to evaluate these assumptions over the years. The aim is to illustrate how models of memory have evolved over the past fifty years, and while theory of autism was divided between theories of memory systems - or theories of memory processes - for much of this time, over the past few years some rapprochement between the two has begun (Gardiner, 2008). Our focus remains firmly on the child with LFA. Our central objective is to establish a theoretical framework and an appropriate method for investigating recognition performance in this child. Our journey begins with an overview of what we mean when we refer to memory, memory systems, and memory processes.

Memory has been described by some as 'a funny thing' (Hobson & Hermelin, 2008: xix). This is unsurprising when you consider that it is something that is used in the present, while required to conjure up the past, while also used to plan for the future. Memory affects how and what we perceive, and how what is perceived is understood, which in turn affects the ways in which we experience and react to our external world (Boucher, et al., 2012; Gardiner, 2008; Hobson & Hermelin, 2008). Undoubtedly, memory is a crucial aspect of who and what we are and the ways in which we understand and behave during our day-to-day lives. However, what is memory *exactly*? Is it something you can touch or examine like the 'brain' or the 'heart'? Alternatively, is it a construct like the 'soul' or the 'mind'? It obviously stores information and this information can be personal or factual; of what words and sounds signify; what we feel we know is linked with other things; what we once felt; and what we once saw (Hobson & Hermelin, 2008). So, is this information held in a box in our head? Is it one box or a number of boxes? How does information 'get into' the box or boxes, and how do we retrieve the information when we need it?

Obviously, memory is far more complex than the simple analogy of a box in the head, and it is often described in terms of systems and processes (Boucher & Bowler, 2008, 2010; Gardiner, 2008). There are suggestions that encoding and retrieval *processes,* and memory *systems,* are, 'the most fundamental hypothetical constructs in theory of memory' (Gardiner, 2008:4).

A memory system is commonly defined by a given set of criteria, such as the kinds of information it can hold, its rules of operation, its evolved function and, 'the conscious states' it may give rise to in an individual (Gardiner, 2008: 05; Sherry & Schacter, 1987). *Memory processes*, on the other hand, differ from memory systems insofar as processes refer to the ways that information is perceived, assimilated, stored, and retrieved by the individual. Process-related distinctions have previously been drawn between, 'deep and shallow encoding, item-specific and relational encoding; immediate (short-term) and long-term memory (LTM); rapid, single trial learning and slow, repetition-based learning; recollection and familiarity; effortful and automatic retrieval' (Boucher et al., 2012: 459). Currently, while it is acknowledged that contrasts between these two approaches have generated debate over the years, more recently there has been some rapprochement between them, with increasing appreciation that the two are actually quite complementary. For instance, different memory systems will necessarily involve encoding and retrieval processes (Boucher et al., 2012; Gardiner, 2008).

We note that much of what is known about autism arises out of a perspective that conceptualises memory as a set of several functionally distinct systems. Conceptualising memory in this way did not happen overnight however. The assumption that memory functions as a set of evolved and discrete systems, or structures, is theoretically motivated and built upon the findings of studies conducted over past decades.

One of the earliest scientific accounts of memory dates back to Hermann Ebbinghaus (1885). When he wrote the first scientific account of memory, he had no database of previous findings and had limited apparatus to guide his research. He conceptualised memory as, 'an indivisible complex entity' (see Tulving 1999:15). So, in a way, if we revert back to the 'box' analogy it appears that during this period of time, memory was considered much like a 'singular' box with one singular capability, function, and/or purpose (see Solso, Maclin, & Maclin, 2005; Tulving, 1999).

Over time, however, evidence for two memory stores began to emerge, primarily from physiological studies (Solso et al., 2005). For example, Weiskrantz (1966) found that performance by animals on learning trials decreased when the trials were followed immediately by electroconvulsive shock. That this arises while earlier learning remained intact suggested that a transfer from a short-term memory (STM) system to a more permanent memory system must be occurring.

Further support for two memory stores came from studies of patients suffering from amnesia, as these individuals presented with either no memory for the seconds prior to their head injury (short retrograde amnesia) or no memory for events experienced in the more distant past (long retrograde amnesia; see Solso et al., 2005). There was also compelling evidence for more than one aspect to memory, from studies of individuals with selective brain injury. For instance, Milner (1966) reported the case of a patient complaining of severe epilepsy who had surgery to relieve the symptoms, which involved taking part of the hippocampus. After the surgery, although the epilepsy was improved, it became obvious that the patient was profoundly amnesic, with practically no ability to form new long-term memories combined with intact short-term memory (Atkinson & Shiffrin, 1968; Milner, 1966). Combined, these findings dramatically changed the view of memory from that of a singular entity to that of a multi-store model (Atkinson & Shiffrin, 1968). What was also becoming apparent was the role of the hippocampus in the operation of memory (Milner, 1966). It is no surprise therefore to note that around this time, it was speculated that autism might derive in part from developmental amnesia, associated with hippocampal abnormalities (see Boucher et al., 2012; Rimland, 1964).

The Multi-Store Model of Memory

A theoretical framework for memory was proposed by Atkinson and Shiffrin (1968), which comprised a sensory register that received input from the environment, a short-term store (or working memory, which temporarily held information used to perform cognitive tasks), and a long-term store (Fig. 1-1).

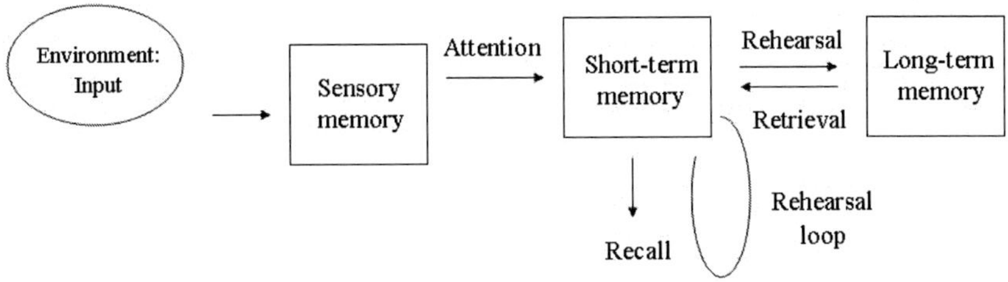

Fig. 1-1 The Multi-Store Model of Memory

Within this, the short-term store (STS) had a limited capacity while the long-term store (LTS) was limitless. The ability to forget from the STS was complete in 30 seconds or less, while forgetting from the LTS was either very slow or information was not forgotten at all (Atkinson & Shiffrin, 1968; Craik & Lockhart, 1972).

A limited set of processes were thought to comprise the encoding of information, certain rehearsal operations, and certain retrieval strategies (Gardiner, 2008). In a way, this multi-store model described memory as a type of system through which information flowed. For instance, via this model information is assumed to be detected by the sensory organs, whereby it then enters sensory memory. If this information is attended to, it enters the short-term memory, and in turn, if this information is rehearsed, it enters the long-term memory. It is further assumed that un-attended to or non-rehearsed material is subject to decay or displacement, otherwise known as forgetting (Atkinson & Shiffrin, 1968).

This model of memory drew criticism particularly in terms of it being a passive and linear model of memory (e.g., Murdock, 1972; Tulving & Patterson, 1968). It was also becoming apparent that the STS could not be considered as a more-or-less unitary system. For example, when tested immediately after material was presented, (and thus tapping the 30 second capacity of the STS), some individuals display no difficulty with the immediate recall of information that was presented visually combined with a poor immediate recall of information that was presented auditorily (Vallar & Baddeley, 1984). The reverse of this finding has also been noted whereby an individual displays difficulty with tasks requiring the manipulation of visual tasks, but no difficulty with the immediate recall of letters heard (Shallice & Warrington, 1974). These particular findings strongly suggest that short-term memory could not be construed as a singular, unitary system.

The Original Working Memory Model of Memory

To replace the more unitary view of short-term memory characterising the distinction between short-and-long term memory, Baddeley and Hitch (1974) developed what is now known as the 'original working memory model of memory' (see Fig.1-2). This model of memory consisted of three components: the central executive, the phonological loop, and the visuo-spatial sketchpad (Baddeley & Hitch, 1974; Baddeley, 2000, 2002).

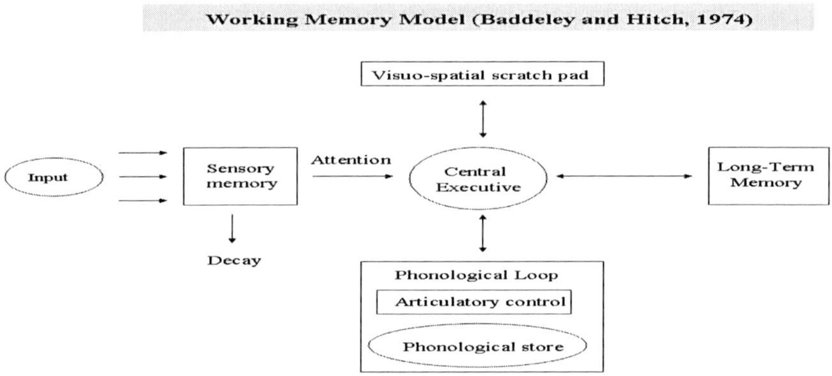

Fig. 1-2 Working Memory as Proposed by Baddeley and Hitch (1974)

The central executive, closely based on the attention control system of Norman and Shallice (1986), is thought to coordinate the operation of the phonological loop and the visuo-spatial sketchpad. The phonological loop has two components: a store, which temporarily holds verbal and acoustic information, and an articulatory rehearsal system capable of converting visually presented information into phonological code (Baddeley, 2006). The visuo-spatial sketchpad parallels the operation of the phonological loop (Baddeley, 2006), but for visual and spatial information (see also Gardiner, 2008).

Later, Baddeley (2000) introduced an additional component to the working memory (WM) system, known as the episodic buffer. The episodic buffer is conceptualised as a limited capacity storage system capable of integrating representations from the phonological loop, the visuo-spatial sketchpad, long-term memory and the perceptual system. Baddeley considered the buffer to be 'episodic' in the sense that it has the ability to integrate information across space and time. In line with Gardiner (2008: 7), the key purpose of the introduction of the episodic buffer is important as it acknowledges an increased understanding that the combination of information in WM, from different sources itself, requires some temporary 'holding mechanism' to bind this information together (see also Baddeley, 2000; Boucher, Bigham, & Mayes, 2012).

The WM model cannot be considered a general model of memory, however, as it only deals with one component of memory. Nevertheless, this model is clear evidence of the way our understanding of memory has evolved significantly over time.

Tulving's Taxonomy of Memory Systems

Over time, Tulving (1985) proposed an even more broad-based and encompassing model of memory. Based primarily on behavioural findings, this model identified *five* memory systems, one of which was working memory, and four of which corresponded to different representations of long-term memory - namely semantic, episodic, procedural, and perceptual representation (Gardiner, 2008: 6) (Fig. 1-3).

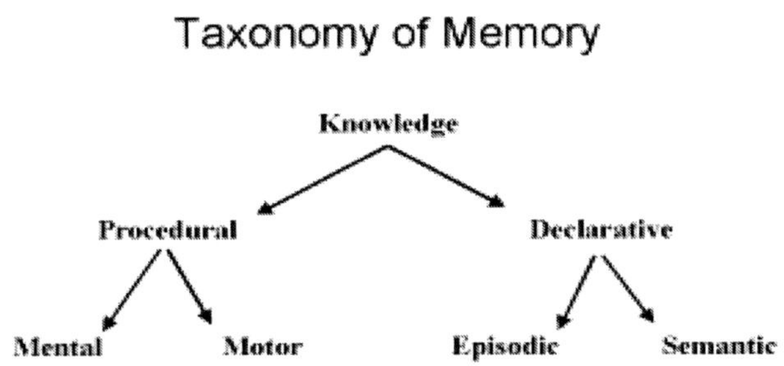

Fig. 1-3 Tulving's (1985) Taxonomy of Memory Systems

In this model, procedural memory refers to the acquisition and use of perceptual, cognitive, and motor skills *and* involves the sensation of 'knowing' how to do something (Tulving, 1985). This type of memory represents accomplished skills and/or behaviours, such as walking, running, cycling, and dressing oneself (Schacter & Tulving, 1994), which is typically acquired through extensive practice (Boucher et al., 2012). Procedural memory, therefore, includes memory for motor, perceptual, and cognitive skills, and various kinds of conditioning, and priming (Mayes & Boucher, 2008). Perceptual representation memory involves the storage of the form or structure of visual objects and words (Schacter &

Tulving, 1994). This too is thought to operate primarily at a level of non-consciousness. Both perceptual and procedural memory form part of the nondeclarative memory system.

Declarative memory is divided into semantic and episodic memory. Consider your own memory for a moment. Can you remember a childhood Christmas, a first day at school, a first kiss, the smell of lemon trees as you holidayed in Sicily? According to Tulving, our memory for personally experienced events is underpinned by episodic memory, which represents one of two components of the declarative memory system. The second component of this long-term memory system is semantic memory, which represents our memory for general knowledge and decontextualized facts (Boucher et al., 2012; Schacter & Tulving, 1994; Tulving, 1985).

The key difference between episodic and semantic memory is thought to be the level of conscious awareness at which retrieval takes place (Gardiner, 2008; Tulving, 1985, 2000; Wheeler, Struss, & Tulving, 1997). Specifically, episodic memory is said to operate at the autonoetic level, and is thought to be characterised by a sense of 'remembering' (Tulving, 1985) or awareness of reliving a previously experienced event (Tulving 1983, 1985). Just to be certain, try recalling those memories of a childhood Christmas, or your school days again. You can probably smell the pine, or remember your teacher's face and maybe even her name. Specifically, it does appear to require effortful and controlled mindfulness at the point of recall. Semantic memory, (e.g., knowing what day Christmas Day falls on), operates at a more automatic, or noetic, level and is better characterised by a sense of 'knowing' (Tulving, 1983, 1985). In particular, this type of memory only requires recalling the date without having to bring to mind any memory of how, or when, you acquired that knowledge.

It is suggested that semantic memory is evolutionarily older than that of episodic memory (Tulving, 1985, 2002) and, while semantic memory can operate independently of episodic memory, many operations of episodic memory remain dependent on semantic memory (Gardiner, 2008). For example, while information can be 'placed' into semantic memory but not into episodic memory, the reverse cannot happen. This implies a very clear role for semantic memory therefore, insofar as it includes information about personal history, but this is known in a detached, factual way, without any accompanying feeling of mental time travel (Gardiner, 2008; Lind, 2010).

Overall, it would appear that memory is clearly explained via a systems taxonomy, as the findings of a number of behavioural and physiological studies do lend support to the suggestion of particular systems processing different types of information (i.e., perceptual, procedural, episodic, and semantic). Each system tends to differ in their rules of operation (visual versus auditory), and they tend to show some incompatibility in their evolved function (semantic versus episodic memory; Gardiner, 2008). Tulving's (1985) model of memory systems is firmly based on the assumption that aspects of memory, 'constitute the major subdivisions of the overall organisation of the memory complex' and that the, 'operating component of a system consists of a neural substrate and its behavioural and cognitive correlates' (Tulving, 1985: 386).

In line with Tulving's (1985) taxonomy, which of these five systems best supports the capacity of an individual to recognise? Mandler (1980: 252) suggests that recognition can be defined as the, "act of perceiving something as previously known" and according to Bowler (2011: e1), the declarative memory system is the memory system used, 'when an individual actively tries to recollect something.' It is mediated by an area called the medial temporal lobe (MTL), particularly in its interactions with the rest of the cerebral cortex in terms of both stored information and also with sensory cortical areas where new information comes in. According to Bowler, the information from these 'inputs' is processed in the medial temporal lobe (MTL), and then stored in other areas of the association cortex.

One of the most important structures in this mediation process is the hippocampus, a structure within the MTL, which is thought to operate like, 'a kind of neural switchboard, relaying information between different parts of the brain' (Bowler, 2011: e1). Recognition is therefore potentially based on the way information is stored and on how this is organised in the memory, and then retrieved. According to Bowler, if the knowledge is stored atypically—not necessarily because of hippocampal dysfunction, but because some other connections are functioning atypically—then the hippocampus will be, 'doing different things' (Bowler, 2011: e1).

What 'different things' might the hippocampus do that would affect recognition judgements? First, it would appear that what *should* happen if all is well, is that declarative memory—underpinned by episodic and semantic memory—should facilitate accurate recognition judgements by the typical person. Episodic memory should allow us to *recall* not only that we have encountered a place, person, or item before, but it should also underpin our ability to remember where and when we encountered them (i.e., contextual/relational information). Semantic memory, on the other hand, should underpin our ability to 'know' that the place, person, or item is *familiar* and has been previously encountered, without recalling any other contextual information.

However, what happens when the hippocampus is spared, but those other all-important areas of the brain, which are responsible for mediating how information is stored and manipulated, are impaired? Is Bowler correct? Will the hippocampus do 'different things' and will recognition be impaired? Consider the case of N.B., a patient who had regions of the medial temporal lobes (MTL) removed, including the perirhinal cortex and the entorhinal cortex, leaving the hippocampus intact (Bowles, Crupi, Mirsattari, Pigott, Parrent, et al., 2007). Compared to a healthy individual of similar age and education, N.B. could 'remember' or 'recollect' contextual information about people, places, and events from her past, but her sense of 'knowing' or 'familiarity' was significantly impaired (Bowles et al., 2007). This is a striking finding as Tulving (1985) suggested that no information could be stored in episodic memory without being stored in semantic memory first (Gardiner, 2008). As such, it seems odd that N.B. could retrieve information from episodic memory but not from semantic stores, unless, as Bowler suggests, the hippocampus was 'doing different things' and that these 'things' refer to how information between the systems is being *processed*.

Specifically, the findings from the case study outlined suggest that memory (particularly declarative memory) can be understood not only in terms of memory systems, but also in terms of memory processes. This finding, and others of a similar vein, (e.g., Aggleton & Brown, 2006; Jacoby, 1991; Joseph, Steele, Meyer, & Tager-Flusberg, 2005; Migo et al., 2012; Yonelinas et al., 2010) have led to a number of dual process models of memory being proposed. These models assume that recognition is accomplished on the basis of two independent but mutually interactive processes - namely, recollection and familiarity (e.g., Atkinson & Juola, 1974; Jacoby, 1991; Mandler, 1980; Yonelinas, 2001, 2002).

Dual-Process Theories of Memory

Memory processes are somewhat more arbitrary than memory systems (Gardiner, 2008) but in the main, they refer to the means whereby information is 'encoded' and 'retrieved' from memory. While often cast in the form of a dichotomy (i.e., conceptual versus perceptual; deep versus shallow; explicit versus implicit; and effortful versus automatic), some memory processes can be conceived more as a continuum of processing rather than as discontinuous categories (Gardiner, 2008). For instance, a given process can be viewed as a continuous index of memory strength ranging from weak to strong. Consider perceptual versus conceptual processes. In a nutshell, perceptual processing is thought to reflect the implicit, automatic processing of the featural and intra-structural aspects of an event, place, face, or item (e.g., Atkinson & Wescourt, 1975; Posner & Warren, 1972; Rosch, 1973). Conceptual processing is assumed to require more controlled and effortful processes whereby the meaning or relations between aspects of a given stimuli are considered by the individual (e.g., Gardiner, 2008; Jacoby, 1988; Solso et al., 2005; Yonelinas, 2002). For some, the ability to recognise is based on a continuum of perceptual strength whereas for others, there are two processes underpinning recognition memory - namely familiarity and recollection, reflecting perceptual and conceptual processes respectively.

The Atkinson Model

This is precisely what was assumed by Atkinson and Juola (1973, 1974). They proposed a dual-process model of recognition memory, which was conditional in its nature (Atkinson & Juola, 1973, 1974; Atkinson, Hertmann, & Wescourt, 1974). The suggestion was that individuals either make a fast and automatic recognition judgement, based, for instance, on the familiarity of a person or a place, or a slower, more effortful, recognition judgement when the familiarity process evoked an ambiguous response, creating the condition whereby the individual *must* engage in an extended search of memory (Atkinson & Juola, 1973, 1974; Atkinson, et al., 1974).

It is a model, which assumes that familiarity and recollection are reliant on two independent storage systems (Atkinson & Shiffrin, 1973, 1974), but the emphasis is very much on the use to which these systems are put. For instance, familiarity is assumed to reflect the activation of nodes in:

1) A *lexical store* in which each node represents a discrete concept (Collins & Quillian, 1969). Whenever a node is accessed (e.g., on hearing a voice on a phone), it is activated (e.g., a feeling of ‘knowing’ the voice from somewhere) and this activation decreases gradually over time. Atkinson and Juola suggested that on a Test of Recognition, the nodes corresponding to items studied most recently would be more active on average than those corresponding to non-studied items, and that assessment of ‘activation’ could be used to discriminate between studied/old items and non-studied/new items. There is evidence to suggest that a familiarity judgement, at least for words, can be accomplished in one second while recollection requires slightly longer retrieval time (see Yonelinas, 2002).

Crucially, this model is one that considers the process of familiarity as an index of memory strength, which ranges from weak to strong. Their model assumes that individuals will have set a 'familiarity criterion' of sorts and that they will accept stimuli (such as voice) exceeding this criterion as familiar and, as such, recognised (Atkinson & Juola, 1973, 1974; Atkinson, et al., 1974). This model also assumes that only *if* or *when* items fall below this criterion that the individual will engage in a recollection process. Atkinson and Juola assume that they now search:

2) An independent *event-knowledge store* that contains aspects of the stimulus that were encoded when the stimulus was first encountered.

Atkinson and Juola thus propose a conditional search model of recognition and it is one based on some very important assumptions. For example, it is assumed that familiarity is the first process activated by a person engaging in recognising a given stimulus. Because this memory retrieval process occurs first, it is also assumed to be faster than recollection, which is only ever initiated if familiarity results in any ambiguity. This further implies that, at the point of retrieval, familiarity and recollection operate independently of each other.

In a way, this model complements the multi-store model of memory that described memory as a type of system through which information flowed (Atkinson & Shiffrin, 1968). It is one, which leans towards the suggestion that recollection and familiarity reflect conceptual and perceptual processes respectively and that familiarity is facilitated by brain regions that are earlier in the processing stream, such as the parahippocampal gyrus, than regions facilitating recollection, such as the hippocampus (Solso et al., 2005; Yonelinas, 2002). Any of these observations would be consistent with the assumption that familiarity would occur at a faster rate than recollection. However, might both processes not be initiated in tandem?

The Mandler Model

This was the argument of Mandler (1980) who initially argued for a conditional search model whereby recollection was only initiated if familiarity led to a vague response, but subsequently argued that both processes, while independent, operated in parallel (Graf & Mandler, 1984; Graf, Squire, & Mandler, 1985; Mandler, 1979, 1980, 1991; Mandler & Boeck, 1974; Mandler, Pearlstone, & Koopmans, 1969; Rabinowitz, Mandler, & Patterson, 1977).

This assumption is one that potentially sees recollection and familiarity as totally exclusive and independent of each other. Mandler (1980: 253), however, argued that the initial sense of 'knowing' a person, place, or event, could never really be 'context free.' He suggested that this would be a very unusual case, 'occurring infrequently in everyday life' (Mandler, 1980: 253). Rather, he argued that in order to recognise someone, information about that person must be located within the relational network of long-term memory which involves the simultaneous recovery of perceptual and featural aspects of that person *and* its relation to other, 'subordinate and superordinate concepts' (Mandler, 1980: 253). This model is one, which seems to imply that recollection and familiarity - though distinct - may be more mutually interactive than a systems approach might suggest. Possibly, one way of testing this assumption would be to find conditions or manipulations that influence recollection without influencing familiarity and vice versa. By contrast, if the two processes are dependent, such dissociations should not be possible (Yonelinas, 2002: 541). One such condition would be the amount of attention given over to studying stimuli at the point of encounter. It would be expected that a person's name, or other contextual information, would not be remembered if one did not spend time tagging this information as important in the first instance.

Mandler's model emerged at more or less the same time as the levels-of-processing (LOP) framework by Craik and Lockhart (1972). According to this framework, individuals often processed information at various 'depths'. At times, information is processed in a superficial or shallow way, possibly just taking on board the surface characteristics of a given stimulus. At other times, deeper levels-of-processing are engaged, whereby the individual makes associations, or semantic links, between the information at hand. The LOP assumes that deeper levels of effortful and intentional processing makes for stronger more durable memories than shallower, more superficial, levels-of-processing (Craik & Lockhart, 1972). Several studies examined the level-of-processing (LOP) and the results indicated that deep processing did tend to produce an increase in recollection combined with smaller, but very consistent, increases in familiarity in the typical individual (Gardiner,1988; Gardiner, Java, & Richardson-Klavehn, 1996; Gardiner, Ramponi, & Richardson-Klavehn, 1999; Gregg & Gardiner, 1994; Java, Gregg, & Gardiner, 1997; Khoe, Kroll, Yonelinas, Dobbins, & Knight, 2000; Perfect, Williams, & Anderton-Brown, 1995; Toth, 1996; Wagner, Gabrieli, & Verfaellie, 1997). This set of finding implies that recollection and familiarity may be more mutually interactive than we thought. It also implies that these two processes are distinguishable, in terms of intentional control (Jacoby, 1991; Yonelinas, 2001).

The Jacoby Model

Jacoby argued that the ability to recognise was based firmly on the assessment of processing fluency (i.e., familiarity) or on the retrieval of the context and elaboration given to an item when it was initially studied (i.e., recollection) (Jacoby, 1983, 1984, 1991; Jacoby & Dallas, 1981; Jacoby & Kelley, 1992; Jacoby & Witherspoon, 1982; Jacoby, Kelley, & Dywan, 1989; Kelley & Jacoby, 1990; Whittlesea, Jacoby, & Girard, 1990).

This model of recognition memory moved away somewhat from conceptualising familiarity and recollection - as reflecting perceptual and conceptual processes respectively (e.g., Atkinson and Mandler) - to one whereby familiarity was considered an *intrinsic* characteristic of an item or an event. It was one that assumed familiarity was not limited to perceptual fluency, but rather that it could also reflect conceptual fluency (Jacoby, 1991).

To consider this point further, for instance, take the example of being shown a list of unrelated words such as ‘elephant—bike—citadel—blister—sun’. It is possible that some of these words may be recognised not only on the basis of appearing ‘familiar,’ but also because a particular meaning was associated to them by an individual at the point of encoding (i.e., the *elephant* rode the *bike* past the *citadel* in the *blister*ing *sun*). Using this example, familiarity may not always simply reflect the operation of a memory process distinct from recollection, nor might it always rely on the activation of existing perceptual representations in memory (Jacoby, 1983, 1984, 1991; Jacoby & Dallas, 1981; Jacoby & Kelley, 1992; Jacoby & Witherspoon, 1982; Jacoby, Kelley, & Dywan, 1989; Kelley & Jacoby, 1990; Whittlesea, Jacoby, & Girard, 1990). Rather, both processes could be assumed to rely on detailed memory for prior events. Therefore, Jacoby’s model is one that assumes recollection and familiarity differ in terms of ‘intentional control’ (see Yonelinas, 2001: 361).

There are some similarities between Jacoby and the earlier models of Mandler and Atkinson. For instance, they all assumed that recollection reflected an effortful, consciously controlled process, while familiarity reflected more of an automatic process (Atkinson & Juola, 1973; Jacoby, 1991; Yonelinas, 2002). They all maintained that while the two processes were initiated in parallel, that familiarity occurred at a faster rate than recollection. In addition (and again similar to Mandler), Jacoby assumed that recollection and familiarity function independently at the time of retrieval (see Yonelinas, 2001, 2002). Unlike Mandler, however, Jacoby argued that recollection reflected an *intentional* use of retrieval memory, which would be, 'hampered when memory was divided rather than full at test' (Jacoby, 1991: 513). In contrast, familiarity was conceptualised as more of an 'automatic use of memory,' which would be 'invariant' regardless of full or divided attention during a study period (Jacoby, 1991: 513).

Thus far, the dual-process models of recognition discussed suggest that recollection and familiarity can be separated out in a number of ways: in terms of intentional control (Jacoby, 1991), perceptual fluency (Atkinson & Juola, 1973, 1974), and speed of processing (Mandler, 1980). However, they have all placed a significant emphasis on the role of familiarity in overall recognition judgements. Atkinson, and colleagues, claims that this process occurs faster than recollection but that recollection is only activated as a conditional factor in recognition, while Mandler argued that recognition memory judgments could be based on the assessment of item familiarity *or* on the basis of a memory search process. It would also appear that Jacoby does not consider familiarity to reflect the operation of a system that is distinct from recollection, but rather that both rely on detailed memory for past encounters. Is there any reason to suspect that these three models really perceive recognition as an index of weak to strong familiarity judgements?

The Yonelinas Model

Yonelinas (1994) suggested that recognition could only really be understood as reflecting the contribution of two *separable* memory retrievable processes, namely recollection and familiarity. This model is interesting insofar as it does conceptualise familiarity as a measure of memory strength or stimulus recency (Yonelinas, Aly, Wang, & Koen, 2010: e1). It assumes that all items are considered to evoke some type of familiarity value, but those most recently encountered will produce, on average, more familiarity than those not encountered/studied before. It is further assumed that if the responses of participants on a Test of Recognition were graphed, that the diagram would form a Gaussian type distribution (Yonelinas et al., 2010: e3).

Recollection, on the other hand, is not ignored as an aspect of recognition, or seen as a conditional factor for recognition; rather, it is seen as different in terms of the *type* of memory information that it provides (Yonelinas, 2002). For instance, Yonelinas suggests that, 'individuals do not recollect information about every event that they have studied.' Instead, he argues that there are times when recollective strength will fall below a certain threshold and fail to produce any discriminating evidence that the event/item was previously encountered.

This dual process model of recognition memory is one in which familiarity and recollection differ, not only in terms of the *type* of information that they provide, but also in the *extent* to which each process influences recognition confidence in a person (Dobbins, Kroll, Yonelinas, & Liu, 1998; Yonelinas, 1994, 1997, 1999, 2001a, 2001b; Yonelinas, Kroll, Dobbins, Lazzara, & Knight, 1998; Yonelinas, Kroll, Dobbins, & Soltani, 1999; Yonelinas, Dobbins, Szymanski, Dhaliwal, & King, 1996). In terms of 'type,' familiarity is assumed to reflect the assessment of quantitative memory strength while recollection reflects the retrieval of more qualitative information about past events. In terms of 'extent,' it is assumed that familiarity will support a range, or continuum, of confidence responses from an individual, whereas recollection will most likely support relatively high confidence recognition decisions.

Similar to the Atkinson, Mandler, and Jacoby model, it is assumed that familiarity is faster than recollection (Yonelinas & Jacoby, 1994, 1996), and that recollection could be expected to diminish with hippocampal damage, whereas familiarity should be reduced only if additional temporal lobe structures (i.e., the MTL) are damaged (Yonelinas et al., 1998). In a way, this appears to bring us back to the role of memory *systems* and the role of 'connectivity' in the hippocampal-frontal-cortical system for achieving recognition (Bowler, 2011).

The Tulving Model

As noted previously, Tulving argued that there are several functionally distinct memory systems (Tulving, 1985, 1982; Tulving & Schacter, 1990; Tulving & Markowitsch, 1998; Nyberg, Cabeza, & Tulving, 1996; Wheeler, et al., 1997), including declarative memory. In this framework, the declarative memory system includes episodic memory, which evokes the conscious experience of 'remembering,' and semantic memory, which evokes the conscious experience of 'knowing.' While 'systems-based,' in its approach, 'remembering' is often equated with the process of 'recollection,' and 'knowing' with the process of 'familiarity' (see Bigham et al., 2010; Boucher et al., 2012).

This model assumes that information must pass through the semantic system before it is encoded into the episodic memory and, as such, the acquisition of episodic memories (and therefore remembering) is reliant upon the semantic system. It further assumes that, at the point of retrieval, the two systems will operate independently *and* in parallel in the sense that information can be retrieved from either of the two systems separately (Tulving, 1985, 1995; Tulving & Markowitsch, 1998).

All systems models of memory assume that the operation of different systems is dependent upon the functioning of different neural substrates (see Gardiner, 2008), and this model is no exception. It assumes that the episodic system relies heavily on the medial temporal and frontal lobes, and, as such, any damage to these regions can lead to diminished recollection (Schacter & Tulving, 1994; Yonelinas, 2002; Wheeler, et al., 1997). However, a further distinction within the temporal lobes is proposed, in which the hippocampus is considered crucial for episodic memory (and therefore 'remembering'), whereas the surrounding temporal lobe regions are considered crucial for semantic memory (and therefore 'knowing') (Tulving & Markowitsch, 1998). This suggestion resonates with the findings of the case study N.B. by Bowles et al. (2007) who 'remembered' material from her past but found familiarity a challenge following damage to the MTL. In addition, this model assumes that retrieval from episodic memory is dependent on the right prefrontal regions while retrieval from semantic memory is dependent on left prefrontal regions and for the encoding of information into episodic memory (e.g., Nyberg, Cabeza, & Tulving, 1996).

Tulving's model appears to be very much grounded in memory systems, but it views recollection and familiarity as operating sequentially at the point of encoding and functioning independently at the point of retrieval. Tulving also assumes that the process of familiarity arises from semantic memory, and that familiarity may not be limited solely to perceptual information (Schacter & Tulving, 1994; Tulving, 1985; Yonelinas, 2002).

Summary

Our conceptualisation of memory has evolved considerably since the writings of Ebbinghaus in 1885. For instance, memory is no longer perceived as a singular, indivisible entity, but rather as an amalgamation of memory systems and memory processes. Our focus is on a particular aspect of memory known as recognition memory, which refers to the ways a person might perceive something as having been previously encountered (e.g., Mandler, 1980). Our particular interest is in the ways the child with autism might recognise certain stimuli, especially voice.

From one perspective, recognition performance will reflect either spared or impaired systems of memory (i.e., Atkinson & Shiffrin, Baddeley & Hitch, and Tulving). One system of particular relevance to recognition memory is the declarative memory system (Bowler, 2011; Tulving, 1985). It is understood that this particular system is mediated by the medial temporal lobe, an area of the brain thought to interact with the rest of the cerebral cortex in terms of stored information, and also with sensory cortical areas where new information comes in. Specifically, the hippocampus is a structure located within the MTL, which functions much like a Post Office in the brain. It is suggested that much of the difficulties a person with autism may have, with memory, are because of some kind of hippocampal dysfunction (Bowler, 2011). Not because there is something wrong with the hippocampus itself, but because some of the other connections are working atypically. For instance, information may not be stored properly, or if it is, it may not be retrieved properly at the point of making a recognition judgement. If this set of assumptions were correct, from a systems perspective, we would conclude that some aspect of declarative memory is impaired in the individual with autism, and that is why recognition is not fully operational. However, what methods are used to evaluate these assumptions? Moreover, how much of the full story will they reveal? These questions form the next part of our discussion.

Measuring Memory and Testing Assumptions

If we take the argument of Bowler (2011) that the declarative memory system is of particular relevance to the functioning of recognition memory, it is important to discuss the methods used to assess this aspect of memory. Declarative memory can be assessed using tests of free recall, cued recall, tests of recognition, or via source memory tasks (Boucher et al., 2012). A number of these tests have been conducted with individuals who have a diagnosis of autism, and these will be discussed now. The main objectives of this section are:

(a) To describe the tests outlined
(b) To discuss the findings of same when conducted with individuals diagnosed with autism
(c) To consider that the relative contributions recollection and familiarity may be contributing to overall performance on these tasks.

The overall aim is to evaluate these methods in terms of their ability to test recognition memory in very young TD children, children with developmental-delay (DD) and the child with low-functioning autism.

Free Recall and ASD

Tests of free recall typically involve showing a participant a list of items and then asking them to recall the items in any order (e.g., Boucher et al., 2012). Memory performance can then be deduced by measuring the percentage of items the participant is able to recall (Goldstein, 2011). For example, if a child recalled five of the ten items at test this would represent fifty percent recall. It is also possible to determine patterns in the way items are recalled when using these tests, for instance, when shown lists of zoo, farm, and domestic animals, participant recall can be analysed to determine whether or not they grouped or categorised the animals together (e.g., Bock, 1994; Tager-Flusberg, 1991). In addition, a person can be asked to recall life events, such as activities they participated in during the week or during the day (Baker-Ward, Hess, & Flannagan, 1990). Therefore, tests of free recall are primarily tapping into the episodic memory and thereby what an individual can remember about a previously studied event.

There have been a number of tests of free recall conducted with children with autism, and when interpreted via Tulving's (1985) taxonomy of memory systems the findings provide some valuable insight to autism spectrum disorders. For instance, when individuals with high functioning autism (HFA) are assessed on their ability to recall strings of digits or unrelated word lists, their performance is generally unimpaired (e.g., Ambery, Russell, Perry, Morris & Murphy, 2006; Boucher, Cowell, Howard, Broks, Mayes, & Roberts, 2005; Bowler, Gaigg, & Gardiner, 2008; Bowler et al., 1997; Minshew, Goldstein, Muenz, & Payton, 1992; Mottron, Morasse, & Belleville, 2001; Renner, Klinger, & Klinger, 2000; Smith, Gardiner, & Bowler, 2007; Williams, Goldstein, & Minshew, 2006). This set of findings imply a certain 'strength' in the immediate free recall of sets of items that are familiar, but unrelated in HFA at least.

A distinct lack of an expected primacy effect was noted in the performance of individuals with autism, however, even when repeated trials were used (see Bowler et al., 2008). Known as the serial position effect (Ebbinghaus, 1913; Toichi, 2008), the tendency to recall earlier items is called the primacy effect, while the tendency to recall the later items refers to the recency effect. The assumption is that items presented early in the list will be encoded into long term memory (primacy effect) as the individual will have had time to rehearse the word, or number. Items from the end of a list are encoded into short term memory (recency effect; Baddeley, 1999; Craik, 1971; Murdock, 1962). Items in the middle of the list would have been there too long for them to be held in the short-term memory (STM; due to displacement) and not long enough to be put into the long-term memory (LTM). This finding resonates with the multi-store model insofar as it suggests that when remembering primary and recent information, participants are recalling information from two separate stores, STM and LTM. The primacy effect would be expected to occur in repeated trials of free recall tests as individuals would have a tendency to 'rehearse' the first few items during their initial presentation and throughout the remainder of the study list (Baddeley, 1999; Ebbinghaus, 1913; Toichi, 2008). Moreover, items, which were rehearsed, should have a better chance of being stored in LTM making them available for later recall. This was not the case in some studies of free recall with individuals with HFA.

It was also noted, that the ways individuals with autism organised the words they recalled at test was very different from the ways non-diagnosed individuals did - despite no difference in the amounts recalled by both groups (Bowler at al. 2009). For instance, although demonstrating intact immediate recall of words from a single category, the same participants with HFA showed impaired recall of words from two semantically related categories (Bowler et al., 1997). A similar finding occurred for the free recall of lists of words that were either random or all came from the same category (Tager-Flusberg, 1991). In addition, children with autism who showed unimpaired free recall of random words demonstrated impaired performance for the free recall of sentences relative to children with developmental-delay (Hermelin & O'Connor, 1967; O'Connor & Hermelin, 1967).

Very few studies have assessed declarative memory via free recall in LFA, but those that have suggest that their performance is impaired even when the material to be recalled is non-social and unrelated in its composition (Boucher, 1981; Boucher & Lewis, 1989; Boucher & Warrington, 1976; Fein, Dunn, Allen, Aram, Hall, Morris, & Wilson, 1996; Frith, 1970; Fyffe & Prior, 1978; Millward, Powell, Messer, & Jordan, 2000; Summers & Craik, 1994; Tager-Flusberg, 1991).

Summary: The findings from tests of free recall in HFA are very interesting. When interpreted via a memory systems perspective they suggest a 'strength' in HFA for the recall of unrelated materials, such as random numbers, words, or letters. Of interest however, the individual with autism appears to retrieve the material to be recalled from memory differently than comparison groups. They tend to show a free recall deficit that is apparent at primacy rather than recency, which might suggest an encoding deficit that is limited to the long-term memory (Smith & Gardiner, 2008). There is also a free recall deficit evident when semantic information needs to be drawn upon (e.g., the recall of sentences versus random words, or when words have to be recalled from two semantic categories). From a systems perspective this could be interpreted as a mild impairment of episodic memory in HFA with a potentially more pervasive deficit in LFA.

Cued Recall and ASD

What is recall like when cues or prompts are given to the individual with autism? Cued recall typically involves showing the participant a list of items to remember and later testing them with cues to prompt their recall. For instance, when given a list of people to remember, the tester might provide the participant with either a visual (e.g., a picture of a face to prompt recall of that person's voice) or an auditory cue (e.g., a recording of a person's voice to prompt recall of that person's face). This type of test also assesses episodic memory, as it requires remembering material from a previously personally experienced event. The use of cues as a prompt is interesting however, as it potentially aids retrieval from this particular memory system.

Intact performance has been shown on tests of cued recall conducted with individuals with HFA (e.g., Ambery et al., 2006; Boucher & Lewis, 1989; Gardiner et al. 2003; Mottron, et al. 2001; Tager-Flusberg, 1991), and with LFA (Boucher & Warrington, 1976; Farrant, Boucher, & Blades, 1999; Klin, Sparrow, de Bildt, Cicchetti, Cohen, & Volkmar, 1999; Tager-Flusberg, 1991). In addition, there is evidence to suggest that children with LFA have shown an ability to use written rhyme cues (e.g., 'mat' to cue 'cat') and written category cues (e.g., 'house' to cue 'window') at test (Tager-Flusberg, 1991). One study by Farrant et al., (1999) required children with LFA to recall the location of a picture on a page, using the picture as a cue, and found no impairment in LFA relative to children with developmental-delay without autism. Children with LFA also respond well to phonological cues (e.g., 'Fr' to cue 'fruit') and verbally presented semantic cues (e.g., 'Something you drink from' to cue 'cup'; Boucher & Warrington, 1976).

In a similar vein, when a novel or arbitrary relationship is established between two stimuli during study, and one stimulus is then used to cue recall of the other at test, performance in autism is typically intact. This type of cued recall test is referred to as paired associate learning (PAL), and an example might be where one letter is used to cue another (e.g., what letter went before the letter 'x'?); or an object to cue a location (e.g., where was the shape on the computer screen?); or a face to cue a name (e.g., which person spoke to you at test?). In relation to the first two of these examples, studies have found no impairments of PAL in HFA, whether testing was immediate or delayed (Ambery et al., 2006; Gardiner et al., 2003; Minshew & Goldstein, 2001; Williams, Goldstein, & Minshew, 2005a). Additionally, in a Test of Paired-Associate Learning using non-related word pairs as test stimuli, children with LFA were not impaired relative to age-matched TD children (Boucher & Warrington, 1976).

Source Memory and ASD

What about when individuals with autism not only have to remember studied items, but also information about where the items were studied? Source memory tasks assess memory for contextual information. They are assumed to demand more than 'mere recall,' relying instead on autonoetic awareness and a very specific capacity to retrieve information from episodic memory (e.g., Boucher et al., 2012; Lind, 2010; Tulving, 2001). For instance, a source memory task could involve asking a participant who accurately identified a picture at study to look at three books and answer, 'Which of these books was this picture printed in?'—a source recognition task. Alternatively, the participant might be asked, 'What was the name of the book that picture was printed in?'—a source recall task. Memory tests assessing contextual information in relation to *people* are referred to as 'source monitoring' tasks (Johnson, Hashtroudi, & Lindsay, 1993). Here a participant who has correctly identified a previously heard word might be asked, 'Was it spoken by an adult, or a child?' Arguably, while these tests still tap into familiarity to *some* extent, they are placing greater demands on recollective processes in particular, as they focus heavily on the recall of specific contextual information (Jacoby, 1991; Mandler, 1980; Yonelinas, 1994).

The findings of source *recall* tasks, conducted with individuals with HFA, have shown impaired performance combined with spared source *recognition* in a test conducted by Bowler, Gardiner & Berthollier (2004). In addition, Bigham et al., (2010) reported impaired recall of actions, which had been paired with the presentation of abstract shapes at test by adolescents with HFA. One study reported spared recall of temporal source memory (TSM) in a word recognition task (Salmond et al., 2005), however, the recall of person-related contextual information was reported as impaired in a Test of Source-Monitoring, conducted by O'Shea, Fein, Cillessen, Klin & Schultz (2005).

In relation to LFA, Russell and Jarrold (1999) tested a sample of twenty-two children, with limited verbal ability, using a task in which experimenter and child took turns to place twenty-four picture cards onto a picture lotto board, either on their own behalf or on the behalf of a designated doll. Afterwards, the child had to remember with whom each card had originated and return the card to that person (themselves/experimenter), or the doll (their doll/experimenter's doll). It was found that relative to typically-developing children and children with intellectual disability, children with autism performed less well on this task. Russell and Jarrold also reported that while both comparison groups were better at remembering the correct origin of the cards they had placed on the board themselves (e.g., their cards and their doll partner's cards) than of the cards they had observed the experimenter place (e.g., experimenter's cards and experimenter's doll partner's cards) - with the difference reaching significance in the group with learning disability, but not the typically-developing group - the children with autism were significantly better at 'knowing' the correct origin of the cards they had observed the experimenter place on the board than 'remembering' the cards they had placed themselves. Accordingly, whereas the comparison groups showed a 'self-advantage,' the children with autism showed an 'other-advantage.'

Williams and Happé (2009) recently failed to replicate Russell and Jarrold's (1999) findings. They used a slightly modified version of the original task, in which 32 - rather than 24 - picture cards were used, to test a sample of sixteen children with autism (of mixed intellectual ability) and sixteen comparison children. In this regard, it was found that participants with autism showed both a similar level and pattern of performance to comparison participants. Neither of the groups showed a self-enactment effect, with both groups showing no significant difference in memory for the origins of their own (i.e., their cards and their doll partner's cards) and the experimenter's (e.g., experimenter's cards and experimenter's doll partner's cards) cards.

Lind and Bowler (2009) assessed recognition and self-other source memory in a group of over fifty children with autism who had mixed levels of verbal ability, and fifty comparison children (matched on age and verbal ability). The experimental task involved a picture naming game in which the experimenter and participant took turns to pick up and name picture cards. Following a two minute filled delay, recognition, and self-other source memory were assessed. It was found that although participants with autism showed similar levels of recognition memory to comparison participants, they showed significantly diminished source recall. Crucially, it was found that both groups showed the same *pattern* of performance, with better recognition and source recall for items originally picked up and named by the child rather than the experimenter.

Bennetto, Pennington, and Rogers (1996) reported impaired source memory, as measured via increased intrusions of items from earlier lists in a multi-list free-recall paradigm, while Farrant, Blades, and Boucher (1998) reported no performance deficit when children with autism were asked which of two adults present during testing had uttered a specific word.

Bigham et al., (2010) showed adolescents with LFA a set of everyday objects individually, one of which—presented near the middle of the sequence—was a tube of sweets. At test, participants were asked which of the items had been presented before the sweets, and which had been presented after the sweets. Adolescents with LFA were impaired on this temporal source memory (TSM) task relative to an age-and-ability matched group with developmental-delay, and an ability matched TD group. Once again it is possible to interpret the findings in terms of a mild impairment of episodic memory - potentially as a result of diminished relational memory (Bowler & Gaigg, 2008) - it is also possible to suggest that whereas recollection is mildly impaired in HFA, leaving familiarity intact, both may be impaired in the child with LFA (Bigham et al., 2010).

Recognition and ASD

Tests of Recognition typically involve a forced-choice (FC) or a yes/no procedure (Bayley, Wixted, Hopkins, & Squire, 2008; Boucher et al., 2012; Holdstock, Mayes, Isaac, Gong, & Roberts, 2002). In the yes/no procedure, participants are shown the items and foils one at a time and asked to respond ‘yes’ to the target items and ‘no’ to the foils (Bayley et al., 2008). In the FC procedure, participants are shown a target and a foil at the same time and asked to identify the target item (Holdstock et al., 2002).

Studies using these methods suggest that recognition of non-social stimuli, such as written word lists and spoken words lists, is spared in individuals with HFA (for reviews see Boucher et al. 2012). Similarly, individuals with HFA have shown intact recognition of stories they heard previously (Salmond et al., 2005), pictures of everyday items (Ambery et al., 2006), and abstract shapes (Bigham et al., 2010). Recognition in HFA falters somewhat when the material becomes complex (Williams et al.,

2006), or when the material contains emotion-related stimuli (i.e., family scenes) (see Lind, 2010; Webb, 2008).

Studies have also assessed recognition memory in HFA using memory illusion tasks (Bowler, Gardiner, Saavalainen, & Grice, 2000: 663). It has been suggested that *false* recall and recognition can often exceed *veridical* recall and recognition and, 'can be more persistent than veridical recall and recognition' (Bowler, Gardiner, Saavalainen, & Grice, 2000: 663). What this means is that people often recall or claim they recognise a word that was never actually presented at study, purely on the basis of forming strong associates from words that were presented (see Deese, 1959). As an example, participants might recall the word 'needle' after hearing the words 'thread—pin—eye—sewing—sharp—haystack' even though the word 'needle' was never actually included on the original list of words to be recalled (Roediger and McDermott, 1995). Because participants report actually 'remembering' the non-presented word, false recognition is thought to provide an index of episodic memory.

Studies using this type of paradigm suggest that overall recognition performance ('remember' plus 'know' responses) is normal in HFA for words that were presented auditorily (Beversdorf, et al., 2000; Bowler, Gardiner, Saavalainen, & Grice, 2000a; Hillier, Campbell, Keillor, Phillips, & Beversdorf, 2007; Salmond, Ashburner, Connelly, Friston, Gadian, & Vargha-Khadem, 2005), and those presented visually (Bowler, et al., 2000a; Bowler, Gardiner, & Grice, 2000b). Indeed, it has been reported that the performance of individuals with HFA, on these Tests of Recognition, are 'indistinguishable' from age and verbal ability matched comparison groups (Bowler, et al., 2000a: 669). However, while overall recognition performance does not differ between those with autism and comparison groups, those with autism did make more 'know' than 'remember' responses over all (Bowler et al., 2000a, 2000b).

In relation to low-functioning autism (LFA), four studies have reported impaired recognition performance (Boucher, Bigham, Mayes, & Muskett, 2008; Boucher & Warrington, 1976; Lind, 2008; Summers & Craik, 1994). However, and of interest, when children with autism were allowed to handle the materials to be recognised later at test, their performance was reported as unimpaired (Boucher & Lewis, 1992; Hauck, Fein, Maltby, Waterhouse, & Feinstein, 1998; Hill & Russell, 2002).

Both individuals with HFA and LFA have demonstrated weak recognition for faces (Boucher. Lewis, & Collis, 1998; Webb, Jones, Merkle, Murais, Greenson et al., 2010) and voices (Boucher, et al., 1998), but it is very important to note that vulnerability to impaired memory for social stimuli is 'not absolute' (see Boucher et al., 2012: 467). Face recognition has not consistently been reported as impaired (Boucher, Lewis, & Collis, 2000), and recognition of face parts appears to be spared (Joseph & Tanaka, 2003). In addition, children with autism, just like TD children, are capable of mirror self-recognition at a mental age of 18 months (Dawson & McKissick, 1984; Ferrari & Matthews, 1983; Neuman & Hill, 1978). This suggests that children with autism do possess the ability to recognise the faces of others and their own faces (see also Lind & Bowler, 2009).

The findings from recognition tests conducted with individuals with autism have been variously interpreted, but are typically understood to reflect a mild impairment in episodic memory in HFA. It is less clear whether recognition memory is less robust in those with LFA, or whether the findings are artefacts of the tests used (see Boucher et al., 2012).

Summary

This section has described tests of free recall, cued recall, source memory tasks, and tests of recognition. It has also shown - when the findings from these tests are interpreted via Tulving's (1985) taxonomy of memory systems - how declarative memory in autism is understood to reflect a combination of impaired episodic memory with spared semantic memory (e.g., Ben-Shalom, 2003; Bowler and Gaigg 2008; Bowler et al., 2000; Toichi and Kamio, 2003; Salmond et al., 2005).

This discussion has also highlighted a very important set of observations. For instance, while the individual with autism shows little or no difficulty on tasks where cues or prompts are given (tests of cued recall and some source memory tasks), they appear to struggle somewhat on tasks where no such support is given (tests of free recall). This suggests that the individual with autism may have a deficit at the point of retrieval from memory.

It is also striking that although some studies showed no difference in the overall scores of individuals with autism and comparison groups, that how those with autism achieve these scores is qualitatively different than their counterparts (e.g., Bowler, et al., 2004; Bowler et al., 2000; Lind & Bowler, 2009). For instance, they often display a similar level and pattern of performance to comparison participants alongside significantly diminished source recall (Lind & Bowler, 2009), or more 'know' and less 'remember' responses than their counterparts do (e.g., Lind & Bowler, 2009; Bowler, et al., 2004; Bowler et al., 2000).

Similarly, where free recall performance is found to be unimpaired in autism, it is possible that the individual is drawing heavily on familiarity, a process that is not accounted for when interpreting tests of free recall from a systems perspective. For example, on these tests - where all the stimuli are presented at study and the participant is asked to recall as many as they can after a retention period - as the participant has encountered the items, they all have some familiarity value (Yonelinas, 1994) but the actual contribution of same is not explicitly assessed in these tests.

Taken together, this might imply that interpreting findings from a purely systems perspective may be disguising the very subtle ways individuals with autism use certain processes to achieve 'normal' performance on certain memory tasks. Establishing how much familiarity and recollection contribute to overall recognition is important, as knowing this will inform us about the ways a child with LFA might react to self-voice on a SGD.

Task-Dissociation Methods

How can we use the same test paradigms, but tease out the potential contributions of recollection and familiarity to the overall performance by the child with autism? More importantly perhaps, which process-distinction method best measures the separate contributions of these two processes? After all, while dual-process models of memory agree that recognition is accomplished on the basis of recollection and familiarity, there are critical differences in the ways these models distinguish between these two processes and as a consequence, critical differences in how they are measured (Yonelinas, 2001). In the first instance, methods to assess recollection and familiarity fall into two broad categories, namely task-dissociation methods and process-estimation methods (Yonelinas, 2002).

Task-dissociation methods include response-speed methods, recall/recognition comparisons, and item/associative methods. In a nutshell, the main aim of this set of methods is to locate or identify a task, or a test, condition that can isolate one of the two processes. For instance, response-speed methods are built on the assumption that familiarity occurs at a faster rate than recollection, in the event of recognition (e.g., Atkinson, Jacoby, and Yonelinas). Tasks are then designed to evaluate this assumption, and indeed, studies have shown that familiarity assessments for word lists can be completed by the typical adult in about one second, while recollection required some additional time (Benjamin & Craik, 2001; Yonelinas & Jacoby, 1994). Likewise, recall/recognition methods are based on the assumption that the recollection process, which operates in recognition, is the same as the search process, which occurs in tests of recall (e.g., Mandler and Tulving), so that performance on recall tests can be used as an 'index of recollection' (Yonelinas, 2002: 449). The idea here is to compare recall performance to performance on tests of recognition so that inferences can be made about the effects of different variables on recollection and familiarity. For instance, if the variable has a greater effect on recall than recognition, then it could be said to have a greater effect on recollection than familiarity. The item/associative method is one that is based on the assumption that while familiarity reflects quantitative information (or memory strength) of a study event, recollection reflects the retrieval of qualitative (or contextual information) about a study event (Atkinson, Jacoby, Mandler, and Yonelinas). Accordingly, tests that asked the participant about the co-occurrence of different items or different aspects of the study event, such as item-item associations (e.g., where these two pictures paired together at study?), or item-context associations (e.g. was this item moved by me or the doll?), or item-feature associations (e.g. was the word spoken by a child or an adult?), should be more reflective of recollection. By contrast, tests that discriminate between studied and non-studied items (FC and yes/no paradigms) should be a better index of familiarity (Yonelinas, 2002).

The main issue with task-dissociation methods rests in the fact that often the test conditions are very different, and so too are the type of responses they require from the participant. For example, in tests of recognition, the target stimuli are presented and the participant is asked to make yes/no responses or FC responses (Gardiner & Java, 1999; Tulving, 1985). In tests of recall, the target stimuli are not presented a second time, rather the participant is asked to recall as many as they can from an earlier study period. Arguably, even if the same recollection process is used across the two tests, recollection may operate differently because of the prompts or cues available in the former as opposed to the latter test paradigm.

Task-dissociation methods may also provide imprecise measures of recollection and familiarity. For instance, in the item/associative methods, some associative tasks - which are assumed to tap recollection - may be influenced by a degree of familiarity. Consider the studies by Lind and Bowler (2009), and Williams and Happé (2009), where pictures were used as part of the testing conditions. It is possible that the pictures presented last (recency effect) may have been more familiar to the participants than those presented first (Craik & Tulving, 1975; Toichi & Kamio, 2003). This may also have occurred in the temporal source memory task conducted by Bigham et al., (2010) where items that are more recent were subject to greater degrees of familiarity than those presented earlier. In addition, as discussed earlier, some dual-process theories of recognition memory suggest that familiarity supports the learning of some form of associative learning (e.g., when participants are able to create links between unrelated words, such as citadel and elephant; e.g., Jacoby, 1991). Therefore, in some situations, familiarity may be contributing to source memory/associative recognition tasks, rather than just pure recollection.

Process-Estimation Methods

Process-estimation methods were possibly developed in response to the limitations of the task-dissociation methods; these typically involve developing a set of model equations that can be used together with observed measures of performance, 'to obtain parameter estimates representing the contribution of recollection and familiarity to overall performance' (Yonelinas, 2002: 449). Two of these methods are the process-dissociation procedure (PDP), and the Remember-Know (RK) procedure.

The process-dissociation procedure (PDP; Jacoby, 1991) is one that uses a modification of the item/associative recognition task discussed earlier in which, 'recollection is measured as the ability to remember where, or when, an item was earlier studied' (Yonelinas, 2002: 451). It rests on the assumption that if the participant can recollect a given stimulus (e.g., a voice), then they should be able to ascertain when or where it was first encountered, whereas familiarity should not support this type of discriminatory capacity (Jacoby, 1991; Yonelinas, 2002).

Jacoby's model of recognition memory was one that argued recollection and familiarity differed from each other in terms of intentional control. When he developed this method originally, therefore, participants were first shown a visually presented set of items under incidental encoding conditions, and then asked to study a different list of heard words under intentional encoding conditions to test his assumptions. One of these conditions was referred to as the 'inclusion trial' and the other an 'exclusion trial.' In the former, the participant is instructed to respond 'yes' if the test item was one they recognised from either the seen or heard lists, whereas on the latter the participant should only respond 'yes' to items from the heard list. It is assumed that recollection and familiarity work in concert for the inclusion trial, as they would in an ordinary Recognition Test. In exclusion trials, however, participants are asked only to identify stimuli from one particular presentation list, while treating stimuli from the other list as new. This places recollection and familiarity in opposition, as the participants must recollect information concerning the list membership of the stimulus; responses based solely on familiarity may be incorrect. The proportion of trials in which participants correctly identify stimuli as old in the inclusion trials (P [Inclusion]), and in which they incorrectly identify stimuli as old in the exclusion trials (P [Exclusion]) trials, are then used to estimate recollection: P [Inclusion] – P [Exclusion], and familiarity: P [Exclusion] / (1-Recollection), (Jacoby, 1991).

Might this method work for the child with LFA? The fact that spoken words are used as stimuli is interesting, as we want to assess voice recognition at some point. This method does appear to distinguish clearly between recollection and familiarity, which is important, but it also assumes that the two processes are fully independent of each other, and that the responses for any given trial can only reflect one of the two processes - but never both. However, the responses given may be less reflective of recollection and familiarity, and more to do with the design of the PDP (see Curran & Hintzman, 1995).

For example, the measure of recollection used in the PDP is really quite narrow. It refers primarily to the ability of the participant to determine in which study list the item was presented. The list is defined by the type of encoding condition (e.g., incidental or intentional), modality (e.g., visual or auditory), and list membership (list 1 or list 2), (Jacoby, 1991; Yonelinas & Jacoby, 1996). In this way, if the participant were to recollect *any* of these particular aspects of the study event, they could use this as a means of excluding items and this would be counted as a measure of recollection. However, if they were to recollect some other aspect of the study (e.g., remembering that a door banged shut when the target stimuli was being presented), which would not actually support the required discrimination—sometimes referred to as partial recollection—this would not be counted as a measure of recollection (Yonelinas, 2002).

Yet, a number of studies lend support to the argument that partial recollection can influence parameter estimates, especially when the two study lists are very similar (e.g., the faces and voices of certain people for instance) and participants are potentially able to remember many different aspects of the study episode, which may or may not support list discrimination (Gruppuso, Lindsay, & Kelly, 1997; Mulligan & Hirschman, 1997; Wagner, Gabrieli, & Verfaelli, 1997; Yonelinas & Jacoby, 1996).

Another potential issue with the PDP is that it uses different test conditions for the inclusion and exclusion trials, which could potentially influence the parameter estimates (Yonelinas, 2002). Consider that it is assumed that recollection can occur across both conditions. Given that recollection is necessary in the exclusion trial (i.e., the participant must distinguish between items from the two lists), but not explicitly required in the inclusion trial (i.e., the participant only has to distinguish between old and new items), participants may have to draw on recollection more heavily in the exclusion rather than the inclusion trial. The PDP also assumes that, the contribution of familiarity is held constant across the two conditions, which may not be the case given the different test conditions. Rather, familiarity as defined in the PDP, may not purely be a feeling of 'knowing' or 'oldness,' as the child may be able to recall some other information about a stimulus, which is not relevant to list membership.

Overall then, the PDP may not be the most suitable measure for assessing the contributions of recollection and familiarity to recognition performance in the child with LFA. Indeed, it is proving difficult to identify a method that is useful in discriminating between these two processes; both recollection and familiarity contribute to performance on most standard memory tests (see also Bigham et al., 2010). The PDP seemed promising, but it relies on fairly complex verbal instructions combined with an assumption that the participant has a full understanding of what is being asked of them. It is also characterised by a very narrow definition of recollection.

Assessing Recollection and Familiarity Separately

The Remember-Know (RK) Procedure

The Remember-Know (RK) procedure, however, allows a much broader pool of responses to be included under the heading of recollection. This model is not often, 'described as a dual-process model of recognition' (Yonelinas, 2002:446) as it conceptualises memory comprised of several functionally distinct memory systems (Tulving, 1985, 1982; Tulving & Schacter, 1990; Tulving & Markowitsch, 1998; Nyberg, et al., 1996; Wheeler, et al., 1997). It has evolved to assess recollection and familiarity separately, however, and thus, is highly relevant to this discussion (Bigham et al., 2010; Gardiner & Java, 1993).

In the RK procedure, participants make experiential judgments about their memories for recognised items, categorising them as remembered (R) or known (K). Participants make R responses when they are able to recollect any specific information about the encoding event associated with a target stimulus. This information may include thoughts that the stimulus evoked, associations that the participant made between stimuli - or any other detail - of the encoding event. Participants make K responses when they believe that they have seen an item before, but are unable to recall any information about the encoding event. Some revised and modified studies also include Guess (G) responses (e.g., Gardiner, Java, & Richardson-Klavehn, 1996; Konstantinou & Gardiner, 2005), and this is aimed at ensuring that K responses are uncontaminated by guessing.

Tulving (1985) argued that recollection arises from an episodic memory system, whereas familiarity is a product of a semantic memory system. While the RK procedure does not directly test these two systems, R responses are presumed to accompany old/new judgments based on episodic memory, while K responses are presumed to accompany old/new judgments based on semantic memory.

The RK Procedure and LFA

Is the RK procedure the most suitable method to use with the child with LFA? It is a model of memory that appears to embrace the interplay of memory systems and memory processes. The standard tests of recall and recollection do not seem to be able to separate out the precise contributions of recollection and familiarity, 'whether the material to be recognised relates to a personal experience event or to a decontextualised fact, word, single item, or scene' (Bigham et al., 2010: 879). The RK procedure however, is one that is specifically designed to assess recollection and familiarity separately (Gardiner & Java, 1993; Migo, Montaldi, Norman, Quamme, & Mayes, 2009; Migo, Mayes, & Montaldi, 2012; Tulving, 1985).

This paradigm has also been criticised, and this criticism requires some discussion before reaching a decision on the suitability of this method for use with the child with LFA. One serious critique is that it does not discriminate between the contributions of recollection and familiarity, 'as satisfactorily' as first appeared to be the case (Bigham et al., 2010: 879; Dunn, 2004; Migo et al., 2009). For example, in the RK procedure participants are asked to make experiential judgments about their memories for recognised items, categorising them as Remembered (R) or Known (K). The proportion of remember responses should therefore provide a measure of recollection (Tulving, 1985). However, Migo et al., (2012: 1446) argue that when participants are asked to remember something, 'their explanations can vary and are not easy to categorise.' For instance, on showing a participant a photograph of a face studied previously, the participant might say that they remember the nose. This would not be considered as a clear and definitive R response. Migo et al., (2012: 1446) cautions that on occasions, therefore, 'high confidence familiarity can be 'mislabelled' as remembering, by participants and researchers alike.'

There are also concerns that people may correctly report recollection and familiarity, but that recollection is 'much more closely associated with confident/strong recognition' (Migo et al., 2012: 1438). If this is the case, people are not making process distinctions; rather they are making judgements on *just* recollection. For instance, participants may use RKG responses to reflect differences in confidence, with R responses, K responses, and G responses being applied to decisions made with high, medium, and low confidence respectively (Donaldson, 1996; Dunn, 2004; Rotello, MacMillan, Reeder, & Wong, 2005; Migo et al., 2012).

Gardiner, Ramponi, and Richardson-Klavehn (1998) reject this argument however. They asked participants to provide explanations for their RKG judgments, and analysed the content of these explanations. Only R responses were accompanied by reports of recollective experience; K responses were accompanied by reports of just knowing, and by feelings of familiarity. K responses were also sometimes associated with quite high confidence. These findings appear to suggest that participants are able to understand and apply instructions meaningfully in the RK paradigm. However, it is also possible that the participants in that particular study were more stringent in their RKG judgments, as they knew that they would have to explain these decisions. Participants in standard RKG experiments may be more likely to use confidence as a means of making RKG judgments (Rotello et al., 2005; Migo et al., 2012).

There is also some discussion around the analysis of RKG responses (Gardiner et al., 1996; Konstantinou & Gardiner, 2005). The recollection process is easily estimated from R responses, as participants will make an R response whenever they recollect an item. Estimating familiarity is more complex, as participants will only make K responses for items that are familiar, but not recollected. However, it has been suggested that the familiarity process will almost certainly contribute to the recognition of recollected items, and K responses could potentially underestimate the contribution of familiarity to recognition (Gardiner et al., 1996).

Another potential limitation for using the RK procedure is its reliance on complex verbal instructions and, as such, a need for good verbal understanding. This makes the RK paradigm somewhat unsuitable for testing young children, children with developmental-delay, or the child with LFA.

Assessing Recollection and Familiarity in LFA

The focus of our investigation is the child's ability to recognise self-voice on a SGD. This child is one that is both linguistically and intellectually challenged, making the goal to find a suitable method for assessing recognition memory rather difficult. While, of course, it is entirely possible to present the child with a number of recorded voices via headphones (e.g., Schuster, 1991; Strömbergsson, 2009) and ask them to indicate their recognition of self-voice via a standard Test of Recognition, what is clear at this point is that the child's performance may be masking some subtleties in how they may achieve this goal. Our aim is to understand the ways familiarity and recollection may be used by the child with autism in the first instance, and - once this is established - to decide whether paradigm's, using cues and prompts to support retrieval, are best when we progress to assessing voice recognition in the future.

Recently, Bigham and colleagues (2010) developed a temporal source memory (TSM) task to assess recollection, and a shape recognition task to assess familiarity in adolescents with autism. The initial aim was to develop these tests for use with both high- and-low-functioning autism but, 'despite extensive piloting of a variety of methodological modifications' this proved impossible (Bigham et al., 2010: 880). Instead, a Test of Recollection was developed and conducted with LFA only, while a Test of Familiarity was designed and conducted with HFA only.

To assess recollection, the TSM task involved showing participants a set of 16 everyday items one at a time for five seconds before removing them from sight. A tube of sweets was presented as item 10. The participants were then shown the 16 items again (but in a different order to that used at study), and asked if they had seen the item before, or after, the tube of sweets. The type of response required from children included the clear placing of the target items onto a before and after strip, but, if unwilling, or unable, to do so, 'a clear indication of a choice' was accepted and the tester placed the item to the side indicated by the child (Bigham et al., 2010: 881). To ensure that these were cognitive, and not motor, responses, a number of practice tests were conducted prior to the main test.

This method is one that draws heavily on the assumptions of Jacoby (1991), as it assumes that recollection reflects the retrieval of the context, and elaboration, given to an item when it was initially studied. Of course, the 16 items have all been encountered by the child at study, and thus will have some familiarity value (e.g., Yonelinas, 1994), but the fact that the child must remember *where* they saw them at test places a much greater demand on recollection than familiarity. Essentially, successful recollection of items placed before and after the sweets will be dependent on intentional control (Jacoby, 1991) and the depth of encoding at the time of study (Craik & Tulving, 1972).

The results showed that not only were children with LFA impaired - relative to age and ability matched children with intellectual disability (ID) *and* ability-matched typically-developing (TD) children - but that impaired recollection was specific to LFA (Bigham et al., 2010). This is a very important finding, and one with significant implications for the present study. Their finding was based on a singular trial however, making generalisations of the children's performance difficult. In addition, the possibility that impaired familiarity may have contributed to the impaired performance of the LFA group relative to comparison groups, was not explicitly controlled for. As such, it could be that the children with LFA recognised the 16 items used at test less well than the comparison groups, and that this may have adversely affected their performance.

In relation to assessing familiarity in LFA, a Shape-Recognition Test was designed (Bigham et al., 2010). In this test, 16 abstract shapes were used as stimuli. Unlike squares, circles, or triangles for instance, or words, colours, or sentences, abstract shapes are meaningless and difficult to 'rehearse' in STM between the time they are presented at study, and again at test. As such, the child must rely heavily on the feeling they have seen one of the four shapes before.

At test, a Forced-Choice Corresponding (FCC) Test - utilising three foils not easily discriminable from the target stimulus - was incorporated (see Fig 1-4). The shapes used as foils were similar to the target-shapes, as when foils are similar to targets the, 'mean difference in familiarity between targets and their similar foils will be small, relative to the overall level of variability in the familiarity for different targets' (Migo et al., 2009:e2; Yonelinas, 2002; Yonelinas et al., 2010). Accordingly, to succeed on this task, recollection of the study period can contribute little because of the similarities between the target-and-foil shapes.

Why was a FCC paradigm used? There are suggestions that yes/no (YN) and forced-choice (FC) procedures may assess the two processes underpinning recognition memory differently (Aggleton & Shaw, 1996; Bastin & Van der Linden, 2003; Bayley et al., 2008). In other words, a child with autism may discriminate a target from a foil on a FC Test on the basis of relative familiarity, but on a yes/no Test, their success might involve a greater degree of recollection (Bayley et al., 2008). In FC tests, there can be either a forced-choice corresponding (FCC) paradigm or a forced-choice non-corresponding paradigm (FCNC). The FCC version is one whereby target items are presented with very similar foils, and the FCNC is one where each target item is presented with foils that correspond to other targets (Hall, 1979; Tulving, 1981) (Fig.1-4). So why choose the FCC paradigm?

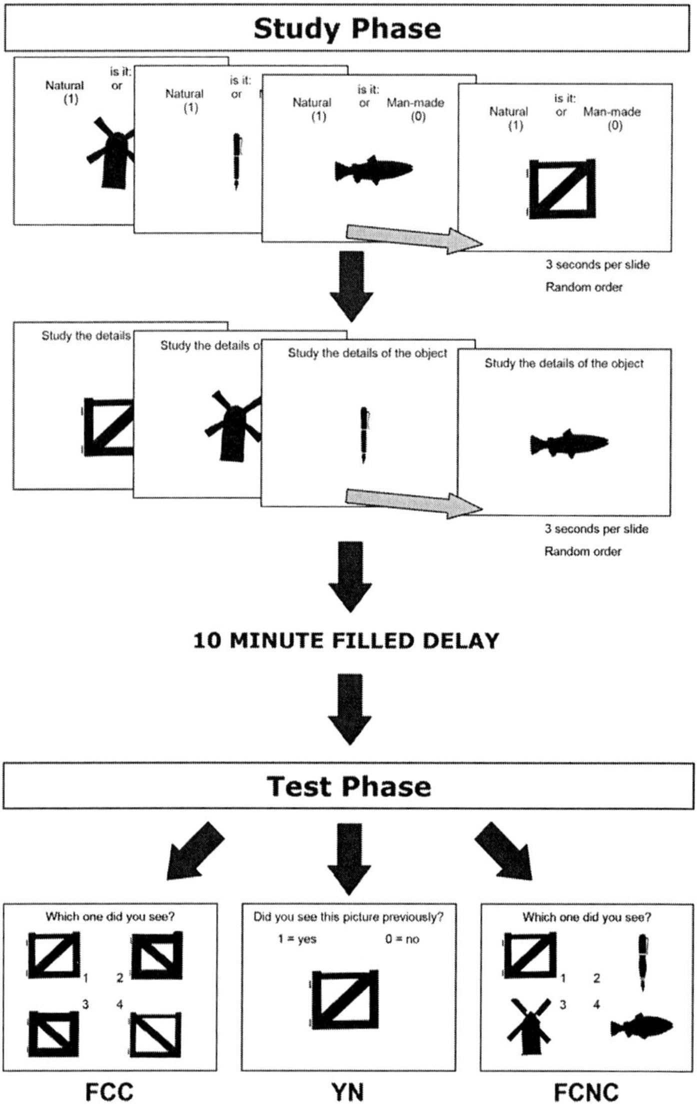

Fig. 1-4 An Example of the Experimental Procedures of FCC, YN, and FCNC. Reproduced from Migo et al. (2009).

Familiarity may be more useful to the child in FCC tests as opposed to YN tests, because when foils are similar to targets the, 'mean difference in familiarity between targets and their similar foils will be small, relative to the overall level of variability in the familiarity for different targets' (Migo et al., 2009:e2; Yonelinas, 2002; Yonelinas et al., 2010). Because of this, it is proposed that familiarity distributions associated with targets and foils will overlap considerably, but, because there is strong covariance in the familiarity values primed by targets and their corresponding similar foils, targets should be, 'reliably more familiar than their corresponding foils' (Migo et al., 2009: e2).

By contrast, on a YN Test, each target item is presented separately and the participant must set a, 'familiarity criterion' in order to choose whether that target item is old or new (Migo et al., 2009; Yonelinas, 2001, 2002). Using meaningless shapes increases the need that familiarity, not recollection, will be used by the child on one hand, but in the other - because they are so similar to each other - it may not be possible, 'for a single criterion to separate the distributions' (Migo et al., 2009:e3). Correspondingly, the YN discriminations - on the basis of familiarity alone - will potentially be very poor.

The FCC appears an appropriate method to use with the child with autism, as each target (e.g., 3s) is assessed by that child relative to its own corresponding foil, rather than the other foils (e.g., 1s, 2s, and 4s). It is assumed that the child will distinguish targets from foils in FCC by, 'consistently accepting the most familiar item on each trial' once the resolution of familiarity is, 'sufficiently fine' (Migo et al., 2009: e3).

In addition, the FCC paradigm is more suitable than the FCNC paradigm. In the latter, each target is presented with foils that correspond to other target items and, therefore, the child cannot, 'utilise the reliable familiarity difference between a target and corresponding foils' because, as with YN recognition, those items are not presented simultaneously (Migo et al., 2009:e3). Instead - much like the YN Test - rather than relying on familiarity alone, on a FCNC Test the child would have to try to *recollect* that item they have seen before *and* discriminate on that basis, rather than on the basis of pure familiarity.

Summary

This discussion has described how our understanding of memory has evolved from a singular and indivisible entity, to one comprised of several functionally distinct memory systems (e.g., Tulving, 1985). How memory is conceptualised at any given time dictates how it is documented, how it is measured, and how the findings are interpreted. It is clear, that while memory in autism has been extensively researched in the past fifty years, more often than not, the findings have been interpreted via Tulving's (1985) taxonomy of memory systems. This has been an informative approach, and has elucidated the very important role of declarative memory for recognition. This approach has highlighted, that while episodic memory may be mildly impaired in HFA, semantic memory is intact. In terms of recognition, it is possible to infer then, that while the child with HFA might know a voice on a SGD, they may not remember whose voice it is.

Of course, the focus of our discussion is the child with LFA, and this step of the overall journey has highlighted a number of important points. Firstly, the findings from a number of tests - used to assess recall and recognition in autism - show little or no difference between the performance of *these* individuals and individuals from matched comparison groups. However, it is clear that the individual with autism struggles with aspects of memory where little or no cues or prompts are given, which has led to the hypothesis that there is a deficit at the point of retrieval (Bowler et al., 2000). Even more importantly, we cannot be sure when using standard tests of recognition, just how much familiarity, and recollection may be contributing to the child's overall performance.

SGDs are expensive, and more importantly, they may be the only way a non-verbal, or minimally-verbal, child with autism has to express themselves vocally (Shane et al., 2011; van der Meer & Rispoli, 2010). We need to be very sure that any new design features will enhance the child's desire to communicate with others, rather than cause them to abandon communication and lose the opportunity to have a voice. Designing a SGD that mimics the child's voice is a novel and exciting feature, created with the aim of promoting AAC use (van Santen & Black, 2009). It is also predicted on the assumption that the child can recognise this voice and, further, that they will prefer to use this voice to communicate, over that of any alternative voice available on the device.

Rather than simply assess voice recognition with a FCC or yes/no format, it may be prudent to first consider the cognitive capacity of the child and their ability to recognise a voice on the basis of familiarity and recollection. For example, it may be that the child will simply recognise the voice as familiar, and this will be sufficient reason for them to accept and identify with the personalised device. However, they may 'know' that the voice sounds familiar, but on the basis of not being able to recollect whose voice it is, abandon the device as any self-reference effect hoped for is thus lost.

Having established a theoretically motivated framework for assessing recollection and familiarity separately in any child with autism, our next steps involve actually testing these concepts experimentally.

CHAPTER TWO

TESTING OUR ASSUMPTIONS ABOUT MEMORY AND AUTISM

This chapter presents the findings of two empirical studies, investigating familiarity and recollection in the child with LFA. The main aim of this chapter is to explore the potential consequences of one, or both, of these two memory retrieval processes being impaired in the child with LFA. The rationale for assessing recognition memory, via a dual-process framework, rests in its potential to separate out the contributions of recollection and familiarity to children's overall recognition judgements. If the child relies more on familiarity than recollection during recognition, it is likely that they may know that the voice on the SGD is one they have heard in the past, but they may not remember that the voice is their own. Implicit in this is that the sound of their own voice will be a 'familiar' to them as that of any other voice, raising the questions as to just how reinforcing self-voice as opposed to any other voice on the SGD is for the child with LFA.

Our First Study: Testing Familiarity in Children with Low-Functioning Autism

This was a Test of Recognition designed specifically to assess the contribution of familiarity to the child's overall performance using a forced-choice paradigm. In this, participants were presented with a number of non-meaningful - or abstract - shapes at study. These target-shapes were then presented alongside three fairly similar foil shapes at test. The task for the child was to identify, which of the four shapes they could recognise from having encountered them previously at study.

It has been argued that to succeed, on this type of Recognition Test, the child must rely heavily on the feeling that one of the four shapes has been seen before: Recollection of the study period will contribute little because of the similarities between the to-be-remembered shapes and the foils - amongst which the target-shapes are presented at test (Bigham et al., 2010; Holdstock et al., 2002; Migo et al., 2009).

The decision to use a FC paradigm, rather than the more standard YN paradigm typically used on recognition tests, was based on the finding that when foils are similar to targets the, 'mean difference in familiarity between targets and their similar foils will be small, relative to the overall level of variability in the familiarity for different targets' (Migo et al., 2009:e2; Yonelinas et al., 2010; Yonelinas, 2002). Because of this, it is proposed that familiarity distributions associated with targets and foils will overlap considerably, but, because there is strong covariance in the familiarity values - primed by targets and their corresponding similar foils - targets should be, 'reliably more familiar than their corresponding foils' (Migo et al., 2009: e2).

A number of studies described in the literature review have illustrated that individuals with HFA typically demonstrate unimpaired performance when standard recognition tests are used. Very few tests of recognition have been conducted with LFA, and those that have provided mixed findings (e.g., Boucher et al., 1998; Boucher et al., 2000; Joseph & Tanaka, 2003). On the basis of these findings, we predicted that familiarity would be somewhat less robust in the LFA group relative to comparison children.

What We Did and How We Did It

Participants

A total of ninety-three children were invited to participate in this study.

General Procedural Points

All our children were tested in their respective schools in a quiet, familiar room. Testing typically took place over a two to three day period. The child was seated to the right-hand side of the tester, at a school desk. Verbal input from the tester during testing was restricted to phrases, such as 'well done' or 'good work' if any child's attention appeared to wander. A pre-prepared score sheet was used to record the children's correct scores. Children were thanked, and praised, for their work on conclusion of the Test.

The Materials we Used and Procedures we Followed

A practice phase was conducted first, to ensure that all participants knew how to respond on this type of Test (Bigham et al., 2010; Boucher et al., 1998; 2000).

Practice stimuli: For this practice phase, a set of eight laminated white A4-sized cards was prepared. On the first four cards, one abstract shape was printed in blue ink via 'auto-shapes' on the computer. These cards were the target-cards. On the second set of four cards, four abstract shapes were drawn in blue ink. One of the four abstract shapes was the target-shape, and the other three were foils (see Fig 2-1). These cards were the target-foil-cards. Each of the target-cards had a number from 1 to 4 printed clearly on the back, in the top right hand corner. The target-foil-cards also had a number from 1 to 4 printed on the back. This was done for two reasons. First, as the tester would be holding the target-cards facing out to the child, and away from themselves, this numbering system ensured the four cards were presented to the child facing the right way up at all times. Second, it meant that the presentation of the target-foil-cards followed the same sequence, as had the presentation of the target-cards.

Fig. 2-1 An Example of the Experimental Procedures of FCC, YN, and FCNC. Reproduced from Migo et al., (2009).

Practice Phase: The practice phase was carried out primarily to ensure that all children fully understood what they were required to do, which was to point clearly to the shape on the target-foil-card that had been presented at study. The procedures used at practice were the same as those described below for the Main Test. If a child hesitated, or made a mistake, a correct response was elicited by using prompts. When the child achieved three consecutively correct identifications unassisted, the practice materials were removed and testing began. Two children in the DD group, and three from the LFA group, showed mild distress and were excluded from the Main Test phase. All remaining participants (n = 88) correctly identified at least three shapes on two of the three practice runs.

Test stimuli: For the Main Test a set of 16 white laminated A4-sized cards were created, each with 4 abstract shapes in black ink printed on them. One of these 4 abstract shapes was the target-shape whilst the other

3 shapes were foils. The 48 foils were (3 on each of the 16 target-plus-foils cards) were all unique. Next, a second set of 16 A4-sized white laminated cards was created. This set comprised of target-shapes only. The back of each target-card and each target-plus-foils card had the numbers 1-16 printed on them to facilitate presentation of the all cards in a predetermined order and orientation at test. For the current study, abstract shapes were printed in blue ink onto white A4-sized cards for the practice phase. In an effort to differentiate between the practice phase and the Main Test, a different set of abstract shapes were used and these were in black ink on a background of white A4-sized card.

Procedure: The 88 children who progressed from the practice phase were asked to engage a second time, but told that this time there would be more cards. The tester began by saying, "*Let's play that game again, but this time the game is a little harder. I have lots more shapes to show you and they are different from the ones I just showed you*"—(i.e., the cards used at practice phase). The tester then said, "*Try to remember exactly what each shape looks like. They all look a bit the same so you need to look at each one carefully. Are you ready*?" Each of the 16 target-cards was placed on the table in front of the child, in a predetermined order of 1-16, facing the right way up.

According to the literature, a familiarity assessment can be completed in the typical participant in about 1 second, while recollection requires extra time (Toth, 1996; Yonelinas & Jacoby, 1994, 1996). As our participants are very young or have a diagnosis of DD or LFA, each target-card was presented for five seconds, which allowed the child 3-4 seconds viewing time.

When all of the 16 target-cards had been presented, the tester said to the child, "*Ok, let's see how many of those shapes you remember. I am going to show you a card with four shapes. One of these shapes you saw before, but you have not seen the other three. They are 'pretending' to be the correct shape. Aren't they naughty? I want you to point to the one you think you saw before. That is the correct shape. Are you ready?*" The children were encouraged to point to the correct shape. When a clear indication of choice was made, the tester placed that card face down and presented the next one. If a child hesitated, or seemed reluctant to make a choice, the tester said, '*Just guess as quickly as you can.*' If a child perseverated, (defined here as choosing the same position on the laminated card more than 3 times in a row) the tester said, '*It's not always this side'* (indicating), '*It could be here, or here, or here'* (indicating).

A short run of procedures to be conducted at the Main Test, confirmed that the presentation of all 16 stimuli in a single run was overwhelming for the participants with LFA. It was decided, therefore, to present the target-cards in sets of four-at-a-time, rather than the entire 16 at once. Thus, all participants were shown just 4 of the 16 target-cards one-at-a-time for three to five seconds in a predetermined order and orientation. Each card was shown for approximately five seconds before being placed face down in a pile to the left of the tester.

When four cards had been presented (e.g., 1-2-3-4), the tester placed the first of the four corresponding target-foil-cards on the table (e.g., 1) and asked the child to point to the shape they had seen before (see Fig. 2-2).

A) The child is presented with this set of four cards, one-at-a-time, for 3-5s viewing time each.

Target-Card 1 **Target-Card 2** **Target-Card 3** **Target-Card** 4

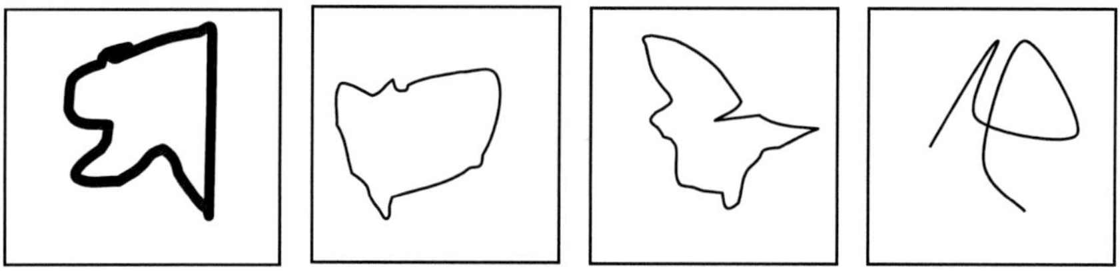

(B) The child is shown a target-foil card corresponding to target card 1 and is then asked to point to the shape they have seen before.

Target-Foil-Card 1

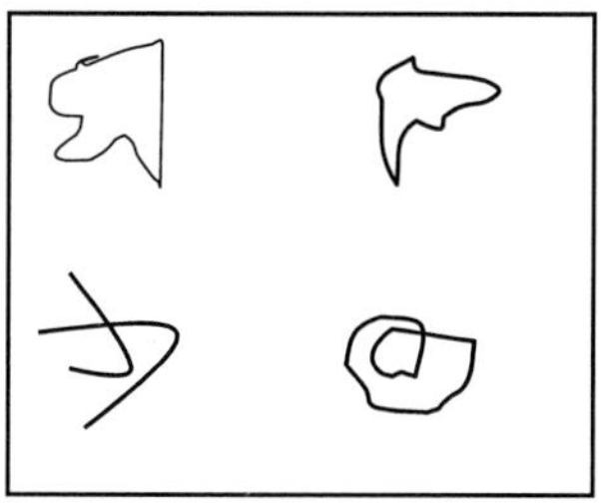

Fig. 2-2 A Diagram Showing the Procedure Followed During Study 1 (please note that Target-Card 1 and the shape in Target-Foil-Card 1 are shaded purely for the purpose of this example).

When the participant had responded, the target-foil-card was removed from the table and the next one (e.g., 2) was presented. If a child hesitated, or was reluctant to make a choice, the tester elicited a response by saying, "*Just guess as fast as you can.*" No child failed to make a choice in a timely fashion (i.e., a time-frame of five to ten seconds was decided on by the tester), and there were no instances in which a participant perseverated to a particular location.

In line with Mandler (2008: 04), familiarity is a, 'subjective response' and as such, a familiarity judgment should be a 'first response to an event and not dependent on subsequent search, recall or insights.' As this Test was one where the child must select the correct item from one of four abstract shapes presented, it was important to calculate the chance success level - or the proportion of correct answers - that could occur if all children were to guess randomly at the answer (Robson, 2002). For example, for a five-response option multiple-choice item, each child would have a 1 in 5 chance of getting the item correct by simply guessing. The chance success level for this item would be 20%. In knowing the chance success level for each item, it is possible to estimate the chance level raw scores for the Test – the range of scores that could have been achieved by randomly marking answers to each test item (Robson, 2002). This Test represented a four-response option multiple-choice item and, as such, the chance success level for this Test was calculated at 25%. On a pre-prepared score card, each correctly identified target-shape from the target-foil-card was awarded one point, and incorrect responses were not awarded any points. Scores ranged from 0 -16.

What We Found Out About Familiarity in Autism

Mean or average scores for the three groups on the Test of Familiarity are shown in Table 2-1. Floor effects (defined here as scoring 4 or less) occurred within the developmental-delay (DD) group, however all three groups scored significantly above chance on this task.

Table 2-1 Descriptive Statistics for the LFA and Comparison Groups: Study 1. A Test of Familiarity

	Study 1	**A Test of Familiarity**	
Characteristic	**LFA**	**DD**	**TD**
Maximum Score (20)			
n	30*	25*	33
M	11.4	12.8	15.2
SD	2.87	3.0	1.2
Range	9 - 16	8 - 16	12 - 16
Median	10	13	16
n at ceiling	7	9	23
n at chance	0	2	0
CA in years			
n	30	25	33
M	10.5	10.6	6.1
SD	3.1	2.9	0.7
Range	5.0-15.4	6.0-16.6	4.6-7.1
NVMA in years			
n	29**	24**	33
M	5.1	5.3	5.9
SD	1.6	1.7	0.4
Range	3.1-8.5	3.1-7.9	5.0-6.8
IQ			
n	29	24	33
M	50.32	53.88	97.84
SD	11.57	13.48	7.58
Range	24.3-85	26.5-76.2	82.3-114.2

MA/CA X 100 = IQ; * 3 children with LFA and 2 with DD were distressed at practice and therefore excluded from the Main Test; ** It was not possible to calculate the NVMA and therefore the IQ of 1 child with LFA and 1 child with DD via the BPVS.

A one-way between-groups analysis of variance (ANOVA) was conducted to investigate the effect of diagnosis on the children's scores. The effect sizes between the groups were calculated using Cohen's (1992) tables. The results of this Test showed that the effect of group (LFA/DD/TD) was significant F (2, 85) = 19.72, p = .0005. The difference in mean scores between the groups however was moderate, with the effect size calculated using eta squared at .31. Post-hoc comparisons using the Tukey honest-significant-difference (HSD) Test indicated that the mean scores for levels of Familiarity for participants with autism (m = 11.40, SD =3.02) differed significantly from both the participants with developmental delay (m = 12.8, SD = 3.0) and the young typically-developing children (m = 15.2, SD = 1.2).

A two-way ANOVA was conducted to explore the effect of gender on scores of familiarity across the three groups. There was no statistical significance for gender in relation to the children with autism or the TD group, although the mean difference in scores across males (m =14.0, SD = 3.0) and females (m = 11.3, SD = 2.4) for the participants with developmental delay was significant at the p = < .05 level on the Test of Familiarity: F (1, 23) = 5.5, p = .02. The effect size, calculated using eta squared was small at 0.1.

The relationship between IQ and scores on this Test in the LFA group was investigated using the Pearson product-moment correlation coefficient. There was a negligible, negative correlation between the two variables, r = -044, n = 32, p .81, with greater familiarity associated with lower IQ scores.

Finally, the three groups of participants were matched for NVMA scores and this score was significantly correlated with performance on the Test of Familiarity (r = .11, n = 87, p = < .29), yet entering NVMA score as a covariate did not affect the overall result.

Discussion

This first study involved conducting a relatively pure Test of Familiarity with participants diagnosed with low-functioning autism (LFA), an age and ability matched group of children and teenagers with developmental-delay (DD), and an ability matched group of young typically-developing (TD) schoolchildren. The Test involved showing the three groups of children 16 abstract shapes, which were used as target stimuli, and a forced-choice test consisting of three foils, which were very similar to the target stimuli (Bigham et al., 2010; Holdstock et al. 2002; Migo et al. 2009). To do well on this Test the participant must rely heavily on the feeling that they have seen the target stimuli before, as recollection of such meaningless images from study would be far too difficult (Holdstock et al., 2002). Some ceiling effects (scores of 16) and some floor effects (scores of 4 or less) occurred. No floor effects occurred in the group of children with LFA, indicating that this entire group understood the task required of them.

It could be argued that the children with autism performed moderately less well than controls in this Test, as a function of the chosen stimuli. As mentioned previously, Williams et al., (2006) previously argued that memory in autism is most impaired when stimuli are complex. The stimuli here were not simplistic, comprising of a range of abstract shapes, yet all 30 participants with low-functioning autism (LFA) performed above chance (scores of 4 or less), with 7 ($m = 3$; $f = 4$) scoring at ceiling (scores of 16) - only moderately less well than an age and ability matched group of participants with developmental delay. Moreover, a FCC format was used because it is established that when foils are very similar to targets the, 'mean difference in familiarity between targets and their similar foils will be small, relative to the overall level of variability in the familiarity for different targets' (Migo et al., 2009:e2; Yonelinas et al., 2010; Yonelinas, 2002). Using a FCC paradigm would have therefore advantaged the children with autism, as the strong covariance in the familiarity values primed by targets and their corresponding similar foils would result in target-shapes being 'reliably more familiar than their corresponding foils' (Migo et al., 2009: e2). On these grounds, it is argued, therefore, that the impaired performance of children with LFA on this task was not an artefact of the stimuli used.

Significantly, the results of this Test of Familiarity imply that not only is a sense of familiarity impaired in LFA - something that has not previously been tested via this particular forced choice paradigm - but that this impairment is specific to the children with LFA as opposed to children who are typically-developing and children who have developmental delay without autism. Therefore, the results are significant and consistent with predictions made by Bigham et al., (2010: 879).

Nevertheless, caution should be exercised when interpreting these results as the Test procedures used here were modified from original procedures set down by Bigham et al., (2010), where the performance of HFA children and teens (n =18; mean mental age 117 months) were compared to an ability matched TD (n = 29; mean mental age 110 months) cohort. Within the Bigham et al., (2010) study, one child from each group performed at ceiling, which prompted the researchers to suggest a recalibration of the paradigm for future use with participants of that age.

To this effect, a slight adaptation of the original procedures was made whereby the 16 target-shapes were shown in a series of 1-4 cards rather than in a sequence of 1-16. This recalibration possibly over-simplified the task for the TD children whilst also facilitating easier recall of the target stimuli in TD working memory (Craik & Lockhart, 1972). However, given the mean scores of children with LFA, and those with DD, in this study, any increase in the presentation rate would have negatively impacted upon these two groups, thus potentially inflating floor effects.

Gender differences were not reported in the study by Bigham et al., (2010), and, in this study, there were no significant differences in the mean scores of males and females in either the group with LFA, or the TD group. A large difference in mean scores for males and females was noted in the group with DD though, with females scoring significantly less well than their male counterparts. This finding merits further research in subsequent studies.

Previous research suggested that the similarity of the foils and target stimuli could be increased or decreased to recalibrate difficulty levels across experimental and control groups (Bigham et al., 2010). While logical in its approach, this alternative may once again disadvantage or advantage participants with learning difficulties and TD groups respectively. As such, it may not be possible to reconfigure this particular Test for use with typically-developing children and individuals with LFA simultaneously (even if matched for mental age).

Mandler (2008) suggested that familiarity is subjective and, as such, a familiarity response should be a first response only, free from any further attempts, which would likely involve recall of more intentional thinking. As such, only the first identification of a shape was recorded, and used, within the analysis of this study.

In sum, therefore, the findings of this Recognition Test suggest that familiarity is somewhat impaired in low-functioning autism relative to age-and-ability matched comparison groups. In terms of placing a recording of self-voice on a SGD, a deficit or impaired sense of familiarity may make this speech output option less relevant to these children. In terms of their ability to recognise self-voice on a speech-generating device as personally relevant therefore, this finding has quite serious implications.

Of course, recognition memory depends on recollection as well as familiarity (Atkinson & Juola, 1974; Jacoby, 1991; Mandler, 1980; Tulving, 1985; Yonelinas, 1994). As noted previously, recollection can be defined as a kind of recall in which a recognised stimulus (e.g., a voice on a SGD) cues recall of diverse types of contextual information (e.g., where that voice was heard last, what was said, and in what tone of voice) experienced within the episode in which the stimulus was initially encountered (Gardiner & Java, 1993; Tulving, 1985). While familiarity is thought to be dependent (at least in part) on intact function and connectivity of perirhinal and entorhinal MTL cortex (Aggleton & Brown, 2006; Montaldi, Spencer, Roberts, & Mayes, 2006), recollection is said to be dependent on intact hippocampal function and connectivity, and possibly also on intact function and connectivity of dorsolateral prefrontal cortex and other regions of the prefrontal cortex (Aggleton & Brown, 2006; Kirwan, Wixted, & Squire, 2008; Mayes, Montaldi, & Migo, 2007). Perhaps, therefore, even though familiarity is impaired in some children with LFA in this study, recollection might be intact.

Our Second Study: Testing Recollection in Low-Functioning Autism

In this study, we used a temporal source memory (TSM) recall task to measure recollection of contextual information in children with LFA. Their performance was compared with performance in a group of young TD children matched with the LFA group for NVMA, and an age matched group of children with DD also matched with the LFA group on NVMA.

A study of TSM is useful for separating out familiarity from recall as the child has to do more than just recall - whether they have encountered the item before (familiarity) and instead recollect contextual information, such as where the items were placed at test also (e.g., Boucher et al., 2012; Lind, 2010; Tulving, 2001).

This was a modification of an earlier temporal source memory (TSM) task used to assess recollection in relatively able adolescents with LFA (Bigham et al., 2010). One modification involved extending the singular trial, used by Bigham, to ten trials in an attempt to obtain more data, and the second involved allowing the children to handle the to-be-remembered items prior to testing, as this can enhance recall (e.g., Lind & Bowler, 2009).

Previous TSM tasks conducted with individuals with HFA (Bennetto et al., 1996) and LFA (Bigham et al., 2010) have found impaired performance. Based on these findings it was predicted that: (1) The children with LFA would be impaired relative to the TD children; (2) the children with LFA would be impaired relative to the children with DD; and (3) there would be a difference between the performance of the TD and DD groups.

What We Did and How We Did It

Participants

All 93 children were invited to participate in this study.

General Procedural Points

General procedural points were the same as those used in the first study, but this time the materials to be used included 12 everyday items (see Appendix D). These items were stored in a box, which was located on the desk to the left-hand side of the tester. Verbal input from the tester was restricted to 'well done' and 'good work' to ensure the child stayed on task. A pre-prepared score sheet was used to record correct scores, and children were praised on completion of the testing period.

What We Did, and the Procedures We Followed

Training materials: A series of pre-tests were given prior to the Main Test, and the materials for these comprised a strip of card with three rectangles drawn on it. This card had the words 'BEFORE' and 'AFTER' printed in the left and right hand rectangles, leaving the central rectangle empty. Also used were a 'Memory' board game (http://www.sesame street.org), and a set of plastic fridge magnet numbers. Finally, a glass paperweight was used for the third pre-test.

Test materials: For the TSM task twelve everyday objects, such as a spoon, a pencil topper, and a crayon were used (Appendix D). Also used was the before/after strip used at pre-test and a blue wooden cat.

General procedures: To ensure that children with LFA would not recognise the everyday items to be used at test less well than the comparison groups (i.e., they might experience a less strong sense of familiarity) it was decided that they would be allocated the items 48 hours prior to testing. It is also suggested that handling the to-be-remembered items can enhance recall at study (Lind & Bowler, 2009).

It was also considered important to ensure children's understanding of what we meant by 'before' and 'after.' A fun and yet educational way of reinforcing their current understanding of these words was to introduce the song 'After Me' - from the popular television show 'Sesame Street' - to the children's classrooms. To do this, several audio-visual copies of this song, stored on USB keys, were also given to teachers in the LFA classrooms (Appendix E). Teachers were encouraged to engage the children with the twelve everyday items frequently over the next 48 hours. Teaching staff also agreed to incorporate the '*After Me*' song in class throughout this period.

Three pre-tests were conducted before the Main Test, to ensure that all participants fully understood what was expected of them. The first Test took approximately five to eight minutes to administer and involved ensuring participants' general understanding of 'before' and 'after.' The second Test was devised to ensure participant understanding of a stimulus to be presented 'just before' and 'just after' an object, and took five to eight minutes approximately. Finally, practice in the actual procedure to be used in the Main Test was given to ensure fully that all participants understood what was expected of them. One child with LFA, called Nita, was unwell on the day of testing but the remaining 92 participants continued with this study.

Training Test 1: Understanding Before and After

The central aim of this Test was to ensure participant understanding of '*Before*' and '*After.*' A 'Sesame Street' board game (http://www.sesame street.org) was chosen as the best means by which to do so. For this game, a bowl of sand was placed in front of three small toys with a card placed in front of each toy. The first card had 'Before' printed on it, the second card had 'Between' printed on it and the third card came with the word 'After' printed on it (see Figure 2.3).

Fig. 2-3 An Example of the Materials Used at Pre-Test in the Test of Recollection

The first step involved the tester pointing to each card clearly saying the words, '*before, in between, and after.*' The tester then said, '*Look at this toy*' pointing to the toy nearest the bowl of sand, '*this toy will play in the sand BEFORE all the other toys.*' The tester then pointed clearly to the last toy saying, '*Look at this toy, this toy will play in the sand AFTER all the other toys.*' Finally, the tester pointed to the middle toy saying, '*And this toy is in between.*' Secondly, the toys were placed in the sand one-by-one by the tester as the tester said, *'Look, he got to go BEFORE the others. This one was in between. And look! This one went AFTER all the others.*'

The third step saw the tester place the toys back in a row at the bowl, making sure they all took different positions in the line. This was to ensure that the participant could see that the labels 'before' 'between' and 'after' did not apply to a specific toy, but rather to a position in the line.

The tester now said, '*Can you show me who will go BEFORE the other toys? Who is in between, and who will go AFTER all the other toys?*' Three practice runs were given, with prompting and support given on the first run if needed to ensure correct responding. Any child who failed on more than one response in each of the practice runs was considered unable to understand the procedure. All children passed this pre-test, which took between 5 and 8 minutes to complete.

Training Test 2: Understanding What Comes Immediately Before and Immediately After an Object

For this pre-test, a laminated strip of card with three rectangles printed on it was placed on the desk in front of, and facing, the child. The words BEFORE and AFTER were written on the left and right rectangles with the word BETWEEN in the central rectangle. The tester pointed to each word saying, *'Look, here are those words again! This is the word before, this is the word after, and this one says the word between.'*

A set of plastic fridge magnet numbers 1, 2, 3, 4, 5, 6, 7, 8, and 9 were placed approximately two inches apart along the middle of the desk, above the before-and-after strip. The tester proceeded to place the plastic (fridge magnet) number 5 in the central rectangle.

The tester pointed to the group of numbers 1-4 saying, '*Look, all these numbers come BEFORE the number 5!*' Then the tester pointed to the group of numbers 6-9 saying, '*And all these numbers come AFTER the number 5.*' The tester then picked up the number 4 and said clearly, '*However, THIS number comes JUST before the number 5.*' The tester then placed the number 4 slowly and deliberately on the rectangle of the laminated strip, printed with the word BEFORE. The tester proceeded to pick up the number 6 and slowly placed it on the rectangle of the laminated strip, printed with the word AFTER, saying, '*And this number comes JUST after the number 5.*'

After five seconds viewing time, the numbers 4, 5, and 6 were removed from the before-and-after strip and returned to their rightful place, amongst the numbers 1-9 located in the middle of the desk. The tester then said, *'Let's play again with different numbers. Will you help me this time?'* The number 5 was placed back on the central rectangle of the before-and-after strip, and the participant was prompted to pick up the number that comes just before (i.e., the number 4), and just after (i.e., the number 6), that number. Verbal praise was given to promote good response.

Next, the tester placed the number 2 on the centre of the before-and-after strip. The tester pointed to the number 1 (slightly separated from the numbers 3-9) saying, *'Oh look, this comes before the number 2.'* The tester pointed to the group of numbers 3-9 saying, *'And all these numbers come after the number 2.'* The tester then looked at the child and asked, *'Can you show me which number comes JUST before the number 2?'* The participant was encouraged to place the correct number (i.e., the number 1) on the rectangle of the laminated strip printed with the word BEFORE, but pointing, or a clear indication of choice, was considered acceptable. This procedure was repeated to encourage the child to place the correct number (i.e., the number 3) on the rectangle of the laminated strip with the word AFTER printed on it. Prompting was given if required.

Two further practice runs were given with no prompting on these occasions. Any child who failed to indicate either the number coming just before, or the number to come just after, the appointed number in each of the practice runs was deemed not to understand the Test and was thus excluded from the Main Test, however, all children passed this Test, which took approximately five to eight minutes to complete.

Training Test 3: Practice in the Procedure to be Used in the Main Test

Practice in the procedure to be employed in the Main Test was then conducted to ensure the participants full understanding of what was expected of them. Six of the twelve everyday items (see Appendix F) to be used as stimuli in the Main Test were used, plus a glass paperweight, and the laminated 'before and after' strip. The procedures, used at this juncture, were exactly as those outlined below for the Main Test. Participants were allocated three practice runs, with prompting given on the first run to facilitate errorless learning. When the child made 3 consecutively correct responses, it was considered appropriate to continue to the Testing phase. This Test took approximately eight to ten minutes. No participant failed this procedure.

Main Test

For the Main Test, the full set of 12 everyday objects was introduced to the child (Appendix D). The laminated before/after strip was also used for this Test. In addition, Dettmer, Simpson, Myles, and Ganz (2000) suggest the use of visual and auditory cues to signal transitions between activities in autism spectrum disorder and, on the foot of this, the glass paperweight - used at pre-test - was replaced with a blue wooden cat, and the tester said, *"I've got a whole lot of new things, different things, to show you. And somewhere amongst this lot, there will be a blue wooden cat! No glass paperweight this time, but a blue wooden cat instead. What you have to do is try to remember if you see the items before or after you see the blue wooden cat. Are you ready?"*

The items were placed one at a time on the table, with each being removed from sight before presentation of the next item. Each item was presented facing the child and in a predetermined order (Table 2-2). Also, because short-term memory is mediated primarily through auditory, or phonological, components (Baddeley, 1999), each item was named aloud by the tester as they were presented. The presentation of each item took approximately 3-5 seconds. The blue wooden cat was presented as item 10 in the first presentation, as item 8 in the second presentation, and as item 6 in the third (Table 2-2). The reason for moving the cat systematically across the trials was based on the finding that when people are tested on word lists, they typically show superior recall for the first and last words presented relative to words presented in the middle (Ebbinghaus, 1913; Murdock, 1962). This phenomena is known as the primacy and recency effect whereby performance in the primacy and middle regions of the serial position are thought to reflect long-term memory while performance in the recency region contain both short-term memory and long-term memory components (Craik, 1971). It was of interest to consider if participant recollection of the one item (which came before/after the wooden cat) was influenced by the number of other items (also presented before/after the wooden cat). It was also of interest to see if the child with LFA showed any recall advantage for items shown just before of just after the cat, relative to comparison groups of children. There was no retention interval, other than the time taken to give the Test instruction.

Table 2-2 The Order of Presentations over 10 Separate Trials: A Test of Recollection

	Item 1	***Item 2***	***Item 3***	***Item 4***	***Item 5***	***Item 6***	***Item 7***	***Item 8***	***Item 9***	***Item 10***	***Item 11***	***Item 12***	***Item 13***
Trial													
1	Comb	Pen	Crayon	Spoon	Cellotape	HLPen	Duck	Eraser	**Watch**	**XX**	Topper	USB	Candle
2	Comb	Pen	Crayon	Spoon	Cellotape	HLPen	Duck	**XX**	Eraser	Watch	Topper	USB	Candle
3	Comb	Pen	Crayon	Spoon	Cellotape	**XX**	HLPen	Duck	Eraser	Watch	Topper	USB	Candle
4	Comb	Pen	Crayon	**XX**	Spoon	Cellotape	HLPen	Duck	Eraser	Watch	Topper	USB	Candle
5	Comb	**Xx**	Pen	Crayon	Spoon	Cellotape	HLPen	Duck	Eraser	Watch	Topper	USB	Candle
6	Comb	Pen	**XX**	Crayon	Spoon	Cellotape	HLPen	Duck	Eraser	Watch	Topper	USB	Candle
7	Comb	Pen	Crayon	Spoon	**XX**	Cellotape	HLPen	Duck	Eraser	Watch	Topper	USB	Candle
8	Comb	Pen	Crayon	Spoon	Cellotape	HLPen	**XX**	Duck	Eraser	Watch	Topper	USB	Candle
9	Comb	Pen	Crayon	Spoon	Cellotape	HLPen	Duck	Eraser	**XX**	Watch	Topper	USB	Candle
10	Comb	Pen	Crayon	Spoon	Cellotape	HLPen	Duck	Eraser	Watch	Topper	**XX**	USB	Candle

XX represents the wooden cat

Procedures: On completion of each trial, the before/after strip was placed centrally on the table and the blue wooden cat placed in the central rectangle of the strip. The tester said, *"Let's see if you can remember which item you saw before the wooden cat, and which you saw after the wooden cat. Are you ready?"* In order that the child's working memory is not over-loaded (Miller, 1956), just six of the twelve items were placed back on the table and the child was asked to indicate the item that they thought had come just before the wooden cat. The six items always included the two items, which had been presented just before and just after the blue cat, and all six were presented together on the table in front of the child about two inches apart from each other.

The children were encouraged to place the items onto the before/after strip, but if unwilling to do this, pointing - or a clear indication of a choice - was accepted, and the tester placed the object to the side indicated by the child. If the child made a correct choice, a score of 1 was awarded. If the child made an incorrect judgement, the tester picked up the correct item and placed it on the strip saying, "*I think it must be this one,*" and a score of 0 was awarded. This procedure was then repeated for the child to choose the item, which had been presented after the blue wooden cat. If a child hesitated, or seemed reluctant to make a choice, they were encouraged to make a response, the Tester saying, *"Just guess, quick as you can."*

A pre-prepared scoring cared was used at test. This consisted of 10 lines with two circles on each line. The circle to the left was marked with a B for 'before' and the circle to the right was marked with an A for 'after'. If the child chose the item that had been presented before the cat, the circle with B was crossed off, and if the child chose the item that came after the cat, the circle with the A was crossed off.

The format of this Test meant that the child was firstly tasked with selecting one correct item (i.e., before item) from a set of six items presented together, and then tasked with selecting one correct item (i.e., after item) from the remaining set of five items, which were also presented together. For the former task, the child had a one in six chance of getting the answer right by just guessing, therefore the chance success level for this item would be 33%. For the latter task, the child had a one in five chance of guessing the right answer and, as such, the chance success level for this item would be 20%. There was no retention level other than time allocated to test instructions. Participants scored 1 point for any of the just BEFORE, and 1 point for any of the just AFTER, items correctly noted with a chance-level raw score of 2.

What We Found Out About Recollection in Autism

Two hypotheses were made in this section: (1) That participants with LFA would likely be impaired relative to both the children with DD and the TD children, in relation to their recall of contextual information; and (2) that participants with LFA would be impaired in recalling the sequencing of items shown just before and just after a target stimulus. It was also predicted that there would be a difference between TD and DD groups on this Test, with TD children performing better than children with DD.

Mean scores for each of the three groups in Study 2 are shown in Table 2-3. One child with LFA, called Nita, was unwell on the day of testing. Some ceiling effects (scores of 20) and some floor effects (scores at chance, defined as 2 or below) were noted. Despite one child with LFA scoring at chance, all three groups scored significantly above chance on this task.

Table 2-3 Descriptive Statistics for the LFA and Comparison Groups: Study 2 A Test of Recollection

	Study 2	**Test of Recollection**	
Characteristic	**LFA**	**DD**	**TD**
Maximum Score (20)			
n	32*	27	33
M	10.7	16.2	17.9
SD	5.0	2.7	1.7
Range	2-20	10-20	14-20
Median	10	16	18
n at ceiling	2	5	10
n at chance	1	0	0
CA in years			
n	32*	27	33
M	10.5	10.6	6.1
SD	3.1	2.9	0.7
Range	5-15	6-16	4 -7
NVMA in years			
n	32**	27	33

M	5.0	5.3	5.9
SD	1.5	1.6	0.4
Range	3-8	3-7	5.0-6.8
IQ			
n	32**	27	33
M	50.	54.9	97.8
SD	11.3	15.4	7.5
Range	24.3-85.	26.5-93.8	82.3-114.2

MA/CA X 100 = IQ; *1 child with LFA (Nita) did not participate on the day of testing; ** It was not possible to calculate the NVMA of 1 child with DD via the BPVS making it impossible to subsequently calculate his IQ.

None of the measures, on which the children were matched (CA, NVMA), correlated significantly with performance on this TSM task and, therefore, none of these measures were entered as covariates - following the guidelines set down by Miller and Chapman (2001). In addition, a Pearson product-moment correlation coefficient analysis revealed a very small, negative correlation between IQ and scores on this Test by the LFA group, $r = -.27$, $n = 33$, $p = .121$, with higher recollection associated with lower IQ scores.

A one-way analysis of variance was conducted to investigate group differences (LFA, DD, and TD) on the TSM task. The effect of the group was significant, $F\,(2, 90) = 39.2$, $p = .0005$. The effect size calculated using eta squared was large at 0.46. Post hoc comparisons using the Tukey Test indicated that the mean score for the children with LFA (m = 10.7, SD = 4.9) was significantly different from the DD group (m =16.2, SD = 2.7), and the TD group (m = 17.9, SD = 1.7), supporting prediction one.

Next, a paired-samples t-test was conducted to evaluate the children's recollection of items presented just before the wooden cat as opposed to those presented just after the cat.

Table 2-4 Descriptive Statistics for the LFA and Comparison Groups: Recalling Items Presented before versus after the wooden cat

Characteristic	LFA	DD	TD
Max score 10			
n	32*	27	33
Before Scores			
M	3.36	7.66	9.03
SD	3.30	2.1	1.35
After Scores			
M	7.30	8.55	8.93
SD	2.6	1.9	1.32
Mean decrease between conditions	**-3.9**	**-.88**	**.09**
Eta square statistic	-0.7	-0.1	.001

***1 child with LFA (Nita) did not participate on the day of testing**

A one-way ANOVA was conducted to explore the effect of the group (LFA, DD, and TD) for recollection of items presented after the wooden cat. There was a statistically significant difference for the three groups: F (2, 90) = 5.72, p = .003 but the actual difference in mean scores, calculated using eta squared, was small at .01. Post hoc comparisons using the Tukey Test indicated that the mean score for the children with LFA (m = 7.30, SD = 2.6) was significantly different from the TD children (m= 8.93, SD = 1.3). The children with DD (m = 8.55, SD = 1.9) did not differ significantly from either the children with autism or the TD children.

In terms of the effect of the group on the children's recall for items presented before the wooden cat, there was a statistically significant difference for the three groups: F (2, 90) = 48.62, p = .0005. The difference in mean scores between the groups, calculated using eta squared, was 0.5. Post hoc comparisons using the Tukey Test indicated that the mean score for the children with LFA (m = 3.36, SD = 3.3) was significantly different from the children with DD (m= 7.6, SD = 2.1) and the TD children (m = 9.0, SD = 1.3).

Six of the 12 everyday items used at Main Test had been used at pre-test, and it was important to consider if this procedure influenced participant recall at Main Test. Over the 10 trials, the children saw the watch, the duck, the tape, the crayon, the comb, the pen, the spoon, the highlighter pen, the eraser, and the topper, presented '*just before*' the blue wooden cat. Of these ten items, the children had seen - and handled - (1) the highlighter pen, (2) the spoon, (3) the crayon, (4) the tape, and (5) the comb, previously. A paired-samples t-test showed a statistically significantly greater recall of these 5 items (m = 3.35, SD = 1.82) than for the 5 items encountered at Main Test (m = 2.68, SD = 1.49), t (92) = 6.78, p <. 0005. The mean decrease between the two conditions was .66 with a 95% CI ranging from .47 to .86. The eta squared statistic was 0.3.

Over the 10 trials the children saw the watch, the duck, the tape, the crayon, the comb, the pen, the spoon, the highlighter pen, the eraser, and the topper, presented as the item '*just after*' the wooden blue cat. Of these, the children had seen - and handled - (1) the highlighter pen, (2) the spoon, (3) the crayon, (4) the tape, and (5) the comb, previously. A paired-sample t-test showed a statistically significantly greater recall for these five items (m = 5.10, SD = 1.57) than for the 5 items encountered at Main Test (m = 3.90, SD = 1.31) t (92), p = .0003. The mean decrease between the two conditions was -1.20 with a 95% CI ranging from -1.50 to -.90. The eta squared statistic was -0.2.

Recollection of 'Before-Items' by Group

We have established that over the course of the 10 trials the children saw 10/12 everyday items as being the item presented 'just before' the wooden cat. We have also established that participant recall of these ten items was enhanced for five of the items with which they had encountered at a pre-test phase. To investigate the impact of the group (LFA, DD, and TD) on the children's recollection - of those 5 items they had seen at pre-test, as opposed to those encountered at the Main Test - a one-way ANOVA was conducted. This showed that there was a statistically significant difference for the three groups: F (2, 90) = 45.2, p = .0005. The difference in mean scores, calculated using eta squared, was large at 0.5. Post hoc comparison, using the Tukey HSD, indicated that the mean score of the children with LFA (m = 3.06, SD = 3.1) was significantly different from both the children with DD (m = 7.11, SD = 1.96) and the TD children (m = 8.15, SD = 1.17).

Recollection of the 'After-Items' by Group

We have also established that, over the course of the 10 trials, the children saw 10/12 everyday items as being the item presented 'just after' the wooden cat. We know that participant recall of these ten items was enhanced for five of the items with which they had encountered at a pre-test phase. To investigate the impact of the group (LFA, DD, and TD) on the children's recollection - of those 5 items they had seen at pre-test as opposed to those encountered at the Main Test - a one-way ANOVA was conducted. This showed that there was a statistically significant difference for the three groups: F (2, 90) = 6.35, p = .003. The difference in mean scores, calculated using eta squared, was small at 0.1. Post hoc comparison using the Tukey HSD indicated that the mean score of the children with LFA (m = 7.84, SD = 3.0) was significantly different from both the children with DD (m = 9.44, SD = 2.18) and the TD children (m = 9.81, SD = 1.55).

The Effect of the Classroom on LFA Recollection

A one-way ANOVA was conducted to consider whether attending different classrooms made a difference - whereby familiarisation with the 12 everyday items to be recalled at test, or the teacher's presentation of the 'After Me' song (http://www.sesamestreet.org) - may have influenced the recollection scores of the children with LFA. This showed that there was no statistically significant effect for classroom change on the children's scores: F (4, 27), = 1.26, p = 0.3.

Table 2-5 Descriptive Statistics for the LFA and Comparison Groups: Test 1 and 2

No	LFA name	Sex	CA yrs.	NVMA yrs.	IQ	T1	T2	DD name	Sex	CA yrs.	NVMA yrs	IQ	T1	T2	TD name	Sex	CA yrs	NVMA yrs	IQ	T1	T2
1	*Frank*	**M**	**7.4**	**5.0**	**67.4**	**15**	**12**	*34*	F	15.5	7.9	51.0	12	20	*61*	*M*	*4.9*	*5.0*	*101.6*	14	18
2	*Jim*	**M**	**11.4**	**4.8**	**42.3**		**19**	*35*	F	14.0	5.8	52.2	13	16	*62*	*F*	*4.6*	*5.3*	*114.2*	14	18
3	*Peter*	**M**	**6.5**	**3.8**	**58.2**		**16**	*36*	F	11.8	7.0	59.8	10	16	*63*	*M*	*4.7*	*5.1*	*108.7*	12	17
4	*Edward*	**M**	**9.5**	**3.7**	**39.8**	**10**	**17**	*37*	F	12.1			8	15	*64*	*F*	*6.0*	*6.2*	*104.0*	16	20
5	*Rachel*	**F**	**5.0**	**4.2**	**85.0**	**9**	**10**	*38*	M	12.0	5.5	45.8	16	20	*65*	*M*	*6.5*	*5.8*	*106.0*	16	18
6	*Jake*	**M**	**7.2**	**3.1**	**43.6**	**12**	**15**	*39*	M	12.6	5.3	42.1	8	20	*66*	*F*	*7.0*	*6.0*	*85.7*	16	20
7	*Francis*	**M**	**10.5**	**5.5**	**51.9**	**10**	**10**	*40*	F	12.4	5.6	45.6	11	20	*67*	*F*	*7.0*	*5.8*	*82.3*	12	16
8	*Jason*	**M**	**6.5**	**3.2**	**50.0**	**11**	**12**	*41*	M	15.2	4.2	27.8	12	15	*68*	*F*	*6.2*	*5.8*	*93.3*	14	16
9	*Linda*	**F**	**14.3**	**7.8**	**54.6**	**16**	**8**	*42*	M	16.6	4.4	26.5	16	17	*69*	*M*	*6.3*	*5.8*	*92.1*	16	17
10	*Anthony*	**M**	**13.8**	**5.5**	**40.3**		**7**	*43*	M	12.0	7.5	62.7	16	16	*70*	*M*	*6.2*	*6.5*	*104.0*	16	16
11	*Tim*	**M**	**11.5**	**5.3**	**46.0**	**9**	**20**	*44*	M	13.1	5.0	37.9	16	16	*71*	*M*	*6.5*	*6.1*	*93.6*	16	18
12	*Alan*	**M**	**6.5**	**3.1**	**43.6**	**9**	**8**	*45*	F	12.2	5.0	40.8	14	17	*72*	*F*	*5.7*	*5.8*	*101.0*	16	19
13	*Brendan*	**M**	**10.7**	**5.9**	**55.0**	**9**	**8**	*46*	M	10.5	4.9	46.4	16	18	*73*	*M*	*6.5*	*6.2*	*96.1*	16	18
14	*Paddy*	**M**	**11.5**	**5.8**	**50.3**	**10**	**5**	*47*	F	8.6	5.5	64.4	14	15	*74*	*M*	*5.6*	*5.8*	*102.0*	16	20
15	*Ida*	**F**	**12.4**	**4.2**	**34.2**	**10**	**4**	*48*	F	9.4	6.1	65.4	15	14	*75*	*M*	*5.4*	*5.6*	*104.0*	16	17
16	*Richard*	**M**	**12.8**	**5.1**	**40.2**	**9**	**12**	*49*	M	8.9	6.1	69.1	16	15	*76*	*F*	*6.1*	*6.1*	*100.0*	14	16
17	*Robbie*	**M**	**14.0**			**16**	**8**	*50*	F	8.2	6.1	74.7	10	11	*77*	*F*	*5.6*	*5.8*	*102.9*	16	18
18	*Ann*	**F**	**13.4**	**7.9**	**59.0**	**9**	**9**	*51*	M	8.1	5.5	68.3	16	16	*78*	*M*	*7.0*	*6.2*	*88.2*	16	20
19	*Nita*	**F**	**13.2**	**8.5**	**64.7**	**16**		*52*	F	7.5	4.9	65.5	10	19	*79*	*M*	*6'0*	*5.8*	*97.2*	16	15

20	Lucy	F	10.6	4.9	46.0	9	8	53	M	6.5	3.7	57.6	16	20	80	M	5.5	5.6	101.0	16	16
21	Maggie	F	11.9	7.1	60.1	10	12	54	M	6.6	3.1	47.5	9	16	81	M	5.1	5.4	104.0	16	14
22	Bob	M	15.4	3.7	24.3	16	16	55	M	7.1	5.3	74.4		13	82	M	5.8	5.8	100.0	16	17
23	John	M	8.0	5.1	63.9	12	9	56	M	8.0	7.5	93.8	16	17	83	M	5.9	5.8	98.5	14	20
24	Mark	M	15.0	6.1	40.8	16	11	57	F	8.0	6.1	76.2	10	18	84	F	6'8	6.0	87.8	16	20
25	Rebecca	F	6.3	3.1	50.0	11	9	58	M	6.0	3.1	52.0	10	11	85	F	7.0	6.0	86.4	16	18
26	Dermot	M	6.1	3.2	52.7	9	11	59	M	12.2	7.5	61.9	13	12	86	F	7.0	5.8	84.7	16	18
27	Fiona	F	6.6	3.1	47.5	9	16	60	M	12.3	5.0	40.5		16	87	F	6.2	6.2	100.0	16	15
28	Kevin	M	13.5	7.9	58.2	9	10								88	M	6.6	6.5	108.7	16	20
29	Sandra	F	10.7	5.9	55.0	16	6								89	M	6.8	6.2	91.4	16	20
30	Paul	M	8.0	3.7	46.3	10	16								90	M	6.6	6.5	97.5	15	20
31	David	M	15.3	6.1	40.2	10	8								91	M	6.8	6.5	95.1	14	19
32	Ger	M	8.1	3.7	45.9	9	2								92	F	7.1	6.8	95.3	16	10
33	Connie	F	11.3	4.9	43.3	16	20								93	F	5.2	5.3	101.5	12	19
				Maximum	Scores	7	2						9	5						23	9

LFA refers to Low-Functioning Autism; DD refers to Developmental-Delay; TD refers to Typically-Developing; CA refers to chronological age; NVMA refers to non-verbal mental age; IQ is calculated via MA/CA X 100; T1-5 refers to Tests 1-5 whereby T1=Test of Familiarity; T2 =Test of Recollection

Discussion

This second study involved conducting a temporal source memory (TSM) recall task with participants diagnosed with low-functioning autism (LFA), an age and ability matched group of children and teenagers with developmental delay, and an ability matched group of young typically-developing schoolchildren. Recollection was assessed across a series of ten trials in which participants had to recall which of sixteen everyday items had been presented '*just before*' a blue wooden cat and the item which had been presented '*just after*' the blue wooden cat.

The overall results of the TSM recall task are interesting and important as it appears that memory for temporal contextual information is not only impaired in LFA, but that the impaired sense of recollection is also *specific* to LFA. Because the two measures on which children were matched (CA/NVMA) were not correlated with performance on this task; it is also possible to suggest that the impaired performance by the children with LFA was not a function of their age or ability, but rather a consequence of impaired recollection in this instance. The results of this study are consistent with previous studies showing impaired recollection in children and adolescents with low-functioning autism (Bigham et al., 2010).

The fact that the participants attended a range of schools and classrooms in this study is another methodological concern when interpreting the results. It could be argued that the teachers in the ASD classrooms may have played the '*After Me*' song differentially across all five classrooms, catering only for students with autism. Equally it could be argued that the ASD classrooms were hugely advantaged over the DD and TD classrooms due to the time the pupils with LFA had with items to be used at test, and the exposure to the song '*After Me.*' In relation to these two issues, it may be wise to allocate the 12 everyday items and copies of the '*After Me*' song to all participants equitably. However, this may cause ceiling effects in more able participants.

Nonetheless, it is noteworthy that performance on the TSM task in this study *did not* increase in the LFA classrooms as opposed to the DD or TD classes. Nor was there any effect noted across classes teaching students with autism only, implying that enhanced exposure to the '*After Me*' song, and the 12 everyday items to be used at test, failed to increase overall scores of recollection for this group.

It was further noted on this TSM recall task that participants with LFA demonstrated significantly better recall for items presented '*just after*' the blue cat than those presented '*just before*' the cat. This effect was specific to the LFA group as opposed to the participants with developmental delay and the young typically-developing children. Before concluding that participants with LFA have an uneven or atypical strategy for recall, it could be argued that as participants really only had to concentrate on recalling two of the entire set items presented on each trial (i.e., the item '*just before*' and the item '*just after*' the blue cat), the DD and TD group may have used verbal mediation during the study phase ('comb' before, and 'crayon' after), which contributed to their more even recall of items encountered before and after the cat.

This is a reasonable argument given that the literature does suggest that typically-developing (TD) children are capable of storing visually presented material in memory, via verbal mediation, from the age of four (Alegria & Pignot, 1979). Yet, less than 30% (i.e., 9) of the TD children scored at ceiling in this task, with less than 20% (i.e., 5) of the DD group demonstrating maximum scores. Further, all children were matched on NVMA in this research affording all participants with equal ability to use verbal mediation strategies.

This research argues therefore that the poor recall of items '*just before*' the blue cat, in the LFA group, may reflect an impoverished serial position effect in this particular group (Boucher, 1978, 1981; O'Conner & Hermelin, 1967; Toichi & Kamio, 2003). Serial position effect refers to the finding that recollection accuracy varies as a function of an item's position within a study list (see Toichi & Kamio, 2003). When asked to recall a list of items in any order (free recall), participants tend to begin recall with the end of the list, recalling those items best (the recency effect; see Toichi & Kamio, 2003). Among earlier list items, the first few items are recalled more frequently than the middle items (the primacy effect). Moreover, recall of items encountered earlier in the test may be considered more indicative of greater use of long term memory (Craik, 1971), while recall of items encountered later in the test may reflect greater use of short-term memory (STM) systems. Could this observation imply that participants with LFA in this research suffer from impoverished ability to store and retrieve information from LTM?

Further evidence for this argument rests in the fact that the set of everyday items used in this TSM recall task were all clearly named aloud by the researcher at test, and research suggests that the short-term memory (STM) is mediated mainly through auditory or phonological components. LTM, on the other hand, is mediated primarily through semantic components (Baddeley, 2002) and as we have seen, the participants with LFA in this study have shown impairments in areas subserved by short term memory (familiarity and automatic consciousness), but not to the extent that their long term memory (source memory and controlled thinking) appears to be impaired in the present study.

Furthermore, and in a related argument, the participants with LFA within this study may have a specific deficit in time-related thinking (Boucher, Pons, Lind, & Williams, 2007). Pons and Montangero (1999) suggest that time-related thinking is a particular skill *independent* of other skills typically considered as indictors of intelligence (Bigham et al., 2010). As such, and in line with previous observations by Bigham et al., (2010), the low scores in overall recollection - demonstrated by the LFA group in this study - may be more reflective of a specific impoverishment in temporal information processing than a specific impairment of recollection. Finally, any suggestion that the high floor effect, in the LFA group, resulted from failure to understand the task is unlikely given that all 33 children and adolescents with autism passed the series of pre-tests, designed to ensure participant understanding prior to undertaking the Main Test.

A significant limitation to this Test is that errors were not recorded. In hindsight, it would not only have been of interest to see whether children who were asked to choose the item they remembered as coming before or after the blue cat , while not choosing the ones that were 'directly' before or after, still chose one that had been presented prior to or after the blue cat. Future research should consider modifying the scoring card to take note of this valuable information.

General Discussion: Studies of Recollection and Familiarity in Low-Functioning Autism

There is increasing consensus that recognition memory is underpinned by two separate, but interrelated, processes, namely recollection and familiarity (e.g., Atkinson & Juola, 1974; Jacoby, 1991; Joseph et al., 2005; Mandler, 1980; Migo et al., 2012; Yonelinas et al., 2010). Recently, it was proposed that a combination of impaired recollection with spared familiarity 'fits well with the uneven profile memory' often associated with high-functioning autism (HFA) (Bigham et al., 2010: 879). Additionally, it has been suggested that impaired recollection is consistent with impaired performance on test of episodic memory, and that spared familiarity is consistent with good recognition memory in individuals with HFA (Bigham et al., 2010).

These findings led Yonelinas et al., (2010: e1) to suggest that the hippocampus is particularly important for recollection, while familiarity appears to depend on regions outside the hippocampus and 'reflects a by-product of repeated neural processing.' This is consistent with findings of relatively impaired episodic memory in HFA (an aspect of memory known to be supported by hippocampal brain regions), leaving semantic memory (an area of memory supported by extra-hippocampal rhinal and temporal cortex) spared in HFA (see Aggleton and Brown, 2006).

Very little research has been conducted with children with LFA in terms of recognition memory (Bigham et al., 2010; Boucher et al., 2012). It has been predicted, however, that while recollection is somewhat impaired in individuals with HFA - leaving familiarity intact (Joseph et al., 2005) - both recollection and familiarity are impaired in individuals with LFA (Bigham et al., 2010).

The present study tested recollection and familiarity separately in 33 children and adolescents with LFA, an ability matched group of 27 young typically-developing schoolchildren, and an age and ability matched group of 33 children with learning difficulties. Results support the predictions of both Bigham and Joseph, showing that both recollection and familiarity are impaired in children with LFA relative to controls. Nevertheless, wide variation occurred across the scores of the children with autism in this study and this merits further discussion.

In line with the dual-process single-detection (DPSD) model (Yonelinas, 1994; Yonelinas et al., 2010), familiarity is assumed to reflect a 'signal detection process' or a process whereby all items have some familiarity value, 'but items that have been recently studied are, on average, more familiar than those that were not studied' (Yonelinas et al., 2010: e2). It is not reliant on the hippocampus, or episodic memory, instead familiarity reflects a 'by-product of repeated neural processing' (Yonelinas, 2001, 2002; Yonelinas et al., 2010: e2). Familiarity also appears to be supported by semantic memory. This is important, as semantic memory is characterised by noetic (knowing) rather than autonoetic (self-knowing) awareness (Lind, 2010; Tulving, 1985). It follows therefore that familiarity is best associated with noetic awareness in the child with autism (see Lind, 2010) and noetic awareness means that the child need only involve re-experiencing the 'self' as the object of experience (i.e., the 'I') when retrieving information at test.

This means that 7 of the 33 children with autism, in this study, show evidence of a spared non-autobiographical memory. In line with the theories of Lind (2010) therefore, these seven children likely possess a rudimentary self-concept and, as such, the foundations necessary to encode self-relevant, autobiographical episodic memory. This speculative observation of a spared basic self-concept in autism may seem at odds with research stating that 'individuals with ASD have self-concepts...

which are impoverished, relative to individuals without autism' (see Lind, 2010: 450). In general, research suggests that any deficits in self-concept in ASD are confined to psychological domains rather than the physical domains (Lind, 2010). These seven children may be able to hold a particular type of belief about the 'self' (e.g., I am a girl, I have two hands and two feet, I am sleepy), while simultaneously experiencing difficulties with other aspects, with 'the me,' or the psychological aspects (e.g., the *voice* I am hearing on that SGD is me). Significantly, and in line with Mandler (1980), the child with LFA may experience 'recognition by familiarity' but not 'identification by recollection.' If correct, this would have implications for the recording of a child's own voice onto a SGD (see van Santen & Black, 2009).

Recollection was also tested. There are a number of different theories, which distinguish between recollection and familiarity, but typically recollection is thought to reflect more effortful and intentional processing (Jacoby, 1991), a longer latency (Atkinson & Juola, 1974; Jacoby, 1991; Mandler, 1980), and a more autonoetic sense of awareness (see Gardiner, 2008; Lind, 2010) than that of familiarity. Recollection is thought to be heavily reliant on the hippocampus and therefore, the episodic memory systems (Joseph et al., 2005).

When asked at test to recall which of 12 everyday items that had been presented at study, the children - in this study - were tasked with mentally representing and being aware of their 'continued existence across subjective time' (Lind, 2010: 421). Their recall of what they saw at test was thus dependent on their ability to have a self-concept at the point of encoding, and their ability to re-experience the 'self' as the object of experience (e.g., the 'me') at retrieval (Lind, 2010).

The results showed that while ten TD children and five children with developmental delay achieved maximum scores in a TSM task in this study, just two with LFA managed to do so. One of the children with autism - Connie, who was aged 11 years and 3 months at the time of testing with an NVMA of 4 years and 9 months on the BPVS (Dunn et al., 1997) - had also scored at ceiling on the Test of Familiarity.

Depending on the dual-process model consulted, it is possible to infer that the children with LFA are, on average, less likely than either age and ability matched children with DD, or ability matched young TD children, to pay attention at the point of encoding, and this lack of deep processing (LOP; Craik & Lockhart, 1972) makes their recall less viable at the point of retrieval (Jacoby, 1991). Alternatively, they may be able to draw on quantitative information about an event, but not on sufficient qualitative information, such as is required to achieve full recollection (Yonelinas,

2001, 2002). Perhaps some of the children in the TD and DD groups were making arbitrary associations between the two items to be remembered on each trial, which would have enhanced their familiarity and recollection (Mayes, 2007), but that this was not a strategy employed by the child with autism. One other inference is that a number of children with LFA, in this case, have diminished higher-order awareness of psychological aspects of 'self' (Lind, 2010). In particular, they may be less able than others to understand their place in, and continued existence through, time (Povinelli, 2001). According to Lind (2010: 433), it is here that the 'bi-directional relationship between memory and the 'self' becomes apparent.' In other words, if the child with LFA struggles to understand that the 'self' encompasses representations of present, past, and future states of 'self,' their episodic memories may be at least impoverished, if not impaired. In any event, it does appear that only two children from the LFA group managed to achieve maximum scores on this task, with Connie - the only participant with autism - to obtain full scores on both the Test of Familiarity and Recollection.

Taken together, the children's scores on the Test of Familiarity, and the Test of Recollection, conducted here indicate that children with LFA are impaired in terms of their recognition memory, relative to other children. This finding raises concern about the likelihood of a SGD with a personalised voice having the ability to create a sense of owness for any communications in that child (see van Santen & Black, 2009). If the child cannot recognise the voice programmed onto the device as that of their own, why would they be motivated to communicate more via that voice over any other speech output option available to them? Yet, some children tested in this regard performed at ceiling on both tests, which not only reflects the heterogeneous nature of autism generally, it also suggests that at least some of these children show the potential to recognise a recording of their own voice on a personalised SGD. To consider this in more detail, the next chapter will present and review the literature on voice recognition in autism spectrum disorder.

CHAPTER THREE

VOICE AND AUTISM

Perhaps no sound in our auditory environment is as important as the human voice. It is the sound that we devote most of our time listening to every day, whether in face-to-face interaction or over different media, such as phone, television, radio, or Skype (Belin et al., 2004). When we attend to speakers, we do not 'simply' listen to the content of their speech, we utilise a host of processing strategies to analyse the wealth of paralinguistic information transmitted in their voices. Much like reading a face, we read the voice for biological (age, gender, ethnicity) and linguistic (pitch, tone, affect) cues, which allow us to recognise others and their emotional states. Even in the absence of actual speech, for instance, a squeal or a shout - through a wall or from a distance - most adults can decipher whether they are sounds of alarm or sounds of joy, and are able to identify which sounds are those of their children, regardless of how many other children are present (see Belin et al., 2004). Voices are unique markers of identity. No two children ever sound the same and no two utterances from the same child will ever be identical (Ambridge & Lieven, 2011). It is easy to appreciate, therefore, the rationale for placing a natural voice, more like that of the child, on a speech generating device for the child with autism (see Van Santen & Black, 2009).

Overview

This chapter examines the range of developing abilities involved in perceiving paralinguistic information carried on the human voice. It reveals how recognition of familiar voices differs qualitatively from the ways unfamiliar voice and our own recorded voice is recognised across the lifespan (Bartholomeus, 1973; Mann et al., 1979; Rosa et al. 2008). The aim is to show how different factors, such as memory, age, gender, maturation, and diagnosis, affect how voice is perceived. The point thereafter is to explore the relation between recording a voice on a SGD and its meaning for the child with low-functioning autism.

Defining Voice

Voice is old. Speech appeared relatively recently in evolution as a 'particularly complex and abstract use of voice by the human species' (Fitch, 2000; Hauser, 1996). Vocalisations were prominent in the auditory environments of vertebrates for 'millions of years before speech emerged' (Fitch, 2000: 258). The ability to decode accurately the information contained in conspecific vocalisations had great importance for survival (Fitch, 2000). This ability is retained by a number of social and territorial creatures today, and by the typical human being (Perrachione, Del Tofu, & Gabrieli, 2011).

Voice is the result of a source in the larynx filtered by the supra-laryngeal vocal tract (Belin et al., 2004; Fitch, 2000). The chest, throat, tongue, lips, and weight, all affect the sound quality of a person's voice (Cavarero, 2005). Minute inter-and-intra-individual variations around those structures mean that each voice is as different as each being that sends their vocalisations into the air. It is directly influenced by age, gender, culture and vocal habits (Spence, Rollins, & Jerger, 2002). No two people ever sound the same, and no two utterances by the same person are ever identical (Ambridge & Lieven, 2011). This has led Cavarero (2005: 173) to propose that voice 'manifests the unique being of each human being.'

Given this 'particularity' of voice, it might appear a relatively simple task to recognise a person on the basis of hearing their voice alone. Yet, a body of research suggests that the ability to recognise individual conspecific as a result of their vocalisations is a non-trivial process, and one influenced by a listener's age, gender, and diagnosis (Bartholomeus, 1973; Mann et al., 1979). On foot of a paucity of research, little is known about the abilities involved in perceiving voices, but there is reason to believe that different types of vocal information are processed in 'partially dissociated pathways' (Belin et al., 2004: 129; Belin et al., 2011). There are three different types of vocal information, namely: speech information, identity information, and affective information (Belin et al., 2004, 2011).

In relation to identity information, the voice is directly influenced by *static* factors, such as age and gender, and also by *dynamic* factors, such as patterns of pronunciation, which can be specific to a region or to a person (Belin et al., 2004). The average human can typically decipher the gender (Belin et al., 2004) and the approximate age (Belin et al., 2004; Hartman & Danahuer, 1976) of a speaker, even in the absence of speech sounds. The ability to accurately recognise other identity markers, such as height, weight, and ethnic background, from voice is also reported, but with less empirical evidence to support it conclusively (Belin et al., 2004, 2011).

Voice is also rich in pitch, tone, and rhythm, allowing those listening to identify our emotional status (Belin et al., 2004). Laughs, screams, whispers, and roars, contain rich affective information and 'can be viewed as the auditory equivalent of facial emotional expressions that typically accompany them' (Belin et al., 2004: 130). As in the case of identity information, emotional information can be transmitted via static features, such as the tone of an angry voice, or via more dynamic features, such as the 'melodic' contour of a particular utterance (Belin et al., 2004).

Taken together, these findings suggest that the ability to analyse and categorise the three main types of information, carried in the human voice, rely on neural underpinnings (see Grossman, Oberecker, Koch, & Friederici, 2010). Furthermore, and of equal importance, recognising voices is likely underpinned by a developing *interest* in vocalising others and *active listening* to people across time (see Kuhl, 2004). It seems, therefore, that successful voice recognition is accomplished by the interactions of both social and biological factors in the developing child.

A Model of Voice Perception

Despite the very different nature of their physical make-up, faces and voices carry highly similar types of social information about the identity of a person (Belin et al., 2011). Both contain linguistic and biological information, facilitating the recognition of a person and, as such, the voice is often considered as an 'auditory face' (Belin et al., 2004; 2011). On foot of this comparison between the two modalities, it has been suggested that the nature of computational complexity - imposed on the brain when processing faces and voices - is probably very similar (Belin et al., 2011). This suggestion has prompted the development of a model of voice perception (see Figure 3-1 below) based on Bruce & Young's seminal model of cerebral face processing (Bruce & Young, 1986; see also Young and Bruce, 2011).

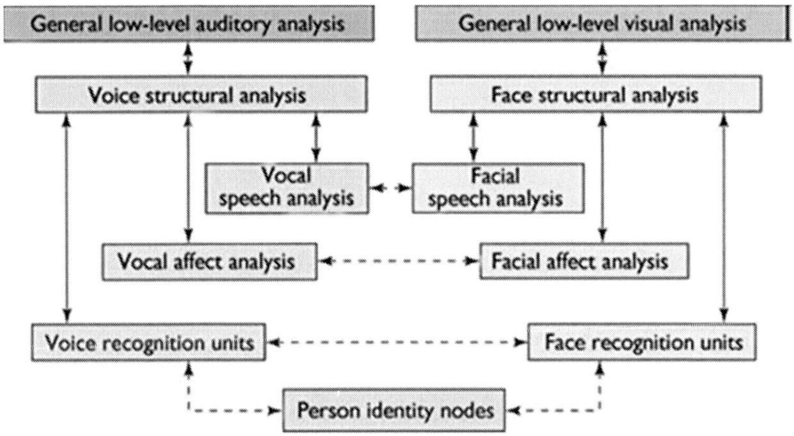

Fig. 3-1 A Model of Voice Perception. Reproduced from Belin, Fecteau, and Bédard (2004).

Via this model, it is possible to conceptualise voice recognition beginning as a low-level type of analysis occurring within the core regions of the auditory cortex, after which, voices are processed at the more 'voice-specific' stage of structural encoding (see Belin et al., 2011). It is here that the three main types of vocal information are extracted and further processed in three interacting, but somewhat separate, functional pathways. The first pathway deals with speech analysis, and is underpinned primarily by the left cerebral hemisphere. During sound and speech processing, this left hemisphere (LH) shows enhanced sensitivity to segmental or phonemic information in particular (see Bourguignon, Nadig, & Valois, 2012). As such, the LH is the dominant hemisphere for speech and language processing (Gazzaniga & Hillyard, 1971).

This area of the brain is underpinned by minicolumns, or what are known as 'vertical bundles of approximately 100 neurons that constitute the basic units of information processing in the brain' (Bourguignon et al., 2012: 128; Mountcastle, 1997). Among other functions, these assemblies constitute basic units of information processing in the brain, and bind their temporal activity via 'different levels of oscillatory coherence, allowing for top-down sensory integration across distant cortical areas' (Bourguignon et al., 2012: 129). It is suggested, that during sound and speech processing, there is both an asymmetric and hierarchal temporal sensitivity of auditory cortices to phonemic information (e.g., c and b in cat and bat), but that there is greater tuning to syllabic information in the right temporal and auditory cortices (see Luo & Poeppel, 2007). Other studies suggest that neurons in the right hemisphere (RH) are more biased toward pitch (Belin, McAdams, Smith, Savel, Thivard, et al., 1998) and slower tones in sounds more typical of musical and prosodic sounds (Belin, McAdams, Thivard, Smith, Savel, et al., 2002). This hemispheric asymmetry is considered a consequence of differences in the 'structure and physiology of neuronal assemblies' in the LH and RH (Bourguignon et al., 2012: 129; Giraud, Kleinschmidt, Poeppel, Lund, Frackowiack, & Laufs, 2007). Typically, minicolumns in the LH contain a greater number of 'large pyramidal neurons than those in the right' (see Bourguignon et al., 2012: 128; Hutsler, 2003). Given their specific role in the processing of speech sounds, these larger LH neurons typically fire at higher temporal frequencies than the smaller neurons on the right hemisphere.

The second pathway is said to be dedicated to the analysis of vocal affective information; a domain thought to be under the remit of the right hemispheric (RH) specialisation, and thus, the nondominant hemisphere during the processing of speech (Belin et al., 2011). It is in this that more basic acoustic features, such as prosody and pitch discrimination, are thought to be processed (see Bourguignon et al., 2012). The large pyramidal cells of the LH are thought to form 'long-range connections between anterior and posterior language areas' of the brain (Bourguignon et al., 2012: 130; Hutsler, 2003). It is presumed, that decreased amounts of these larger LH cells, with the smaller RH minicolumns, would result in impoverished - if not disconnected - long-range connectivity required in normal voice analysis (Casanova, Buxhoeveden, & Gomez, 2003). Additionally, Casanova et al., (2003) argue that this is precisely the difficulty underpinning many of the social and communicative deficits in autism. Nevertheless, and in line with the model of voice perception under discussion here, the third pathway of this model is one thought to be committed to voice recognition. This area is comprised of 'voice recognition units,' each of which is activated by any given voice known to a person (Belin et al., 2011: 712).

Of course, voice recognition is not always restricted to the voices of people who are *familiar* to a person. It also relies on the ability of a person to make an *unfamiliar* voice familiar, that is, 'to encode a voice and store some representation of it in long-term memory' (Mann et al., 1979: 153). Our discussion now turns to these two aspects of voice recognition in the developing child.

Recognising Familiar Voices

Foetus, Neonate, and Infant

Evidence from foetal studies strongly indicates that from twenty weeks gestation the foetus is sufficiently developed to listen to auditory sounds, and from six months gestation, attends preferentially to the sounds of the mother's voice (see Karmiloff & Karmiloff-Smith, 2001). Moreover, while the developing foetus cannot understand what is being said, it does appear that from long before their birth, the unborn child is growing increasingly familiar with the sounds of the mother's voice (Karmiloff & Karmiloff-Smith, 2001). Already equipped with some experience of what voice sounds like, the newborn comes into the world prepared to pay special attention to that particular auditory sound.

Evidence of foetal 'eavesdropping' is found in a host of behavioural studies, which indicate that infants of one hour old show reliable recognition of their mother's voice (DeCasper & Fifer, 1980, 1986; Eisenberg, 1976; Karmiloff & Karmiloff-Smith, 2001). Although infants come to reliably prefer the characteristics of infant-directed speech (IDS), initially the newborn infant can prefer their mother's adult-directed speech (ADS) to her IDS as it is the voice they have become familiar with in utero (Cooper, Panneton, Abraham, Berman, & Staska, 1997; Hepper, Scott, & Shahidullah, 1993). At three days old, high amplitude sucking (HAS) procedures show that infants recognise their mother's voice over that of any other female voice presented to them (DeCasper & Fifer, 1980), and - from one week - infants show overt recognition of the language(s) spoken by that of their mother, as opposed to other languages they are exposed to (Mehler et al., 1978). In addition, infants show recognition of passages of prose that they heard their mother read repeatedly in the last weeks of her pregnancy (DeCasper & Spence, 1986).

Music can be carried on voice also, and Satt (1984) and Panneton (1985) found that newborns showed recognition of a lullaby that mothers had repeatedly sung during the last trimester of pregnancy, over that of a lullaby the infants had never heard before. Similar results have been found for voice with accompaniment, or instrumental music (Hepper, 1991). Infants born to mothers who watched an Australian soap opera with a catchy musical theme daily while pregnant, exhibited a decrease in heart rate, a decrease in movements, and the adaption of an alert state when exposed to that music. Newborns whose mothers had not watched the soap opera before did not exhibit any significant changes in heart rate or movements, and very few showed recognition upon hearing the music (Hepper, 1991). These studies suggest links between prenatal listening and newborn responses, but, of course, the foetus would not have understood anything that it was hearing in the womb. Rather, it was learning to recognise the melodies and rhythms, or the prosodic qualities that underpin the particularities of the mother's voice.

Prosody is rich in *affective information,* and the way people use prosody is said to be distinct to each individual speaker (Fisher & Tokura, 1996). This means therefore that the infant's early eavesdropping on the mother's voice will have increased their familiarity with how she might raise the pitch of her voice for questioning, and lower it when making statements (Paul, Augustyn, Klin, & Volkmar, 2008). The infant will also be sensitive to how she used prosody when creating boundaries between her words, phrases and sentences, all of which mark *her* as unique, and thus, extremely identifiable to the newborn infant (see Fisher & Tokura, 1996). Clearly, therefore, prosody is a very significant component of the human voice, which serves to make mother very recognisable to the newborn (Karmiloff & Karmiloff-Smith, 2001).

Neonates also show a capacity to recognise differences between vowels and consonants, carried in the *speech* sounds of voices, from a very young age (Streeter, 1976). From five months onwards, this ability of infants to detect phonetic differences between all the world's languages narrows distinctly (Kuhl & Rivera-Gaxiola, 2008). Babies of five months and older, begin to show greater behavioural recognition of voices transmitting words comprised of the phonetic units specific to the language to which they have been most exposed (Kuhl & Rivera-Gaxiola, 2008). From six months onwards, infants show recognition of words such as 'baby' and 'mammy' spoken in their native tongue (Bortfeld, Morgan, Golinkoff, & Rathbun, 2005). By seven months, babies listen longer to voices telling stories containing words in the language they are familiar with than words they have not heard before (Jusczyk & Hohne, 1997). By eleven months, babies show increased recognition of voices speaking words they have been consistently exposed to, than words they had not (Halle & de Boysson-Bardies, 1994).

How does this feat of development occur? Is the human infant born programmed to listen to, and learn, speech? There is evidence to suggest that at birth 'the brain is the most undifferentiated organ in the body' (Siegel, 1999: 14). It has few neural pathways, and abilities, such as face recognition, are not specialised and are thought to be heavily dependent upon social interaction and maturational changes (see Chung & Thomson, 2011; Levine, Banich, & Koch-Weser, 1988; Wang & Cottrell, 2012). In relation to infant auditory discrimination abilities, studies investigating the brain substrates of the infant's auditory discrimination abilities - by measuring cerebral blood flow - lend support to an incrementally sophisticating pattern of voice recognition in the developing child (Grossman et al., 2010). These studies indicate that, by the age of eight weeks, infants show a left hemisphere (LH) specialisation for spoken language with a right hemispheric (RH) specialisation evident from the age of three months (Grossman et al., 2010). While these lateralisation patterns resemble those in adults, as outlined by Belin and colleagues (2004), they do not show specificity in the infant (Grossman et al., 2010). In other words, babies show little difference in brain regional responses for either their mother's voice, the voice of a stranger, or between forward and backward speech (Grossman et al., 2010). It is only clear that they respond cerebrally to speech sounds at this stage.

By seven months, there is a much clearer LH pattern of response to speech sounds, combined with a clear RH pattern of activity for the emotion carried in voices (Grossman et al., 2010). These neurological findings lend weight to the suggestion that rather than coming into the world pre-programmed to analyse and categorise the information carried in voices, the infant brain must be *'shaped'* through social listening experiences (see Karmiloff & Karmiloff-Smith, 2001).

Behavioural studies with infants who have had at least five months interaction with communicative others, support this hypothesis. For example, Kuhl has suggested a strong associative link between phonetic learning and social interaction in developing children (Kuhl, Tsao, & Liu, 2003). This study showed that when Mandarin tutors interacted socially on a regular basis with nine month old English-speaking American infants, the babies showed active recognition for phonetic contrasts used in that language, that control children - unexposed to Mandarin - were unable to detect (Kuhl et al., 2003). In contrast, same-aged children who listened to exactly the same Mandarin tutelage via a streamed video-link, failed to recognise the phonetic contrasts readily identified by their peers (Kuhl et al., 2003). The findings from this study lend strong support for social interaction in the ongoing encoding of important information carried on voices from a very early age.

Kuhl (2004) has proposed that an increasingly sophisticated pattern of auditory perception, and voice encoding, in infants is based on three important factors: (1) The infant's ongoing interest in listening to voices, and (2) the child's ability to encode auditory patterns of native-language sounds into memory, plus (3) the child's ability to discriminate speakers on the basis of prosodic and phonetic units of speech. So, we are back to a concept of voice recognition that is constituted in a social interest in the sounds of speech carried on the human voice, rather than one achieved purely on the basis of cerebral underpinnings.

The Pre-School Child

The proposal that voice recognition is based on the child's interest in social interaction also presupposes the child is engaging in communication with others, not just through vocalisations, but also through eye contact, joint attention, and play (see Saint-Georges, Mahdhaoui, Chetouani, Laznik, Apicella, Muratori, et al., 2011). The developing child learns a host of verbal and non-verbal cues about people, their emotional states, and their intentions - via both the face *and* the voice (Rochat & Striano, 1999). However, can voice recognition be accomplished via absolute judgements, or is it tempered by more salient identity cues to be found in faces by the very young child?

To investigate this, Bartholomeus (1973) recruited thirty-six nursery school children below the age of six. The children were photographed while recordings of their voices were also collected to use as stimuli at test. The four adult female teachers, employed at the nursery, were also recorded in this manner. First, children were presented with photographs of two of the four teachers at their nursery, and seventeen of their nursery classmates. Voice recordings of the teachers and children were played to the listening child and they had to point to the picture of the person they thought was speaking at that time. Next, in a voice-naming task, the children were simply played the voice recordings of seventeen of their nursery mates and two of their nursery teachers, minus the photographs, and the children were asked to call out the name of the person they thought was speaking. The third condition involved asking the children to listen to the same voices again, but this time the voices were played backwards. The four teachers involved were also given the tests using the visual and auditory stimuli appropriate for their class (Bartholomeus, 1973).

The findings indicated that children below the age of six rely *more* on visual cues (i.e., the information carried in faces) than auditory cues when tasked with recognising people deemed as familiar to them. Bartholomeus suggested that this may be the consequence of a 'smaller number of distinctive features in vocal than in facial stimuli' (1973: 470). Nevertheless, a number of the children showed 'near-maximum speaker identification' abilities, with the highest teacher scores matched by some of the children in this study (Bartholomeus, 1973: 470). Bartholomeus argued that very small (if any) developmental changes occur in voice recognition abilities after the age of four.

Although a few children in the study received near-maximum scores, the average performance suggests that children perform at a lower level of accuracy than adults do (Spence et al., 2002). Additionally, there was wide variation in the scores of the children on all three conditions. One common factor noted amongst the children was that girls consistently outperformed boys, on all aspects of voice recognition. Although difficult to explain, this result may be due to the finding that the female brain functions more bilaterally, as opposed to male brains, which function more unilaterally - at least for face processing tasks (see McGlone, 1980; Proverbio, Brignone, Matarazzo, Del Zooto, & Zani, 2006, but see Sommer, Aleman, Bouma, & Kahn, 2004 for an alternative view). There is also some suggestion that females have, in general, stronger neural connectors in their temporal lobes than boys have. These connectors are thought to lead to 'more sensually detailed memory storage, better listening skills, and better discrimination among the various tones of voice' (Ryan & Cooper, 2007: 343). In addition, it is proposed that the hippocampus is larger in girls than in boys, thereby increasing the learning advantage girls have, especially for language (Gurian & Stevens, 2004; Ryan & Cooper, 2007: 343).

On a separate, but somewhat related note, girls are socialised differently than boys in Western society (see Cheslack-Postava & Jordan-young, 2012). Moreover, there is evidence to suggest that the developing brain is shaped by social interaction (Chung & Thomson, 2011; Karmiloff & Karmiloff-Smith, 2001; Levine, Banich, & Koch-Weser, 1988; Wang & Cottrell, 2012). As such, could early socialisation patterns result in differences between the ways girls and boys listen to, and recognise, voices later in life? For instance, observational studies suggest that mother's spend longer talking to their daughters as opposed to their sons (Page, Wilhelm, Gamble, & Card, 2010). In addition, mother's engage more deeply in more conversations with their young daughters, whereas, the mothers of sons make 'more comments and attentionals,' which are 'typified by instruction rather than conversation' (Clearfield & Nelson, 2006: 127). Mothers also engage in more play with their daughters compared to supervision of their sons (Clearfield & Nelson, 2006), while the findings from a number of studies indicate that adults in general speak differently to infants on the basis of their gender (see Condry & Condry, 1976; Culp, Cook, & Housley, 1983). Is it possible to infer, therefore, that females may have had more opportunities to *familiarise* themselves with the voices of those around them than boys, resulting in better recognition of voices later in life?

It has also been suggested that the use of children's voices as stimuli may have affected the performance values obtained in this study (Spence et al., 2002). The children were tape-recorded repeating the sentence 'Hi. I go to your school. Do you know who I am?' (Bartholomeus, 1973). Children aged between three and five years of age have been observed altering their voices when instructed to speak into a microphone—typically by speaking in an unusually quiet voice (Spence et al.,= 2002; Strömbergsson, 2009). If the recorded sample of some of the children's voices was not representative of their typical speaking voices, then this could have contributed to the variability and/or relatively low performance observed. Alternatively, some very young nursery school children are less verbal or socially skilled than others, and these factors could potentially affect their overall vocal production, and ultimately, the ability their classmates have to encode, and subsequently recognise, acoustic attributes of their voices at test (Spence et al., 2002).

The children in the Bartholomeus study were also better at identifying the voices of their teachers, than that of their peers. This may have occurred because teachers would spend most time talking in class and, therefore, these voices were the most familiar to the children. Easier identification of adult voices would also be expected if voices were analysed and categorised as that of an adult or a child, and then identified from a set of just three adults versus fourteen or fifteen children. Familiar voice recognition in the typical child, therefore, involves 'a hierarchical sequence of judgments in which absolute identification is preceded by categorization of voices with respect to different variables, such as age or sex' (Bartholomeus, 1973: 471). In other words, it is possibly simplest for young children to discriminate between the voice of a child versus the voice of an adult, and between male voices as opposed to female voices. When voices belonging to individuals of the same age and gender are presented together, therefore, the accuracy of familiar voice recognition declines in children less than six years of age.

Self-Voice Recognition

Surely the most familiar voice of all is one's own voice? It is well established that stimuli, encoded in the context of the 'self,' creates a reliable memory advantage (the self-reference effect (SRE) in memory; Rogers, Kuiper, & Kirker, 1977). The SRE is thought to occur as a consequence of the 'enrichment and organisation of incoming information by the framework of stored autobiographical knowledge' (Cunningham, van den Bos, & Turk, 2011: 450).

The years between three and five are crucial to development of autobiographical, episodic memory, 'as it is traditionally tested in children, through verbalized recall of past episodes in their own lives' (Dunphy-Lelii & Wellman, 2012: 212; Lind, 2010). The findings of these type of tests indicate that this type of memory, for personally relevant information only, fully emerges in the fourth year of life, 'when a combination of sociocognitive, linguistic, and brain maturational factors come together' in the TD child (see Dunphy-Lelii & Wellman, 2012: 213; Bauer, 2002). By the age of four, children show the ability to accurately recall novel, episodic memories from more than six months ago (e.g., Boucher & Bowler, 2008; Fivush & Hammond, 1990). While children, younger than three years of age, show an ability to recount both semantic and episodic memories - typically, they do not exhibit autonoetic memory in the sense of 'attaching these memories to a continuous self' (Dunphy-Lelii & Wellman, 2012: 213; Lind, 2010). In addition, children, below the age of four, are less able than children aged four and older to tell the difference between memories they personally experienced from those they were simply told about (Dunphy-Lelii & Wellman, 2012; Gopnik & Graf, 1988). Moreover, before the age of five, children show difficulty in recalling which of two speakers was the source of an utterance (Dunphy-Lelii & Wellman, 2012; Foley & Johnson, 1985). Taken together, these studies imply a developmental aspect to the systems and processes of memory considered responsible for the encoding and storage of personally relevant information, such as self-image and self-voice. It is possible to speculate therefore that, after the age of four, representations of the self-referenced material (i.e., self-voice) are more likely to be retrieved than those of information encoded about other people (Cunningham et al., 2011; Rosa et al., 2008).

Yet, the recorded voice often sounds unfamiliar to people (Strömbergsson, 2009). This is likely because people are used to hearing their voice through air and bone conduction simultaneously as they speak, and as the recorded voice lacks the bone conduction filtering, its acoustic properties are different from what they are used to (Maurer & Landis, 1990). Alternatively, reactions toward hearing a recording of self-voice may not be solely attributable to physical differences between the natural voice and the recorded voice (Holzman, Berger, & Rousey, 1967). It is possible that the self-voice experience can cause a reaction to aspects of personality that they may not otherwise realise when speaking (Holzman et al., 1967). In some instances, this can facilitate recognition of one's own recorded voice, but, in others, can cause interference (Hughes & Nicholson, 2010).

Nonetheless, adults rarely mistake their own recorded voice for someone else's voice (Rosa et al., 2008).

There are very few studies on children's perception of their own recorded voice (Spence et al., 2002; Strömbergsson, 2009). Methods used to assess self-voice recognition, typically involve recording the participants as they read from a pre-prepared script of words (Hughes & Nicholson, 2010; Rosa et al., 2008; Schuster, 1998; Strömbergsson, 2009). Following a retention interval, participants are fitted with headphones and the script of words is played back to them, randomised with the voices of same-age-and-gender matched others. The task for the participant, in this forced-choice recognition task, is to recognise and identify the sound of their own voice.

On occasion, procedures to assess self-voice recognition use voice-face matching procedures. The voice recordings, photographs of target participants, and age-and-gender matched foils, are used as stimuli, and, on hearing a set of the recorded voices, the target participant is tasked with matching the correct voice to the correct photograph at test (Hughes & Nicholson, 2010: 1134; Damjanovic & Hanley, 2007; Hanley et al., 1998). The theoretical basis for this strategy rests in the finding that people are often more capable of retrieving biographical information about a person from seeing their face, than from just hearing their voice 'regardless of how familiar the voice is to the listener' (Hughes & Nicholson, 2010: 1134; Damjanovic & Hanley, 2007; Hanley et al., 1998).

Children have been assessed on their ability to recognise self-voice with and without the use of photographs as prompts for recognition. For example, Shuster (1998) conducted a study where twenty-six children aged seven to fourteen - unable to pronounce the letter 'r' - were recorded when saying a list of fifty words containing that letter. For each participant, half of the word list that he or she had produced was then edited so that the 'r' sounded correct. Listening tapes were then created for each child. Each tape consisted of two presentations of the fifty words with one presentation containing twenty-five corrected versions of the child saying words with 'r' in them, and twenty-five uncorrected versions of the child saying words with 'r' in them. The second presentation on this tape contained the same corrected and uncorrected words spoken by another child, matched for age and gender. This study consisted of two tasks therefore: The child's ability to judge the correctness of the 'r' *and* the child's ability to identify their own recorded voice.

The results showed that most children could recognise their own recorded voice quite accurately. It was found that older children were better at recognising their own voice at test than the younger participants, suggesting that 'the ability to recognise one's own speech on audiotape may improve with age' (Shuster, 1998: 948). However, the findings of this study did indicate that children exhibited a difficulty in recognising their own voice on the corrected version of their own recordings. This led Shuster (1998: 947) to speculate that taped speech - even one's own taped speech 'may not tap into the output lexicon.' Straight (1980) proposed that the sounds children hear (or the auditory characteristics associated with words children can understand), refer to an input lexicon, while the words children produce refer to an output lexicon, and these two types of representation are completely independent. What Shuster (1998) appears to be suggesting therefore is that the recording of children's voices may introduce, or remove, something, which then renders the recording less familiar to the speaker. However, this explanation does not clarify why the children could recognise their own recorded voice except when their voice was edited.

An alternative explanation was proposed by Strömbergsson (2009: e1) who suggested that the one-to-two-week time span between the recording, and the listening task in this study, 'may have made the task more difficult than if the children had heard the 'corrected' version directly after the recording.' To investigate this aspect further, Strömbergsson (2009) conducted a study of voice recognition with forty-five children aged between four and eight years of age. This study found that a span of one-to-two weeks did not affect younger children's ability to recognise their own recorded voice at test, but that older children did perform significantly less well on this task after this time span (Strömbergsson, 2009). As the age of the older children in this Test matched that of the children in the Shuster study, it was suggested that children's difficulties - when judging themselves as the speaker in 'corrected' versions of their own recordings - could be explained by the time span between recording and listening tasks (Strömbergsson, 2009).

Why did the older children perform less well on self-voice recognition than the younger children did? Strömbergsson (2009: e3) speculated that there was a 'developmental aspect to the cues children use when identifying their own voice.' Younger children might attend to more stable characteristics (accent, gender, age) while older children recognise their own voice by other 'more time-sensitive' features. For instance, it was noted that a number of children 'played' with their voice at the time of recording making it 'unlikely that all recordings reflect the children's normal speech behaviour' (Strömbergsson, 2009: e3). Therefore, the time lapse between recording and listening may have rendered the recording as less familiar to the older children at test, a finding consistent with that of Spence et al., (2002).

Overall, the studies described here suggest that children over the age of four can recognise their own recorded voice—nevertheless there is wide variability in performance. There appears to be a developmental aspect to this ability in children, and there is a difference in the way children perform self-voice recognition compared to adults. There are no studies of self-voice recognition conducted with children with ASD.

Recognising Unfamiliar Voices

Necessarily, voice recognition involves more than just identifying people with whom we are *familiar*. Generally, as we progress from infanthood to preschool, and so on, the pool of people to which we are exposed to increases substantially. Accordingly, a second aspect of voice recognition is the ability to *make* a voice familiar, that is, 'to encode a voice and store some representation of it in long-term memory' (Mann et al., 1979: 153). This ability is likely to be underpinned by maturing and sophisticating cerebral systems and processes in the developing child. For instance, children under the age of ten can recognise *familiar* faces just as well as adults (Diamond & Carey, 1986; Mann et al., 1979) and as poorly as adults when the photographs are inverted (Goldstein, 1975; Hobson, Ouston, & Lee, 1988; Tantam, Monaghan, Nicholson, & Stirling, 1989). However, children of this age show a marked impairment in their recognition of *unfamiliar* faces (Carey & Diamond, 1977; Boucher et al., 1998). As faces and voices are both complex stimuli, which contain important social information, encoding of both plays a crucial role in 'the ability to recognise and distinguish individual persons' (Mann et al., 1979: 154). As outlined by Belin et al., (2011) these similarities imply that the development of voice recognition in the child may parallel the development of face recognition.

Recognising Unfamiliar Voices between the Ages of Six to Fourteen

A study conducted by Mann et al., (1979) investigated the encoding and subsequent recognition of voices in children aged six, eight, ten, twelve, fourteen, and sixteen, *plus* a sample of the voices of adults. Participants were first asked to listen to a recording consisting of two unfamiliar voices (one male and one female) played one after the other. They were told the name of the first speaker (i.e., 'Ken') and then the two speakers were presented again. The task was to indicate when they thought one of the voices was that of the previously named speaker (Mann et al., 1979). In a subsequent trial, the participant heard two unfamiliar same-sex speakers with different *accents*. The participant was again told the name of one speaker (i.e., 'Carol') and then asked to try identify her when both voices were presented (Mann et al., 1979). The results showed that the ability to recognise unfamiliar people by voice improved markedly with age. Six year olds did not perform at a level above chance, but recognition improved sharply between ages six and ten, with ten year olds approaching adult levels. After the age of ten, the accuracy of the children declined significantly but reached adult-level performance by the age of fourteen (Mann et al., 1979).

These findings are interesting for three main reasons. First, while Bartholomeus (1973) suggested that the ability to recognise *familiar* voices is subject to minimal change after the age of four, Mann et al., (1979) proposes that the ability to recognise *unfamiliar* voices changes markedly with age. This suggests that tasks requiring encoding of unfamiliar voices 'produce a developmental pattern' distinct from that found in tasks of recognition of voices already stored in long-term memory (Mann et al., 1979: 160).

In the second instance, it was shown that between the ages of ten and fourteen children disimproved in terms of their voice recognition skills (Mann et al., 1979). This decline in performance mirrors that found in studies of face recognition conducted with children in that age range (Carey, Diamond, & Woods, 1980). In neither domain was the decline in performance earlier in girls than in boys. It is possible to speculate therefore that this u-shaped dip in voice and face recognition is a function of maturational changes, but there is a lack of empirical evidence to fully conclude that this is the case. Alternatively, the ability to encode unfamiliar voices is linked to changes in the functioning of the right hemisphere (Belin et al., 2011). There is evidence to suggest that in relation to the encoding of unfamiliar faces, a left visual field advantage does not emerge until age nine and diminishes at ages twelve and fourteen (Leehey, 1977). According to Mann et al., (1979: 162) the 'decline in lateral asymmetry' in Leehey's study appeared at the same time as which a decline in face recognition was observed by Carey et al., (1980). Given the frequent parallels between the development of voice and face recognition, it is possible that changes in the functioning of the right hemisphere underpin the dip in children's scores noted in Mann's study.

Summary of Voice Recognition in the Typically-Developing Child

There are a number of similarities between voices and faces insofar as both carry linguistic and biological information, which serve as bases for person recognition. It is unsurprising therefore to discover that the ability to make new voices familiar follows the same developmental course as the ability to make new faces familiar (Belin et al., 2011). It is suggested that deficiencies in encoding both faces and voices are characterised by functioning of the right hemisphere, implying an important role for cerebral underpinnings. Combined, the findings of both the Bartholomeus (1973) study and the study conducted by Mann et al., (1979) suggest that a social interest in people during the first decade of life could account for the acquisition of schemata supporting efficient encoding of faces and voices in the developing child.

Children aged between the ages of four and fourteen are able to recognise the sound of their own recorded voice but with high levels of individual differences noted in their performances (Schuster, 2008; Strömbergsson, 2009). This form of voice recognition appears to be heavily dependent on the episodic memory system and the self-reference effect (SRE; Rogers et al., 1977). In addition, children with phonological disorders show difficulty on self-voice recognition tasks when their speech has been edited, implying that this process may introduce or remove something to make the recording less familiar to the speaker. No studies of self-voice recognition have been conducted with children with ASD.

Familiar Voice Recognition in ASD

A number of brain imaging studies have investigated the neural substrates of children and adults with autism on tasks of voice processing (e.g., Boddaert, Chabane, Belin, Bourgeois, Royer, Barthelemy et al., 2004; Ceponiene, Lepistö, Shestakova, Vanhala, Alku, Näätänen, & Yaguchi, 2003; Gervais, Belin, Boddaert, Leboyer, Coez, Sfaello, Barthelemy, Brunelle, Samson, & Zilbovicius, 2004; Lepistö, Kajander, Vanhala, Alku, Huotilainen, Näätänen, & Kujala, 2008; Lepistö, Kujala, Vanhala, Alku, Huotilainen , & Näätänen, 2005). In general, these studies have concluded that while children with autism can perceive the human voice, they are not *attracted to* this type of stimuli. Instead, many of these studies suggest that other types of information may be regarded as more salient by the individual with autism and that these non-social stimuli are preferentially attended to and processed to a greater extent than voices

(Heaton, 2003; Mundy & Neal, 2001). Importantly, if the general findings of these studies are correct, increased attention to non-social information by the individual with autism, could then shape the brain towards specialisation on non-social rather than social stimuli, such as faces and voices (Klin, Jones, Schultz, & Volkmar, 2003). If this is the case, placing a natural voice on the SGD for the child with autism may be a meaningless exercise.

Just three studies have focused on the abilities of children with autism in relation to their specific ability to recognise voices via experimental paradigms (see Boucher et al., 1998, 2000; Klin, 1991). The first was conducted by Klin (1991) who recruited ten boys and two girls with autism below the age of six. A group of age matched children with developmental-delay (DD) and a slightly younger group of typically-developing (TD) children also participated. While the control groups were matched on nonverbal mental age (NVMA), the children with autism presented with slightly higher scores in this domain (see Klin, 1991: 33). All children were presented with a device, much like a toy, which at all times contained a choice of two auditory outputs. Children were familiarised with the device, during which time they could listen to it play a well-known song, or a synthetic hum - referred to as 'Babel' (Klin, 1991). For the Main Test, however, the song was replaced with a recording of the voice of the child's mother.

The results of this study revealed that children with autism, and controls, were very capable of discriminating between the song and Babel, with both the experimental and control groups showing a strong preference for listening to the song (Klin, 1991). The three groups of children also discriminated between the sounds of their mother's voice and Babel (Klin, 1991). Yet, it was noted that while the typically-developing children spent twice as much time preferentially listening to their mother's voice as the children with developmental delay did, children with autism spent significantly more time listening to Babel than the voice of their mother, relative to both control groups (Klin, 1991).

This is of interest. The reason being that when tasked with processing voices, children with autism (just like ability matched TD and DD children) do appear to experience the low-level type of analysis known to occur within the core regions of the auditory cortex (Belin et al., 2011). Therefore, some children with autism can quite obviously discriminate between two competing sounds and they can show an obvious preference for one sound over another. Less clear is the child with autism's ability to process the sounds of *speech* at the more 'voice-specific' stage of structural encoding (Belin et al., 2011). A rather complex question, therefore, surrounds whether this lack of processing of voice is a difficulty based at the cerebral level (see Boddaert et al., 2004; Ceponiene et al., 2003; Gervais et al., 2004; Lepistö et al., 2007; Lepistö et al., 2005), or, whether it is a difficulty more primarily based on the lack of social interest found in the child with autism spectrum disorder in general (see Klin, 1991; Kuhl et al., 2005).

Age and its Effects on Voice Recognition in ASD

An acknowledgment of the very diverse nature of autism spectrum disorder runs throughout this study (Waterhouse, 2013). It has been suggested that this phenotypic heterogeneity is 'likely associated with different etiologies' (Fountain, Winter & Bearman, 2012: 2). Moreover, some research has shown differential outcomes as well as a change in autism symptoms over time (Fountain et al., 2012; Howlin, Goode, Hutton, & Rutter, 2004; Seltzer, Shattuck, Abbeduto, & Greenberg, 2004). This research adopts the position that stresses the 'dynamic nature of neural and cognitive development over time' (Karmiloff-Smith, D'Souza, Dekker, Van Herwegen, Xu, Rodic, & Ansari, 2012: 1). A growing number of theorists have abandoned the interpretations of child developmental psychology as one inspired by 'static adult neuropsychological models' (Karmiloff-Smith et al., 2012: 1) for one that recognises that the infant brain is not only differentiated and less modular than the adult brain, but 'that early on, is highly interconnected' (Karmiloff-Smith et al., 2012: 1). This neuroconstructivist approach emphasises how environmental and social factors play a key role in ontogenesis (Karmiloff-Smith et al., 2012). Primarily, this approach acknowledges how developmental cascades always involve both biological and environmental factors. In other words, social interaction will have 'material effects on the developing brain' (Cheslack-Postava & Jordan-Young, 2012: 1670), which in turn will affect the biological substrate at another level. Via this theoretical lens, successful brain development (and thus the ability to recognise voices and faces) is one that relies on social interaction. It is important therefore to consider how the abilities of the maturing child with autism may *change* as a function of increased opportunity for exposure to voices over time and place. Furthermore, given that the typical child shows an incremental increase in the recognition of individuals on the basis of their voices after the age of six (see Mann et al., 1979) perhaps this will also be the case for the child with autism.

Boucher et al.,'s (1998) study of voice processing provides a useful platform from which to begin this discussion. The ability to recognise familiar individuals on the basis of their voices was examined with a sample of nineteen children with autism aged between six and eight years of age, compared to an ability-matched sample of twenty children with developmental-delay (DD). Generally, the voices of famous people or cartoon characters are used for these tasks (see Spence et al., 2002). However, it cannot be ascertained that all children will have had equal exposure to any set of famous characters that might be used. To counteract this, Boucher et al., (1998) selected participants from a school catering for children with autism, and children with DD, where the faces and voices of twenty staff, known to the recruited children, could be used as stimuli. While the children with DD and the autism group were matched on verbal mental age (VMA) in this study, it must be noted that the children with autism were slightly older chronologically. As a result, they would have had a slightly longer time at school and, therefore, relatively more opportunities for exposure to the twenty staff to be included as stimuli (see Boucher et al., 1998).

Similar to the study by Bartholomeus (1973), children in the Boucher study were first assessed on their ability to match familiar faces with familiar voices. After a short training period, recordings of the staff's voices were played to the children who were then invited to point to the picture of the person they thought was speaking at that time (Boucher et al., 1998). On correct identification by the child, the picture was turned over and the trial started again, which resulted in a progressively smaller pool of options from which to choose. In a second condition, children were assessed on their ability to recognise familiar voices from the tape recordings of the twenty staff utilised in the previous face-voice matching condition, without any visual cues (Boucher et al., 1998).

The results of the first study showed that voice-face matching performance did improve somewhat with increased chronological age in the children with autism (Boucher et al., 1998). This finding is consistent with the research of Mann et al., (1979) who suggested that typically-developing children, after the age of six, demonstrate a significant level of progression in their recognition abilities. It also lends support to the neuroconstructivist approach taken within this research, whereby increased social interaction has material effects on the brain, which in turn affects the biological substrate at the next level of development (Karmiloff-Smith et al., 2012). Moreover, a weak correlation was reported between verbal ability and voice-face matching skills in the children with autism, in the study by Boucher. Nevertheless, and in spite of these correlations, children with autism still exhibited significantly less recognition of familiar voices than controls.

In addition, marked floor effects occurred for the children with autism in the next condition, where they were asked to recognise voices without the aid of visual cues (Boucher et al., 1998). While Boucher et al. (1998) did not report the age and gender of the twenty staff used as stimuli in this research, it must be noted that an earlier study with typically-developing children stressed the difficulty children had discriminating voices when the individuals to be identified were the same age and the same gender (Mann et al., 1979). Boucher did introduce significant modifications to her study, whereby the children were presented with the voice recordings *plus* a set of photographs of familiar staff, and another set of photographs of unknown staff (Boucher et al., 1998). On hearing a voice they thought they recognised, the child was asked to 'post' that photograph into a box with a picture of their school on it, while placing the photographs of unrecognised voices into a 'rubbish' box (Boucher et al., 1998). Notwithstanding these modifications, children with autism - aged between six and eight years of age - recognised fewer familiar voices than controls on this Test.

While the results of these two experiments are not promising, with regard to personalising AAC devices for the child with autism, it should be noted that a very small number of children with autism (n =7) were assessed overall. This substantially reduced number of participants occurred as a result of three children failing to meet the training period criterion, while two others were omitted from the Test due to overt distress (Boucher et al., 1998). Clearly the reduced sample in this study makes generalisation to wider populations very difficult (Robson, 2002). Additionally, two children in the control group presented with specific language impairment rather than developmental delay (see Boucher et al., 1998). It could be speculated that the inclusion of these boys who were *'at or above the expressive language ability'* may have inflated the differences between the groups (Boucher et al., 1998: 180), advantaging those participants in the control group in particular. Furthermore, and of central relevance to a neuroconstructivist position, a number of the children with autism in this study had mental ages of three years and six months (Boucher et al., 1998). As noted, two seminal studies in the field of child developmental psychology have strongly implied that below the age of six, the typically-developing child exhibits wide variation in their ability to recognise voices (Bartholomeus, 1973, Mann et al., 1979). Accordingly, for the substantial number of children faced with learning difficulties in the Boucher study the overall task demands may have been overly difficult.

Yet, the finding remains that despite learning difficulties, the children with autism in the present study had had rather more opportunities than the control group for exposure to the staff whose voices and faces were used as stimuli on the study, and it is of interest that this did not translate into greater recognition of familiar adults voices within this group at test.

Unfamiliar Voice Recognition in ASD

Boucher and colleagues went on to conduct another study of voice processing abilities with a somewhat older group of nineteen children with autism, relative to nineteen children with a specific language impairment and nineteen mainstream school children (Boucher et al., 2000). The participants in this study were matched on verbal mental age (VMA) and on non-verbal mental age (NVMA). To be specific, the children with autism in this study presented with a mean NVMA of just below nine years of age, which is an age bracket correlated with much more accurate recognition of voices than children aged six, or less, in the typically-developing child (Mann et al., 1979).

In this study, voice recordings of three familiar and highly recognisable teaching staff, three familiar and highly recognisable children from the participant's classroom, plus three *unfamiliar* adult voices and three computer-generated sounds not previously heard by participants, were used as stimuli. Photographs and pictures of the auditory stimuli to be used were provided also, and - on hearing the given stimuli - children were asked to post the appropriate visual images into one box while assigning unfamiliar images into another (Boucher et al., 2000). The results showed that in this study the children with autism did not differ from controls in their ability to discriminate familiar, from unfamiliar, sounds (Boucher et al., 2000). This is consistent with the finding from studies conducted with TD children (Bartholomeus, 1973), which indicated little or no developmental changes occurring in familiar voice recognition after the age of four.

This study also investigated the ability of children with autism to recognise recently encountered, but previously unknown, voices (Boucher et al., 2000). This ability in typically-developing children is considered a direct function of a maturing and elaborating encoding process, thought to occur across the first decade of life (Mann et al., 1979). Here, the children with autism - with a mean age of nine years and seven months - were matched with a DD group for chronological age (CA), verbal mental age

(VMA), and NVMA, as well as being matched with a younger TD group on their respective VMA (Boucher et al., 2000). For this particular study, one adult person was recorded saying two different things on two separate occasions. This was the target voice. A recording of a different adult of the same gender was also made. This was the foil voice. None of the adults was known to the participants. Children were fitted with headphones, and the target voice was played. They were then invited to listen to the target and foil voices and to indicate their recognition for the target voice (Boucher et al., 2000).

The results of this study showed *no* difference between the groups, with all three groups scoring significantly above chance. These findings are once again consistent with research, proposing that increased age correlates with increased recognition of both familiar and unfamiliar voices up until the age of ten in the typically-developing child (Mann et al., 1979). Accordingly, increased age also seems to be a positive factor, influencing the ability of the child with autism in their respective abilities to recognise people on the basis of voice.

Less clear is the effect of gender in studies of voice processing conducted with individuals with autism. Given the preponderance of male cases in the epidemiology of ASD, it is unsurprising that in both neurological and behavioural studies, the participants with autism are mainly male. However, a lack of female participants with ASD may be skewing the findings of studies of voice recognition in individuals with autism. For example, studies with TD children suggest that the social environment of a female child may provide, on average, more opportunities for social interaction, whether through play, eye contact, or vocalisations (Clearfield & Nelson, 2006; Cheslack-Postava & Jordan-Young, 2011; Page et al., 2010). It is also suggested that paying attention to communicating others (e.g., holding eye contact or responding vocally to questions) is more ‘heavily coached’ in girls (Cheslack-Postava & Jordan-Young, 2011). The point being made here is that girls with autism may have had the same gendered advantages as their TD counterparts during early socialisation. If this is the case, they may, like their TD counterparts, have had more opportunities for familiarisation with the faces and voices of others, and as a result, may show greater recognition of people at test. This suggestion conceptualises development as a ‘looping process’ in which gender is a ‘critical, ongoing factor,’ which shapes initial social and tactile input children receive from communicating with others (Cheslack-Postava & Jordan-Young, 2011: 05). It is one that warrants greater investigation in all future studies of ASD.

On a final note for this section, it is important to note that paradigms using voice-face matching procedures, when investigating voice processing abilities in autism, may be somewhat confounded by face processing abilities in the child with autism (Boucher & Lewis, 1972; de Gelder, Vroomen, & van der Heide, 1991). There is evidence that children with autism recognise affect in the faces of others less well than comparison groups (Capps, Yirmiya, & Sigman, 1992; de Gelder et al., 1991; Fein, Lucci, Braverman & Waterhouse, 1992) and that that they have a difficulty integrating visual and auditory aspects of facial speech (de Gelder et al., 1991).

However, it is important to note that vulnerability to impaired memory for faces is not absolute (see Boucher et al., 2012). Face recognition has not always been reported as impaired (Langdell, 1978), and while studies have shown that the child with autism recognises faces less well than the TD child, there is sometimes 'considerable overlap between groups' in terms of their ability to achieve maximum scores (Boucher et al., 2000:847).

Summary

At this point of the book, three main issues have been established. The first of these factors is the finding that many children with autism can distinguish between two auditory stimuli. This was highlighted in the study by Klin (1991), which clearly showed that before the child with autism is six years old they are able to distinguish the sounds of a song from the sound of white noise, and the sound of white noise from the sound of a voice. That this discriminatory ability is maintained by the child with autism is evidenced in the second study outlined in this chapter. This study was conducted with older children with autism, and it revealed that this group could discriminate known from unknown voices immediately after testing (Boucher et al., 2000). A third study has further confirmed that a number of children with autism show an improvement in their ability to recognise familiar and unfamiliar people, on the basis of voice, as they increase in chronological age (see Boucher et al., 1998, 2000). Secondly, no studies of self-voice recognition have been conducted with children with autism spectrum disorder. A third aspect is the overall lack of research into voice processing abilities in children with low-functioning autism (LFA) as opposed to children with autism that are more 'able.' For example, the two studies conducted by Boucher and colleagues, to examine voice recognition in autism, were conducted with children whose NVMA scores were well 'within the normal range' (Boucher et al.,

2000: 849). Accordingly, we know that the child with HFA has a reasonably good ability when tasked with both familiar, and unfamiliar, voice recognition. The child with HFA is much less likely to require a speech generating device for communicating than the child with LFA (see Goldsmith & LeBlanc, 2004). It is children with LFA who are frequently associated with severe learning and language deficits and who are the focus of this study. Moreover, it is these children who are relatively neglected in the literature (see Boucher, Mayes, & Bigham, 2008). This book is an attempt to bridge that gap.

CHAPTER FOUR

TESTING OUR ASSUMPTIONS ABOUT VOICE AND ASD

In a classic fairy tale by Hans Christian Anderson, the little mermaid is forced to surrender her voice to a wicked sea-witch (http://www.classic fairytales.com). The mermaid asks plaintively 'But if you take away my voice, what will I have left?' It is likely that the little mermaid would be left with the memories of what her voice sounded like, as both linguistic and non-linguistic acoustic attributes of voice are stored in long-term memory (Spence et al., 2002: 215). Furthermore, as a result of the perceptual representation system in memory (Gastgeb, Wilkinson, Minshew, & Strauss, 2011), she will have linked the sounds of peoples voices to memories of their faces, their roles in life, and their names.

This explanation implies a form of implicit encoding/storage of talkers' voices in the nondeclarative memory system (Tulving & Schacter, 1990). This type of processing would involve noetic awareness at the time of encoding, and prompts or cues, such as photographs, should prime the retrieval of memory for identification of a person on the basis of voice at test. This was the method used with typically-developing children in the study by Bartholomeus (1973), Mann et al., (1979) and Spence et al., (2002). This method had also been used when conducting voice recognition studies among children with autism (Boucher et al., 1998, 2000). Studies of self-voice recognition imply a more active role for the declarative memory system however, with a need for the child to have 'tagged' the voice as personally relevant at the time of encoding (see Lind, 2010). Moreover, retrieval of this type of memory would be associated with autonoetic awareness at the time of retrieval entailing the ability of the child to be 'aware of a past state of self' (Lind, 2010: 433).

Overview

This chapter presents the findings of three studies of voice recognition tests conducted with three groups of children (LFA, DD and TD). The first of these studies is a Test of Voice-Face Matching, which explores the child's abilities to recognise the voices of already known people. This is a Test of Familiarity therefore, based on the assumption that the child's recognition of already known people will be accomplished on foot of stimulus repetition, building on perceptual representations of people's faces and voices that may initially have been implicit (see Atkinson & Wescourt, 1975; Mandler, 1980; Boucher et al., 2012). Using photographs as cues, or prompts, the child's memory is tested in terms of the associations they have made in long-term memory for faces, names, and voices (Mandler, 1980).

The second study is a Test of Self-Voice Recognition. This assesses children's *recollection* of personally relevant information from long-term memory. For instance, recognising your own recorded voice assumes that you have the ability to become the object of your own attention (Rosa et al., 2008), an ability which may underlie such 'higher-order capacities as theory of mind and introspection' (see Rosa et al., 2008: 204; Gallup, 1982). This task would be difficult for a TD child younger than four, as this kind of memory only emerges as a combination of 'sociocognitive, linguistic, and brain maturational factors' (see Dunphy-Lelii & Wellman, 2012: 212; Bauer, 2002).

The third study is a Test of Pure-Voice Recognition. This study investigates the child's ability to recognise the sound of their own recorded voice from that of three other children's voices (Strömbergsson, 2009). No photographs will be used as prompts in this study. Typically-developing children between the ages of four and eight can identify their own voice this way, but the variability amongst children is large (Strömbergsson, 2009). The overall aim of this set of tests is to identify a group of children with sufficient voice processing abilities to partake in a semi-longitudinal study designed to assess their preferences for natural voice on a speech generating device.

Our Third Study: Testing Familiar Voice-Face Matching in Low-Functioning Autism

This was a Test designed to assess the ability of children to match voice recordings to photographs using a forced-choice (FC) paradigm. In this, children were presented with a PowerPoint demonstration whereby each of the slides showed the photographs of two people the child knew from school, and the voice of one of these individuals was played. The task for the child was to match the voice recording to the correct photograph.

Previous studies suggest that voice recognition is developmentally sensitive with an incremental improvement in the accuracy of TD children from the age of six to ten, when it reaches adult-level performance (Mann et al., 1979; Shuster, 1991; Spence et al., 2002). Children up to the age of six years show some competence at this task, with their greatest difficulty being when the photographs are of people the same age and/or gender (Bartholomeus, 1973; Mann et al., 1979; Shuster, 1991; Spence et al., 2002).

Studies of individuals with autism suggest that while affect processing is impaired (de Gelder, Vroomen, & van der Heide, 1991), so is unfamiliar voice-face matching (Boucher & Lewis, 1992) that they have previously shown intact performance on voice-face matching tasks (Boucher, Lewis, & Collis, 1998; Ozonoff, Pennington, & Rogers, 1990).

On foot of these findings, and those of Studies 1 & 2, it was predicted that: (1) Children with LFA would be impaired relative to age and ability matched groups of children with DD and TD children; (2) that girls would match voices to faces more accurately than boys; and (3) - given the range of NVMA scores in the two clinical groups - higher NVMA scores would be associated with greater voice-face matching ability.

What We Did and How We Did It

Participants

All 93 children were invited to participate in this study.

General Procedural Points

General procedural points were the same as those outlined in our first study. Some additional points need to be mentioned with regard to this Test of Voice-Face Matching however. For instance, the assessment of familiar voice and face matching, in children with special needs, raises the difficulty that the voices and faces of famous people or cartoon characters - such as are typically used as stimuli in this type of Test - cannot be used, as there is no certainty that children will have had equal exposure to any set of 'famous' people/characters that might be used (see also Boucher et al., 1998, 2000).

In order to overcome this issue, previous researchers have selected participants from schools catering specifically for children with autism and other types of developmental delay (see Boucher et al., 1998, 2000). This enabled them to use - as stimuli - the faces, and voices of staff and/or students from these schools, ensuring the target group and comparison group had comparable exposure to the stimuli.

Within the Republic of Ireland (ROI), educational policy dictates that children with autism are educated separately from children with general special needs and typically-developing children (see http://www.education.ie). The implications of these policies are that there are no staff or pupils that can be used as common stimuli across the three groups of participants in this study who are from the same school. In order to overcome this methodological difficulty, it was decided to use the voices and faces of staff and pupils from the classrooms of each group of children (LFA/DD/TD), within the five participating schools. This meant that each participant had experienced equal exposure to the stimuli used. Although the stimuli for each participant were not the same set of persons *per se*, the relationship between the participants and the persons used as stimuli was the same.

Materials and Procedures

Materials: For each school, and for each group of children in these schools (LFA/DD/TD), the following materials were created.

Practice Stimuli: To ensure that the child knew what was expected of them, a practice phase was designed. Four standard-sized digital colour photographs of faces were taken, and stored on a USB key. Once made part of the PowerPoint slideshow, these images were presented side-by-side and were approximately 6 x 8 inches on a 13 x 11 inch screen. The photographs were of staff working daily at the schools of the participants for more than six months. These included the school secretary, the school principal, the cleaner, and the grounds-man. The individuals were photographed looking into the camera. They were asked to remove all jewellery, but not their spectacles as these are most likely perceived by participants as 'part of the person's face' (Boucher et al., 1998: 173, 2000).

In addition, an audio-list was created by which each of the four staff, whose faces appeared in the practice phase, were recorded on a hand-held digital recorder (http://www.phillips.com) saying "*Hello! Do you know who I am? Can you point to my picture*" (Boucher et al., 1998:173). This particular speech sample was selected to maximise voice recognition cues by providing a sample longer than one second in duration (Bartholomeus, 1973; Bricker & Pruzansky, 1966), and to include both falling and rising intonation (Bartholomeus, 1973).

For the practice phase, the four photographs and their corresponding speech samples were uploaded onto a PowerPoint slideshow. There were four slides, and each displayed two photographs which were presented side-by-side (e.g., A-B, C-D, D-A, B-C). The speech sample of just one of the people shown on these slides was played during each presentation (e.g., A, C, D, B). For each of the 4 slides shown, the two images filled the screen with the caption "Whose voice is this?" always displayed as the heading of the slide shown. A pre-prepared score was used for this practice phase.

Main Test stimuli: For each group (LFA, DD, and TD), at each school, six standard-size colour photographs - similar to those taken for the training phase - were taken, and these were always of people different to those used at the training phase. Typically, these six people consisted of the child's teacher, two special needs assistant's (SNAs), and three pupils from the participant's classroom (see Appendix H). Only staff or pupils who were in the participant's classroom for more than six months were included, in an attempt to ensure the child's familiarity with that person. This procedure was accomplished for each of the 93 participants, as classrooms catering for children from all three groups (LFA, DD, and TD) contained at least three pupils, two SNAs and a teacher.

A separate audio recording of the same speech sample used at training was prepared for each individual photographed. The voices of the three staff and three students were recorded using a hand held recorder (http://www.phillips.com). Care was taken to firstly record the researcher stating which school the recording was being made from; the group of participants this recording was intended for (i.e., the autism group, the DD group, or the TD group); and the names of those individuals recorded. Additionally, for a number of the children with special needs, it was necessary for the researcher to whisper the words, "*Hello! Do you know who I am? Can you point to my picture*" for the child to echo the same. Later, the voice of the researcher was edited out.

When the photographs and audio recordings were completed, a PowerPoint slideshow demonstration was created. This slideshow consisted of 20 slides (see Appendix H). Each slide contained the photographs of two individuals presented side-by-side (see Fig. 9) with the voice of only one of the individuals shown played. For each of the 10 slides shown, the two images displayed side-by-side filled the screen, with the caption, "Whose voice is this?" always displayed as the heading of the slide shown.

There were only six images used throughout this slideshow, and the aim was to arrange these images so that the participants were presented with a number of child/child, adult/adult, and child/adult slides. This predetermined arrangement was motivated by the findings of previous studies suggesting that children show the greatest difficulty matching voices to faces when the persons used as stimuli are of the same age and gender (Bartholomeus, 1973; Mann et al., 1979; Shuster, 1991; Spence et al., 2002). In addition, and in an attempt to control for perseveration, the voice played did not always represent either the photo just on the left hand side of the presentation, or that of the photo on the right. A pre-prepared score sheet was used for this Main Test, which recorded √ for each correct response and x for each incorrect response. Before the Main Test, a practice phase was conducted and this is described in the next section.

Procedure: The practice phase and the Main Test were completed in a single session. The main objective of the practice phase was to ensure children's understanding of the task of matching a familiar voice to a familiar face, as assessed via a PowerPoint demonstration. Children were invited to sit at a desk to the right of the tester. In the centre of the table, facing the child and the tester, a laptop - with the training and Main Test PowerPoint - was located. The laptop was equipped with a wireless-mouse, which was located under the right hand of the tester and out of direct reach of the child. The tester began by saying "*I have some photographs to show you. Look, let's see whose pictures I have on here!*" Using the wireless-mouse the tester then put up the first slide. Showing (A-B) side-by side and pointing at photograph A, the tester named the person, and said, "*You know 'A'. 'A' is the school principal.*" This procedure was repeated until all four individuals, shown in the four slides, were named.

The practice phase PowerPoint slideshow was returned to the first slide showing images A and B side-by-side, and the tester said, "*I'm going to play a recording of a voice next. It will be the voice of one of these people. I want you to point to the person you think the voice belongs to. Will you do that for me?*" The tester then used the mouse to activate the voice of A. If the child pointed to A, the next slide - showing C and D side-by-side - was presented *and* the next recording (i.e., voice C) was played. If the child chose the incorrect photograph, the tester said, "*I think it must be this person*" and moved onto the next slide. This procedure was repeated until each of the four slides (e.g., A-B, C-D, A-D, B-C) had been presented with the voices of A, C, D, B played, and then again with the voices of B, D, A, and C played. When the child had made four consecutive correct responses within the eight presentations, they were deemed to understand the procedure and they progressed to the Main Test. All 93 children passed this criterion.

For the Main Test the child was told there were many more photographs to see, and asked the child if they wished to continue. All children were pleased to progress to the Main Test. The very same procedure used at practice was used, except the faces and voices of different staff and pupils were used as stimuli. Ten slides were used at Main Test with each slide comprised of two photographs presented side-by-side (1-2, 3-4, 5-6, 4-3, 2-4, 6-1, 3-1, 5-2, 4-6, 2-1; see Appendix H). For each slide shown, the voice of just one person played (1, 4, 6, 3, 2, 1, 3, 5, 6, 1). When all ten slides were shown, the PowerPoint was repeated with the voice of the other person played (e.g., 2, 3, 5, 4, 4, 6, 1, 2, 4, 1). This strategy ensured that the voice of each photographed individual was presented once.

Previous studies, conducted with children with autism, showed the participants objects, and/or images, to be recalled for five seconds (3-4s looking time; Bigham et al., 2010; Strömbergsson, 2009), and this was the procedure used here. If a child hesitated, or was reluctant to make a choice, the tester elicited a response by saying, "*Just guess as fast as you can.*" No child failed to make a choice in a timely fashion (i.e., a time-frame of between five and ten seconds was decided upon by the tester). A record was made as to whether the child made a correct voice-face match, or not, across each presentation. If the child correctly matched the voice to the face, a score of 1 was awarded and the next slide was presented. If the child failed to respond (fifteen seconds was the time decided on by the tester), or made an incorrect response, the tester pointed to the photograph and said *'I think it must be this person,'* and a score of 0 was awarded. The child's responses were recorded as either √ (correct), or x (incorrect), on the score sheet and scores ranged from 0-20.

As this was a forced choice response option Test, each child had a 1 in 2 chance of choosing the target photograph by simply guessing (Robson, 2002). The chance success level for this identification would be 50% therefore, and, as such, the chance level raw score for this Test was estimated at 10/20.

What We Found Out About Voice Recognition in Autism

It was predicted that: (1) Children with LFA would be impaired, relative to age and ability matched groups of children with DD and TD children; (2) that girls would match voices to faces more accurately than boys, and; (3) given the range of NVMA scores in the two clinical groups, higher NVMA scores would be associated with greater voice-face matching ability. Mean scores for the three groups on the Voice-Face Identity Matching Test are shown in Table 4-1.

Table 4-1 Descriptive Statistics for the LFA and Comparison Groups: Study 3 A Test of Voice-Face Matching

	Study 3	**Test of Voice-Face Matching**	
Characteristic	**LFA**	**DD**	**TD**
Maximum Score (20)			
n	33	27	33
M	14.48	16.22	18.93
SD	4.01	4.30	1.57
Range	7 -20	5 -20	15 -20
Median	16	18	20
n at ceiling	4	10	21
n at chance	6	3	0
CA in years			
n	33	27	33
M	10.5	10.5	6.1
SD	3.1	2.9	0.7
Range	5.0-15.4	6.0-16.6	4.6- 7.1
NVMA in years			
n	32*	26*	33
M	5.07	5.03	5.09
SD	1.5	1.6	0.4
Range	3.1-8.5	3.1-7.9	5.0- 6.8
IQ			
n	32	26	33
M	50.0	54.9	97.8
SD	11.3	26.5	7.5
Range	24.3-85.0	26.5-93.8	82.3-114.2

ma/ca x 100 = IQ; Chance is defined as scoring at 10 or less; *The NVMA of one child with LFA, and one child with DD, could not be calculated via the BPVS

Some ceiling effects occurred in this Test. It is also clear that some participants (*n* = 8) scored at chance (scores of 10 or below) and it was decided to remove these from the data set prior to conducting any further analysis (see Table 4-1), leaving a remainder of 27 participants with autism, 25 participants with developmental delay and the full set of 33 typically-developing participants. The IQ of the six children, removed from the data, ranged from 40.3 – 60.0, and there was no significant difference between the IQ scores of these children (*M* = 45.71, SD = 5.05) and those scoring above chance (*M* = 51.0, SD = 12.1; *t* (30), *p* =. 31 (two-tailed). The magnitude of differences in the means (mean difference = -5.28, 95% CI: -15.7 to 5.18, was very small (eta squared = -.07).

Table 4.2 Scores on a Test of Voice-Face Matching by Group when Participants Scoring at Chance are Removed from the Data

	Study 3	Test of Voice-Face Matching	
Characteristic	LFA	DD	TD
Maximum Score (20)			
n	27*	25*	33
M	15.8	16.9	18.9
SD	2.9	3.5	1.5
Range	11-20	6-20	15-20
Median	16	18	20
n at ceiling	4	10	21
CA in years			
n	27	25	33
M	10.5	10.5	6.1
SD	3.21	3.0	0.7
Range	5.0-15.4	6.0-16.6	4.6-7.1
NVMA in years			
n	26**	25	33
M	5.1	5.5	5.9
SD	1.6	1.3	0.4
Range	3.1-8.5	3.1-7.9	5.0-6.8
IQ			
n	26	25	33
M	50.78	55.0	97.8
SD	12.0	15.7	7.5
Range	24.3-85.0	26.5-93.8	82.3-114.2

ma/ca x 100 = IQ; *Six children with LFA, and 2 with DD, scored at chance (defined here as 10 or below) and were excluded from the data; **The NVMA of 1 child with LFA (Robbie) could not be calculated via the BPVS

First, although it was apparent that some participants with autism in this study achieved maximum scores in this task, in the main these children successfully matched familiar voices to familiar faces at a lesser rate than did their ability-matched typically-developing (TD) counterparts. Numerically, they also performed less well than age-and-ability matched children with developmental-delay (DD) but this difference did not reach statistical significance. A 'one-way between groups' analysis was conducted to explore the effect of group (LFA/DD/TD) on participants' mean scores of voice-face identity matching.

The Effect of Diagnosis on Participant Ability to Match Voices to Faces

There was a statistically significant difference in voice-face matching scores for the three groups: F (2, 81) = 11.72, p < .0005. Post-hoc comparisons using the Tukey HSD Test indicated that the mean score of the participants with autism, for matching voices to faces (M = 15.85, SD = 2.97), was significantly lower than that of the ability matched younger typically-developing participants on this task (M = 18.93, SD = 1.57). This difference in group means was moderate, with the effect size calculated using eta squared as .22 (Cohen, 1992: 157). As noted previously, the participants with developmental delay (M = 17.37, SD = 2.81) did not differ significantly from either the LFA or the TD groups on this task. Consequently, the results of this ANOVA suggest that the ability to match the voices of highly recognisable people to photographs of their faces was most difficult for the children with LFA.

The Effect of NVMA and Gender on Participant Ability to Match Voices to Faces

A 'two- way (NVMA x gender) between-groups' analysis of variance was conducted. Participants in this study (n = 84) ranged in NVMA from 3.1 years to 8.5 years on the BPVS. To capture any developmental changes in the ability to match voices to faces, they were divided into three groups (Group 1: <= 64 months; Group 2: 65–72 months; Group 3: 73-103 months). The interaction effect between gender and NVMA was not significant F(2, 77) = .926, p = .40). Yet, there was a statistically significant effect for NVMA, F(2, 77) = 8.63, p = .0005), However, the calculated effect size was small (partial eta squared = .18).

Post-hoc comparisons, using the Tukey HSD Test, indicated that the mean score for the youngest group (<= 64 month) (M = 16.06, SD = 3.29) was significantly lower on voice-face matching abilities than both the slightly older 65 – 72 month group (M = 18.64, SD = 1.57) and that of the eldest (73 +) age group (M = 18.07, SD = 2.33). Therefore, there was an incremental improvement in performance of the children based on their non-verbal mental ages. Significantly, children with the highest NVMA of 6 years and over were the most accurate at matching voices to faces at test.

A main effect for gender, F (1, 77) = 4.76, p = .03 also reached statistical significance, but the effect size here was small. Boys (m = 17.62, SD = 3.02) and girls (m = 16.9, SD = 2.9) in this study differed somewhat in terms of their ability to match familiar voices to faces at test, with boys performing better than girls.

The Effect of Repeated Exposure to Stimuli Used at Test

A one-way analysis of variance showed that there was a statistically significant difference in the length of time spent in school for the three groups in this study: F (2, 81) = 46.43, p = .0005. Post-hoc comparisons showed that the number of term attendance for the autism group (m = 10.48, SD = 5.37) was significantly greater than the number of school terms attended by the young typically-developing group (m = 2.0, SD = .00). There was also a statistically significant difference between the number of terms spent in school by the DD group (m = 10.12, SD = 4.46) and the TD group (m = 2.0, SD = .00).

An independent samples t-test was conducted to calculate the actual magnitude of the difference in the mean length of time participants in this study had spent in school. Owing at least in part to their chronological age (e.g., 5-15 years approximately) it was immediately apparent that the children with low-functioning autism had spent much longer in school than the very young typically-developing children (e.g., 4.6-7.1 years approximately), and thus had had much greater exposure to the faces and voices of teachers *and* pupils used as stimuli in this voice-face matching task. The results of an independent t-test confirmed that the magnitude of the differences in the mean number of terms spent in school between these two particular groups (mean difference =8.48, 95% CI: 8.48 to 1.03) was of medium effect (eta squared = 0.53).

The children with low-functioning autism (m = 10.48, SD = 5.37) and the children with developmental delay (m = 10.12, SD = 4.46) had spent similar lengths of time in school and an independent t-test confirmed that the size of differences in the means between these children (mean difference = 0.356, 95% CI: -2.44 to 3.15) was minimal at 0.001. A final t-test in this set of analyses showed that the difference in terms spent in school by the children with developmental delay (m = 10.12, SD = 4.46) and the typically-developing children (m = 2.00, SD = .00) was moderate at 0.59, calculated using eta squared (mean difference =8.12, 95% CI: 6.23 to 10.01).

Clearly therefore, both the LFA and DD groups of children had had, in fact, considerably more opportunities than TD children for exposure to staff and pupils whose voices and faces were used as stimuli - given that they had been in school for longer than the TD group. However, the results suggest that the children with LFA either did not, or could not, utilise these opportunities to recognise the voices of well-known staff and pupils to the same extent as comparison children.

The Principle of Maximum Contrast

Previous research suggests that children over the age of four years are capable of discriminating between individuals on the basis of identity information typically carried in the human voice (Belin et al., 2004, 2011). One such marker of a person's identity, normally transmitted via voice, is that of the person's age (see Bartholomeus, 1973; Mann et al., 1979; Belin et al., 2004). What this means, therefore, is that the typically-developing child can generally *match* a familiar voice to the photograph of a familiar person more easily when the stimuli provided to them at test are between that of an adult and a child presented simultaneously, as opposed to a child with a child or an adult with an adult.

Table 4-3 Descriptive Statistics for the LFA and Comparison Groups when Stimuli Used in Study 3 Comprise Adults and Children Presented Simultaneously

Study 3. A Test of Voice-Face Matching			
Characteristic	**LFA**	**DD**	**TD**
Maximum Score (14)			
n	27*	25*	33
M	11.29	12.08	13.18
SD	1.83	2.18	1.21
Range	8-14	7-14	10-14
Maximum Scores (14/14)			
n	4	10	21

*** Six children with LFA (Jim, Jake, Anthony, Tim, Maggie and Fiona), and two with DD (id no.'s 35 & 37), scored at chance, or below, in the Test of Voice-Face Matching and were excluded from this data**

Fourteen of the twenty slides used at Main Test in the present study presented a photograph of a child next to the photograph of an adult, with the voice of only one individual played. If the literature is correct, participants should have found it easiest to match the correct voice to the correct face in these slides - given the different age information transmitted via their voices (Bartholomeus, 1973). Mean scores of the three groups for this task are shown in Table 4-3. Children who scored at chance remain omitted from the data.

A one-way ANOVA, conducted to investigate the effect of group (LFA/ DD/TD) on participant ability to discriminate between the voices of a child and of an adult when matching familiar voices to familiar faces, revealed a significant difference across the three groups F (2, 81) = 8.9, p =.0005.

Interestingly, compared to almost 64% of the typically-developing children - aged between 4 – 7 years of age scoring at ceiling on this task, and almost 42% of individuals with developmental-delay - less than 15% of children, and adolescents, with LFA consistently discriminated in a successful way between the voice of an adult and a child at this Test. One child, a girl named Connie, was one of the 4 children with LFA who did achieve a maximum score on this Test, and she had also achieved maximum scores on a Test of Familiarity and a Test of Recollection.

The Principle of Minimum Contrast

The remaining six slides of the Main Test comprised the auditory and visual stimuli of either child/child or adult/adult only. As noted earlier, findings from previous research would suggest that the speed and accuracy of speaker recognition decreases somewhat when the stimuli to be discriminated amongst are very alike (see Bartholomeus, 1973; Mann et al., 1979), and this is particularly difficult if the participants making these identity judgements are less than six years of age. To this effect, a second one-way ANOVA was conducted to explore the impact of group on participant's ability to discriminate between familiar individuals on the basis of their voices when those individuals were the same age and gender. The results are presented in Table 4-4 below.

As anticipated, given the established difficulty of this particular task for children, a higher number of all participants scored at chance (defined here as 3/6 or less) when discriminating between the voices of very similar stimuli compared to when the stimuli were quite different. However, and unanticipated in light of previous research (Mann et al., 1979), substantially more participants scored at ceiling (scores of 6/6) also. One of these children, in the LFA group, was once again Connie, and she had achieved maximum scores on all tests conducted thus far (see Table 4-5).

Table 4-4 Scores on a Test of Voice-Face Matching when Stimuli Consist of Similar Stimuli

	Study 3	Test of Voice-Face Matching	Minimum contrast
Characteristic	**LFA**	**DD**	**TD**
Maximum Score (6)			
n	27*	25*	33
M	4.55	5.29	5.75
SD	1.57	0.85	0.66
Range	1-6	3-6	3-6
Maximum Scores (14/14)			
n	11	1	28

*** Six children with LFA (Jim, Jake, Anthony, Tim, Maggie and Fiona), and two with DD (id no.'s 35 & 37), scored at chance, or below, in the Test of Voice-Face Matching and were Excluded from this Data**

Table 4-5 Descriptive Statistics for the LFA Group; Studies 1-3

Id No.	Name	Gender	CA yrs	NVMA yrs	IQ	Study 1	Study 2	Study 3
						Max Score 16	**Max Score 20**	**Max Score 20**
1	**Frank**	Male	7.4	5.0	67.4	15	12	11
2	**Jim**	Male	11.4	4.8	42.3		19	
3	**Peter**	Male	6.5	3.8	58.2		16	12
4	**Edward**	Male	9.5	3.7	39.8	10	17	16
5	**Rachel**	Female	5.0	4.2	85.0	9	10	11
6	**Jake**	Male	7.2	3.1	43.6	12	15	
7	**Francis**	Male	10.5	5.5	51.9	10	10	18
8	**Jason**	Male	6.5	3.2	50.0	11	12	14
9	**Linda**	Female	14.3	7.8	54.6	16	8	14
10	**Anthony**	Male	13.8	5.5	40.3		7	

11	**Tim**	Male	11.5	5.3	46.0	9	20	
12	**Alan**	Male	6.5	3.1	43.6	9	8	14
13	**Brendan**	Male	10.7	5.9	55.0	9	8	15
14	**Paddy**	Male	11.5	5.8	50.3	10	5	16
15	**Ida**	Female	12.4	4.2	34.2	10	4	16
16	**Richard**	Male	12.8	5.1	40.2	9	12	16
17	**Robbie**	Male	14.0			16	8	18
18	**Ann**	Female	13.4	7.9	59.0	9	9	17
19	**Nita**	Female	13.2	8.5	64.7	16		20
20	**Lucy**	Female	10.6	4.9	46.0	9	8	11
21	**Maggie**	Female	11.9	7.1	60.1	10	12	
22	**Bob**	Male	15.4	3.7	24.3	16	16	20
23	**John**	Male	8.0	5.1	63.9	12	9	20
24	**Mark**	Male	15.0	6.1	40.8	16	11	18
25	**Rebecca**	Female	6.3	3.1	50.0	11	9	12
26	**Dermot**	Male	6.1	3.2	52.7	9	11	12
27	**Fiona**	Female	6.6	3.1	47.5	9	16	
28	**Kevin**	Male	13.5	7.9	58.2	9	10	18
29	**Sandra**	Female	10.7	5.9	55.0	16	6	19
30	**Paul**	Male	8.0	3.7	46.3	10	16	18
31	**David**	Male	15.3	6.1	40.2	10	8	16
32	**Ger**	Male	8.1	3.7	45.9	9	2	16
33	**Connie**	**Female**	**11.3**	**4.9**	**43.3**	**16**	**20**	**20**

All names used are pseudonyms; MA /CA x 100 = IQ Study 1: A Test of Familiarity excludes 3 children who showed distress on the day of testing Study 2: A Test of Recollection excludes 1 child who was unwell on the day of testing Study 3: A Test of Voice-Face Matching excludes 6 children with LFA who scored at, or below, chance (defined as 10 or less)

Finally, a one-way ANOVA showed there was a statistically significant difference, for the three groups (LFA/DD/TD), on their ability to match familiar voices to familiar faces at study when the stimuli presented were very similar in age and gender : F (2, 81) = 9.12, p =

.0005. The effect size, calculated using eta squared, was small however at .18 (Cohen, 1992; Ferguson, 2009). Post-hoc comparisons, using the Tukey HSD Test, indicated that the mean score for the children with autism, when asked to match a voice to one of two individuals who were the same age and same gender (*m* = 4.55, SD = 1.57), was significantly lower than that achieved by both the children with developmental delay (*m* = 5.29, SD = .858) and the typically-developing children (*m* = 5.75, SD = .662). The children with developmental delay and the typically-developing children did not differ significantly on this task, implying that the diminished performance noted may be specific to individuals with LFA.

Discussion

This study involved conducting a Test of Familiar Voice to Familiar Face Matching, with participants with LFA; an age and ability matched group of participants with developmental delay (DD); and an ability matched group of typically-developing children. As this was a Test of Familiarity, only the children's first responses were recorded (see Mandler, 1980). Some ceiling effects (scores of 20), and some floor effects (scores of 10 or less), occurred in this study. Despite some floor effects, the majority of participants (n = 84) scored well above chance on this task indicating that participants fully understood what was expected of them.

The overall results of the Voice-Face Matching Test are important as they indicate that the recognition of familiar individuals, on the basis of their voices, is not only impaired in LFA, but also, that impaired voice recognition is specific to LFA as opposed to age and ability matched participants with developmental delay and ability matched young typically-developing children. This result is consistent with previous studies reporting impaired familiar voice recognition in autism even when visual cues, such as photographs, are present for the participant (Boucher et al., 1998).

Furthermore, and consistent with the earlier findings of Boucher et al., (1998), the children with autism in this study had had rather more opportunities than controls for exposure to the adults and children whose voices and faces were used as auditory and visual stimuli - given that they had been in school for longer than the other groups. This finding implies that a number of children with autism either do not, or cannot, utilise such opportunities to achieve *'normal'* familiarity (Boucher et al., 1998: 180).

Significantly, children with low-functioning autism demonstrated a marked impairment relative to age and ability matched controls in their capacity (or inclination) to discriminate between the voice of an adult, and the voice of a child. This finding is important on two counts. First, research suggests that the typically-developing four-year-old child distinguishes between the voices of males and females - adults and children using a relatively low-level 'hierarchal sequence of judgements' (Bartholomeus, 1973: 471). The children with autism, in this study, had a mean chronological age of ten years and five months, implying this task should have been relatively easy for them. This was not the case. Second, as all the faces and voices used as stimuli in these tests were of teachers and pupils in the schools of participants, it is of interest that children with autism - who had the most exposure time to these individuals, and thus, should have benefited from increased familiarity - performed the least well of all participants tested.

In terms of gender, studies with typically-developing children suggest that females tend to do better on voice-face recognition tasks than males (Bartholomeus, 1973; Mann et al., 1979: Rosa et al., 2008). Previous studies of voice processing autism did not report gender differences in the overall scores (Boucher et al., 1998, 2000). Conversely, in the present study, a small main effect for gender on measures of voice-face matching was found across all participants, but with males scoring higher than females. This finding is difficult to reconcile with those of previous studies (Bartholomeus, 1973; Mann et al., 1979; Rosa et al., 2008). However, boys outnumbered girls in this study with twice as many males as females in the group with LFA, which may have skewed the results somewhat.

Previous studies (Ni Chuileann & Quigley, 2013) affirmed that children and adolescents with LFA were significantly impaired, relative to age and ability matched controls on Tests of Familiarity and recollection. In addition, it is well established that both recollection and familiarity underpin recognition memory (Joseph et al., 2005). It is unsurprising, therefore, to note that - in the main - the participants with LFA in this study were significantly impaired on tests of voice-face recognition. Furthermore, this impairment appears to be specific to participants with LFA.

Overall, we had predicted that children with LFA would be impaired relative to other children at matching voices to faces. We further predicted that girls would perform better than boys on this type of task, and that children with higher NVMA scores would be more accurate when matching voices to faces than those with lower NVMA scores. In the event, only two of those hypotheses were supported: The children with LFA scored least well of the three groups of participants at matching familiar voices to familiar faces, and children with higher non-verbal mental ages were more accurate on this task than children with lower

NVMA scores. Unexpectedly, the boys were better at matching voices to faces than the girls.

Caution should be exercised when interpreting these results, however, as the procedures used were different from those described by previous researchers (Bartholomeus, 1973, Mann et al., 1979; Boucher et al., 1998, 2000). Using a computer-based Forced Choice Test design, rather than asking the child to listen to a voice recording and subsequently identify the speaker from an array of photographs, was intended to reduce task demands for the child with LFA (see Wilson, Blades, & Pascalis, 2007). This 'simpler' methodology may have overly advantaged the TD children. Yet, given the mean scores of both the children with LFA, and those with DD, any increase in the number of stimuli presented may have negatively impacted upon these participants, potentially inflating floor effects.

In addition, there was no school in the Republic Of Ireland catering for children with autism; children with developmental delay and typically-developing children, inclusively. As a result, the participants attended one of five different schools, meaning the stimuli used was always three staff and two pupils from the child's class, but were non-comparable across schools. A second consequence of this methodological difficulty is that units catering for children with autism rarely comprise of more than six pupils, with one teacher and two special needs assistants (http://www.education.ie). This meant that a total of five people could be used as 'familiar' stimuli for the children with LFA in any given school, and consequently, for all other participants. Restricting all Test stimuli to such a small group of familiar people may have once again advantaged the typically-developing child, but increasing the number of people the child with LFA is 'familiar' with, for future voice processing work, remains problematic.

On the whole, a computer-based paradigm allows stimuli to be stored, inter-changed, and presented, in a fast, efficient and attention-capturing way for school-aged participants, and is very useful in terms of clarifying the extent of impoverished voice-face matching in the non-verbal child with LFA.

Our Fourth Study: Testing Self-Voice-to-Self-Face-Matching in Low-Functioning Autism

In this study, we used the same 2-choice forced recognition paradigm, utilised in Study 3, to assess the ability of the child with LFA to match a recording of their own voice to that of their own photograph at test. We compared the performance of the 33 children with LFA with performance in a group of young TD children, matched with the LFA group for NVMA and an age matched group of children with DD, also matched with the LFA group on NVMA.

We chose a FC format on the basis that this paradigm enhances familiarity, more so than standard Y/N formats (e.g., Holdstock et al., 2002; Migo et al., 2009). In addition, the use of visual prompts - such as photographs - were used to assess self-voice recognition, using cues to support recognition in the first instance, and if this advantaged certain children with autism, those children could be tested on self-voice recognition minus visual prompts at a later date.

Self-voice-self-face matching has not previously been tested, but, on the basis of findings from Study 3 it was predicted that: (1) Children with LFA would be impaired, relative to age and ability matched groups of children with DD and TD children; (2) girls would match self-voice to self-face more accurately than boys, and; (3) given the range of NVMA scores in the two clinical groups, higher NVMA scores would be associated with greater self-voice-self-face matching ability.

What We Did and How We Did It

Participants

All 93 children were invited to participate in this study.

General Procedural Points

General procedural points were the same as those used in Study 1.

Materials and Procedure

Materials: For each school, the following materials were created.

Practice Stimuli: For each of the 5 participating schools, a set of eight standard-sized digital colour photographs of faces were taken. Three of the photographs were of male pupils from the school of the participants, but not those pupils whose faces and voices were used as stimuli in Study 3. Three were of female pupils from the participant's school, but again, not those children who were involved in Study 3. Two slightly different photographs of the participant (photo A and photo B) were also taken at this juncture. By 'slightly different,' we mean the child's photograph was taken with them looking a little more to the right for photo A and straight on for photo B.

An audio-list was created by which each of the photographed children were recorded on a hand-held digital recorder (http://www.phillips.com) saying, "*Hello! Can you point to my picture?*" (Boucher et al., 1998:173).

This particular speech sample was selected to maximise voice recognition cues by providing a sample longer than one second in duration (Bartholomeus, 1973; Bricker & Pruzansky, 1966), and to include both falling and rising intonation (Bartholomeus, 1973).

For most children with LFA, and some children with DD, to record their voices as audio stimuli the tester needed to sound out the words in order for the child to mimic them. Later, the tester's voice was edited from the voice recording. Editing the recordings of the voices of the children with autism runs the risk of introducing, or removing, some acoustic cues from the process, which may render the recording less familiar to the child at test (see Shuster, 1998). However, transplanting a recording of an autistic child's voice onto a SGD will necessarily involve some form of editing, making the process here valid.

For the practice phase, when the target child was a boy, the photographs of the distracter children were those of same age/ ethnicity male pupils, and vice versa when the target child was a girl. There were four slides, and each displayed two photographs presented side-by-side (e.g., 1-2, 3-4, 1-4, 2-3) with the target child's photograph presented as '3.' For each of the 4 slides shown, the two images filled the screen with the caption, "Whose voice is this?" always displayed as the heading of the slide shown. In addition, a pre-prepared score was used for this practice phase. The speech sample of only one of the two person's shown was ever played on any presentation (e.g., 1, 3, 4, 2).

Main Test stimuli: The set of colour photographs and audio-recordings used as stimuli in the PowerPoint designed for the purpose of Study 3, were used as stimuli for this Test. As per Study 3, the photographs comprised the child's teacher and two SNAs. However, for the purpose of this study, instead of using the voices and faces of three pupils from the target child's classroom, just two were retained for this PowerPoint slideshow. The voice and face (photo B) of the target child replaced that of the third pupil.

Once again, the PowerPoint slide-show comprised 10 slides. Each slide contained the photographs of two individuals presented side-by-side (1-2, 3-4, 5-**6**, 4-3, 2-4, **6**-1, 3-1, 5-2, 4-**6**, 2-1). The photograph of the target child corresponds to position 6 and was therefore shown on three of the ten slides. For each of the 10 slides shown, the two images filled the screen with the caption, "Whose voice is this?" always displayed as the heading of the slide shown. In addition, a pre-prepared score was used for this practice phase. As per Study 3, for each slide shown, the voice of just one person played (1, 4, **6**, 3, 2, 1, 3, 5, **6**, 1). Therefore, the photograph of the target child was shown on three occasions while the voice of the target child was played on two occasions, across the ten slides. The reason for using this order of presentation is that, rather than just play the target child's voice on each occasion their image is shown - and thus increase the child's chance of false positive identification - on at least one occasion, the target face would act as a distractor.

No other study of self-voice-to-self-face matching in autism had been conducted previously, making it difficult to know exactly how many times the target-child's image and voice should be presented. Therefore, while the frequency of self-face and self-voice may appear somewhat low in this study, based on the children's performance here, it could be recalibrated for future studies. The order of the presentations used in Study 3 was replicated here, as it meant the tester only had to replace the image and voice recording of one child used as a stimulus in Study 3 with those of the target-child in Study 4.

Procedure: Training and testing took part in a single sitting. The aim of the practice phase was to ensure children's understanding of the task of matching a recording of their own voice to a photograph of their own face, via a PowerPoint demonstration. The training procedure was as follows: The children were invited to sit at a desk to the right of the tester. In the centre of the table, facing the child and the tester, a laptop with the training and Main Test PowerPoint was located. The laptop was equipped with a wireless-mouse, which was located under the hand of the tester and out of direct reach of the child. The tester began by saying, "*I have some photographs to show you. Look, let's see whose pictures I have on here!*" Using the wireless-mouse the tester then put up the first slide showing (A-B) side-by side and pointing at photograph A, they then named the person, and said, "*You know 'A'. 'A' is in your class.*" After a pause of approximately three seconds, this procedure was repeated for photograph B (see Boucher et al., 1998). The tester then showed the second slide displaying a photograph of the target child and a control child (C-D) side-by-side, and - pointing at the photograph of the target child – said, *"This is a photograph of you."* After a pause of approximately three seconds, the tester pointed to photograph D, and said, *"And this is 'D'. 'D' is in your class."* This naming procedure took approximately five seconds per slide. It was conducted for two reasons. First, to ensure the child recognised all the photographed individuals in the slideshow, including that of their own photo. Second, it is suggested that STM is mediated mainly through auditory or phonological components (Baddeley, 1999) and therefore it was hoped that naming the people used as stimuli in this Test would enhance the child's memory for them later at test.

The tester then drew the child's attention back to the screen and, using the wireless-mouse, returned to the start of the practice phase PowerPoint. The tester then said, '*I'm going to play a recording of a voice next. It will be the voice of one of these people you just saw. I want you to point to the person you think the voice belongs to. Will you do that for me?"* The tester then clicked the mouse to activate the voice of A. If the child pointed to A, the next slide - showing C and D side-by-side - was presented, and the next recording (i.e., voice C) was played. If the child chose the incorrect photograph, the tester said, *"I think it must be this person*" and moved on to the next slide. This procedure was repeated using a different order of voices until each of the four slides (e.g., A-B, C-D, A-D, and B-C) had been played twice and participants had made four consecutive correct responses, two of which were self-voice recognition responses within the eight presentations. All children met this criterion and progressed to the Main Test.

For the Main Test, the child was told there were many more photographs to see and were asked if they wished to continue. All children were pleased to progress to the Main Test. The procedure was the same as used at practice, whereby the child was shown the ten slides and was helped to name the people on the screen to ensure that the children recognised the staff, pupils, and the photo of themselves. The PowerPoint slideshow was then played again, but this time the tester said, "*I'm going to play a recording of a voice next. It will be the voice of one of these people you just saw. I want you to point to the person you think the voice belongs to. Will you do that for me?"* The first slide was shown with the photographs of two individuals presented in a side-by-side format, and the speech sample of one of the individuals was played. Each of the ten slides was shown for a total of five seconds, as this time corresponded with the length of time it had taken to name each photographed person previously. This procedure was repeated until all ten slides were shown. The child would have seen their own photograph on three of the ten slides shown, but the recording of their voice would only have played on two of these three occasions. Therefore, the child had two individual occasions on which they could correctly match their own recorded voice to their own photograph at Main Test.

Proportions of correct responses were praised, and comments, such as, "*Well done!"* "*You are doing great,*" and "*We are nearly finished!"* were used to keep the child motivated and on task. A record was made only as to whether the child made a correct self-voice-face match or not. If the child correctly matched the voice to the face, a score of 1 was awarded and the next slide was presented. If the child failed to respond (more than fifteen seconds), or made an incorrect response, the tester pointed to the photograph of the target child and said, *'I think that was your voice,'* and a score of 0 was awarded (see Mandler, 1980). The child's responses were recorded as either √ (correct) or x (incorrect) on the score sheet, and scores ranged from 0-2. As this was a forced-choice response option Test, each child had a 1 in 2 chance of choosing the target photograph by simply guessing (Robson, 2002). The chance success level for this identification would be 50%, therefore, and, as such, the chance level raw score for this Test was estimated at 1 / 2.

What We Found Out About Self-Voice-Face Matching in Autism

It was predicted that the child with LFA would be impaired in their ability to match a recording of their own voice to that of their own photograph at test, relative to age and ability matched children with DD and ability matched TD children. The results of this Test confirm this prediction as less than 40% of children with LFA were able to recognise their own recorded voice at a level above chance - compared to over 60% of children with developmental delay and almost 90% of typically-developing children (see Table 4-6). Of the 12 children with LFA who succeeded on this task, 8 (66.7%) were males and 4 (33.3 %) were female, and they ranged in age from 6 years 5 months to 15 years 4 months. NVMA scores ranged from 3 years 1 month to 8 years 5 months. One of these children was once again Connie, the young girl who had scored at ceiling on the previous three tests. Two children with developmental delay were absent from school on the day of testing.

Table 4-6 Descriptive Statistics for the LFA and Comparison Groups: Study 4 A Test of Self-Voice-Face Recognition

Study 3. A Test of self-voice-face matching			
Characteristic	**LFA**	**DD**	**TD**
n	33	25*	33
Did not match self-voice to self-face on any trial *n* (%)	16 (84.2%)	3 (15.8%)	0 (0%)

Matched self-voice to self-face on 1 trial *n* (%)	5 (35.7%)	4 (28.6%)	5 (35.7%)
Matched self-voice to self-face on 2 trials *n* (%)	12 (20.7%)	18 (31.0%)	28 (48.3%)
CA in years			
n	33	25	33
M	10.5	13.9	6.1
SD	3.1	2.8	0.7
Range	5.0-15.4	6.0-16.6	4.6- 7.1
NVMA in years			
n	32**	24**	33
M	5.07	5.3	5.09
SD	1.5	1.7	0.4
Range	3.1-8.5	2.2-7.8	5.0- 6.8
IQ			
n	32**	24**	33
M	50.0	56.4	97.8
SD	11.3	14.8	7.5
Range	24.3-85.0	26.5-93.8	82.3-114.2

ma/ca x 100 = IQ; *Two children with DD (id no.'s 40 & 41) were absent from school on the day of testing; **The NVMA of 1 child with LFA, and 1 with DD, could not be calculated via the BPVS

A Kruskal-Wallis Test revealed a statistically significant difference in self-voice-to-face matching across the three groups of children (LFA, $n = 33$; DD, $n = 25$; TD, $n = 33$), $\chi 2$ ($n = 91$) = 22.37, $p = .0005$. The children with LFA recorded a lower median score (*Md* = 1.0) than the other two groups of children, which both recorded median vales of 2.0.

A second Kruskal-Wallis Test revealed no statistically significant difference in self-voice-to-self-face recognition scores on the basis of gender (LFA, $m = 22, f = 11$; DD, $m = 15, f = 10$; TD, $m = 19, f = 14$), $\chi 2$ ($n = 91$) = .81, $p = .36$. Instead, both males and females recorded median values of 2.0.

Within the LFA group, an independent samples t-test showed no significant difference between those who scored below chance (M = 49.8,

SD = 11.03) and those who scored above chance (M = 50.0, SD = 12.4; t (30), = -.103, p = 91 (two-tailed). The magnitude of the differences between the means (mean difference = -.44, 95% CI: -9.19 to 8.30) was very small (eta squared = .006).

Finally, a two-way ANOVA was carried out to examine the effects of gender and NVMA on scores of self-voice-face recognition. Participants were divided into three groups according to their NVMA scores (Group 1, <= 62 months; Group 2, 63–72 months; Group 3, 73+ months). While the interaction effect between NVMA and gender was not statistically significant, F (2, 84) = 2.23, p = 1.1, and there was no main effect for gender, F (1, 84), = 1.50, p = .22, there was a statistically significant effect for NVMA on participant scores for matching their own voice to photographs of themselves at test, F (2, 84) = 3.47, p = .03 with a very small effect size (partial eta squared = .07). This suggests that while males and females did not differ in their ability to match self-voice to self-face in this study, there is a small difference in scores for those with an NVMA of 62 months or less; those with an NVMA between 63 and 72 months; and those with an NVMA of 73 months and more.

Table 4-7 Descriptive Statistics for the 33 Children with LFA: Studies 1-4

Id No.	Name	Gender	CA yrs	NVMA yrs	IQ	Study 1	Study 2	Study 3	Study 4
1	Frank	M	7.4	5.0	67.4	15	12	11	
2	Jim	M	11.4	4.8	42.3		19		2
3	Peter	M	6.5	3.8	58.2		16	12	2
4	Edward	M	9.5	3.7	39.8	10	17	16	
5	Rachel	F	5.0	4.2	85.0	9	10	11	
6	Jake	M	7.2	3.1	43.6	12	15		2
7	Francis	M	10.5	5.5	51.9	10	10	18	1
8	Jason	M	6.5	3.2	50.0	11	12	14	1
9	Linda	F	14.3	7.8	54.6	16	8	14	
10	Anthony	M	13.8	5.5	40.3		7		
11	Tim	M	11.5	5.3	46.0	9	20		
12	Alan	M	6.5	3.1	43.6	9	8	14	
13	Brendan	M	10.7	5.9	55.0	9	8	15	
14	Paddy	M	11.5	5.8	50.3	10	5	16	
15	Ida	F	12.4	4.2	34.2	10	4	16	
16	Richard	M	12.8	5.1	40.2	9	12	26	1
17	Robbie	M	14.0			16	8	18	2

18	**Ann**	F	13.4	7.9	59.0	9	9	17	2
19	**Nita**	F	13.2	8.5	64.7	16		20	2
20	**Lucy**	F	10.6	4.9	46.0	9	8	11	1
21	**Maggie**	F	11.9	7.1	60.1	10	12		
22	**Bob**	M	15.4	3.7	24.3	16	16	20	2
23	**John**	M	8.0	5.1	63.9	12	9	20	2
24	**Mark**	M	15.0	6.1	40.8	16	11	18	2
25	**Rebecca**	F	6.3	3.1	50.0	11	9	12	
26	**Dermot**	M	6.1	3.2	52.7	9	11	12	
27	**Fiona**	F	6.6	3.1	47.5	9	16		
28	**Kevin**	M	13.5	7.9	58.2	9	10	18	2
29	**Sandra**	F	10.7	5.9	55.0	16	6	19	2
30	**Paul**	M	8.0	3.7	46.3	10	16	18	1
31	**David**	M	15.3	6.1	40.2	10	8	16	
32	**Ger**	M	8.1	3.7	45.9	9	2	16	
33	**Connie**	F	11.3	4.9	43.3	**16**	**20**	**20**	**2**
				Maximum	**Scores**	**7**	**2**	**4**	**12**

All names used are pseudonyms; MA /CA x 100 = IQ; Study 1: A Test of Familiarity excludes 3 children who showed distress on the day of testing; Study 2: A Test of Recollection excludes 1 child who was unwell on the day of testing; Study 3: A Test of Voice-Face Matching excludes 3 children with LFA who scored at, or below, chance (defined as 10 or less)

Discussion

The findings of this study were largely expected. It was anticipated that children with LFA would show some difficulty in the recognition of their own recorded voice even when visual cues were available. Children with LFA showed a significant impairment of self-voice recognition relative to comparison children, something which has not previously been documented. The findings also suggest that this impairment is specific to LFA.

Consistent with the suggestion that the development of autobiographical episodic memory is sufficient for the recall of information in four year olds, almost ninety per cent of the typically-developing schoolchildren recognised their own voice. Additionally, as self-recognition is often compromised in atypical populations (Christiana, Malcolm, Johnson, & Keenan, 2008; Rosa et al., 2008) it was unsurprising to note that one third of the children with developmental delay did not succeed on this task. Just

12 children with LFA matched their own voice to their own photograph at test.

It might be assumed that the differences between self-voice recognition in typical, versus atypical, groups here result solely from low intellectual ability. However, verbal and non-verbal abilities in the three groups of children were controlled for by matching procedures. Despite this, more severe recognition impairments are noted in the children with autism. This does not mean that learning difficulties do not contribute to memory and processing impairments in autism and children with developmental delay. Rather, it means that some additional factor(s) are required to explain these differences as they emerge in relation to memory in LFA and ability-matched comparison groups. One such factor appears to be low NVMA scores. This study shows that participant ability to recognise self-voice increased exponentially with increased NVMA scores. Moreover, the twelve children with autism - who performed at ceiling in this task - had slightly higher NVMA scores than their twenty-one counterparts who did not score above chance-level. This finding is consistent with general voice-face processing studies in children with autism by Boucher et al., (1998, 2000) and with typically-developing children (Mann et al., 1979).

It might be that the low scores of the children with autism reflect a lack of motivation or attention to this particular task, yet, great care was taken to ensure this Test was as autism-friendly as possible. For instance, rather than more traditional methods to assess voice recognition in children (Boucher et al., 1998, 2000) a computer-based paradigm was used, as it is well accepted that the child with autism enjoys interacting with technology (Dautenhahn, 1999). In addition, a forced-choice paradigm was used, as this particular method places significantly less task demands on children with ASD (Wilson et al., 2007). Despite these measures, children with LFA still performed less well than either the child with developmental delay or the very young typically-developing child in this study.

It could be argued that the recorded voices of the children with autism were subjected to editing, which may have introduced - or eliminated - something, making the recording less familiar to the child (see Shuster, 1998). In a similar vein, it could be argued that the children with autism were the most linguistically challenged group in this study, thereby making this group the least familiar with the sound of their own voice than any of the other participants. There are several reasons for arguing that these factors did not significantly contribute to the poor performance by children with autism in this case. In the first place, the proposal that a natural voice on a SGD will better suit the child with ASD is predicated on a voice being recorded onto the device. This process will necessarily involve some form of editing as conducted here, making testing - using an edited recorded voice - ecologically valid. In the second place, children between the ages of three and five are notorious for altering their voices when asked to speak into a microphone (Pollack, Pickett, & Sumby, 1954; Spence et al., 2002). The young typically-developing children here, and the children with DD with an NVMA of five, most likely engaged in similar processes (e.g., speaking unusually softly), making their voices less familiar at test. Therefore, the recorded voices of all the children in this study were relatively comparable in terms of their sound quality for all participants. Rather, it is possible to speculate that while the children found their voices *familiar*, they were unable to *recollect* whose actual voice it was (e.g., Jacoby, 1991).

Summary of Studies 3 and 4

The aim of these studies was twofold: First to establish not only the ability to recognise the voice of an already known person in LFA, but also to assess the ability of children with autism to recognise their own recorded voice. Whereas the first study was a measure of implicit knowledge and noetic awareness in LFA, the second was an assessment of episodic memory, and, as such, a sense of 'I was there', and thus self-concept and ways in which aspects of the 'self' are experienced in LFA (see Lind, 2010). It was found that children with LFA are significantly impaired in both instances, relative to TD children and children with DD.

The second aim of these two studies was to identify children with autism, in this sample, for whom the allocation of a personalised SGD over a twelve-week period would be meaningful. It was assumed that children who could recognise familiar voices and/or their own self-voice would benefit most from a SGD programmed with the voice of a child similar to them in age, gender, and accent, or that of their own recorded voice.

Next, it is important to assess the child's ability to recognise the sound of their own voice in the absence of visual stimuli. The reason being that while standard SGD comes with a range of synthesised speech output options - such as adult, child, male, and female voices (http://www.toby-churchill.com) - there are no visual cues, such as photographs, to prompt the user to choose these options. Generally, speech output options are denoted by small symbols on the unit itself and are fully explained in the user-guide, which accompanies the device (http://www.toby-churchill.com). It is necessary, therefore, to assess whether children are able to recognise their own recorded voice as their own when it is presented together with three other child voices, without any visual cues.

Our Fifth Study: Testing Self-Voice Recognition in Low-Functioning Autism

In this experiment, we used a 4-choice forced recognition task to assess self-voice recognition in LFA. We compared the performance of twelve children with LFA - who had achieved maximum scores on a Self-Voice-Self-Face Matching Test in Study 4 - to a group of children with LFA who also took part in Study 4, but did not achieve maximum scores.

In this Test, we wanted to investigate the child's ability to recognise the sound of their own voice when no visual cues were provided as prompts. As the study of children's self-perception of their own recorded voice in the absence of visual cues is 'relatively unexplored' (Strömbergsson, 2009:e1), appropriate and effective methods are therefore difficult to ascertain and come mainly from research into speech and language pathologies (Schuster, 1998; Strömbergsson, 2009).

Typically, the voices of target participants and the voices of a comparison group are recorded reading from a pre-prepared script. Following a retention interval, the script is played back to them via headphones and participants are required to identify the sound of their own voice from those of the foils (Hughes & Nicholson, 2010; Rosa et al., 2008; Schuster, 1998; Strömbergsson, 2009). This procedure reflects an assessment of familiarity and recollection, as the child is required to identify a voice they have heard previously and is thus familiar with, and also to recollect which voice is actually that of their own. Using the FCC method over that of a YN should also make the task easier for participants, as all the voices will have some familiarity value (Yonelinas, 2001, 2002), but their own should evoke the strongest sense of recognition (Rogers, Kuiper, & Kirker, 1977).

Both Shuster (1998) and Strömbergsson (2009) recorded participants as they read from a pre-prepared reading script. At test, the children's recorded voices were played back to the children, alongside the recorded voices of other children, and the task for the participant was to identify their own recorded voice.

No studies of this type have been conducted on the child with autism, but it was predicted that the children from the target group would perform at a statistically significantly better rate, on this Test, than the children from the randomly chosen comparison group.

What We Did and How We Did It

Participants

Twelve of the thirty-three children with LFA had matched a recording, of their own recorded voice, to a photograph of themselves at a level above chance in Study 4: A Test of Self-Voice-to Self-Face Matching. These twelve children were considered to be the children most likely to succeed on a Test of Self-Voice recognition where no visual cues, such as photographs, might be used. Seven of these children were attending School A, and the remaining five were attending School B.

A further seven children from School A, and five from School B (all from the original sample of thirty-three children with LFA), were chosen randomly on the day of testing and invited to participate in this study of self-voice recognition as a comparison group.

General Procedural Points

The general procedural points were the same as those used in Study 3.

Materials and Procedure

For each of the two schools the following materials were prepared:

Training stimuli: A slideshow consisting of six slides was created on PowerPoint (http://www.microsoft.com). Each slide showed a set of four identical 'smiley faces' across the top (Fig. 10). These smiley-faces were downloaded from an app store (http://www.mileythetalkingsmiley.com). They could be customised to play sounds, words, or music, and the colour and size could be adjusted as required.

Six sounds from clipart were downloaded as stimuli and these comprised (1) a drum roll, (2) a dog's bark, (3) an ambulance siren, (4) a doorbell, (5) a jingle bell, and (6) a baby crying. In addition, the target children were recorded on a handheld recorder (http://www.phillips.com) saying the word, "*Hello*." These seven sounds comprised the audio list accompanying the training phase PowerPoint slideshow.

There were six slides in total and each one comprised the four smiley faces as shown in Fig. 10. For each of the six slides, four of the seven sounds were recorded (in a random fashion) onto the four smiley faces by following the instructions accompanying the app (see Fig. 4-1).

The voice of the child was recorded onto one of the four faces on each of the six slides, but, to avoid preservation, this recording was randomised across the four faces on each of the slides.

Fig. 4-2 An Example of a Slide Used at Training During Study 5

Test stimuli: For each of the two schools, a PowerPoint demonstration was created for the Main Test consisting of ten slides in total. Each of the ten slides displayed four 'smiley faces' from the app 'mileythetalking smiley,' but, to avoid interference (Ebbinghaus, 1913) or feature overlap (Yonelinas, 2002), they were different faces from those used for the training phase. Underneath the four smiley faces, the slides showed a picture, which was different for each of the ten slides used (Fig. 4-2).

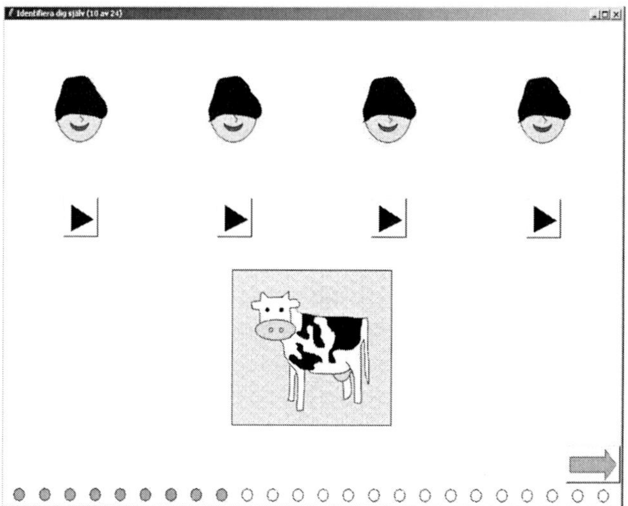

Fig. 4-2 An Example of the Slides Used at Test in Study 5 (Adapted from Strömbergsson, 2009)

A reading script of ten single syllable words corresponding to these ten pictures (e.g., a cow, a dog, a house, a spoon, a car) was created, and each participant with LFA was recorded via a digital hand held recorder (http://www.phillips.com) saying these ten words. Typically, the researcher or a teacher said the word and the child repeated it. Later the adult's voice was edited out, leaving a script of ten words just of the child's voice.

To create a set of foil voices, two male (male voice 1 and male voice 2) and two female (female voice 1 and female voice 2) TD children - from School B (from the original sample of TD participants) - were recorded reading the same ten words.

For this PowerPoint demonstration, the recordings of the children (i.e., target and foils) were recorded onto the 4 smiley faces across 10 slides (see Fig. 12), firstly for School A and then for School B. The target voice appeared on every slide, but was randomised across the four smiley faces on each of the ten slides so as to avoid perseveration.

Procedure: The training and testing for this assessment were completed in a single session. The main objective of the practice phase was to motivate the children to point at the correct location on the screen when they heard a recording of their own voice. For the Training phase, the children were invited to sit at a desk to the right of the tester. In the centre of the table, facing the child and the tester, a laptop with the training and Main Test PowerPoint was located. The laptop was equipped with a wireless-mouse, which was located under the hand of the tester and out of direct reach of the child. The tester drew the child's attention to the computer screen and said, "*Look, here are four smiley faces*" and pointed to each face one after the other. The tester then said, *"Look, they make sound"* and (1) a drum roll, (2) a dog's bark, and (3) an ambulance siren, were activated by placing the cursor on the screen on each smiley face. When the cursor touched the fourth smiley face, the recording of the child's voice was played saying, *"Hello.*" When all four sounds had been played, the tester pointed to smiley face number four and said, *"That was your voice! Will we see if we can find your voice on another slide?"*

The second slide was shown and the same procedure followed, except the child's voice was activated when the cursor was over the third smiley face. When all four smiley faces had produced a sound, the child was encouraged to point to the one that had said, *"Hello"* with their voice. This procedure was repeated for all remaining slides, but the child's voice was randomised across the four smiley faces on the screen. If the child pointed to the correct 'smiley face,' the child was praised and the next slide was shown. If the child pointed to the wrong smiley face, the tester pointed to the correct location on the screen saying, *"I think it must be this one*" and moved on to the next slide (see Mandler, 1980). A criterion of three-out-of-six correct judgements was considered as a level above chance and, thus, sufficient for children with autism to progress to the Main Test. On the day of testing, five of the children from the comparison group showed mild distress and withdrew from the study, leaving a 'target group' of 12 children and a 'comparison group' of 7 children.

For the Main Test the children were instructed there were lots more pictures to see, and the child was asked if they wished to continue. The same procedure used at practice was used, except that ten slides with four smiley faces were used as stimuli. In addition, each of the ten slides showed one picture taken from clip art (http://www.mocrosoft.com), such as a cow, a dog, a spoon, and a house (see Fig. 12). The tester drew the child's attention to the first slide and said, "*I have some more pictures to show you. Look, let's see which pictures I have on here!"* The tester presented the first slide showing the picture of an animated cow and, pointing to that picture, said, "*Look, this is a picture of a cow."* This naming/labelling procedure was repeated until all ten pictures in the ten slides were named aloud. It was anticipated that naming/labelling each picture to be shown would activate the child's STM (Baddeley, 1971), and help the child recognise the items better at test. This naming/labelling procedure took approximately 5 seconds per slide. Next, the PowerPoint slideshow was returned to the first slide. The tester said, "*I'm going to play a recording of some voices next. There are lots of voices, but one of them will be your voice. When you hear your voice, I want you to point to the smiley face that you think it came from. Ready? Here we go!"*

The target child's voice was randomised across the four 'smiley faces,' across each of the 10 slides. The task for the target child was to recognise their own voice when it was presented, together with three other voices. When the child had identified the smiley face associated with their voice the child was praised, and the next slide was presented. If the child was reluctant to respond, the tester elicited a response by saying, "*Just guess, quick as you can"*. At test, there were no instances in which a child perseverated to a particular location. The children's responses were scored on a sheet as '√' for a correct answer, and 'x' for an incorrect guess. Each correctly recognised target item was awarded one point. Incorrect responses were not awarded any points (see Mandler, 1980). Possible scores therefore ranged from 0 to 10.

As this Test was one where the child must select the right voice from one of four voices presented, it was important to calculate the chance success level, or the proportion of correct answers, that could occur if all children were to guess randomly at the answer (Robson, 2002). This Test represented a four-response option and, as such, the chance success level for this Test was calculated at 25%, or a score of 2.

What We Found Out About Self-Voice Recognition in Autism

It was predicted that the children from the target group would show a significantly better rate of voice recognition than, the group of children in the comparison group who had been chosen randomly on the day. Mean scores for the target and comparison groups are displayed in Table 4-8. Some ceiling effects (scores of 10) occurred. No participants scored at chance (scores of 2 or below).

Table 4-8 Descriptive Statistics for the Target and Comparison Groups of Children with LFA Participating in Study 5: A Test of Pure-Voice Recognition

Id No.	Name	Gender	CA yrs	NVMA yrs	IQ	Max Score SVRT 2	Max Score PVRT 10
Target	Group	(n =12)					
2	Jim	M	11.4	4.8	42.3	2	10
6	Jake	M	7.2	3.1	43.6	2	10
3	Peter*	M	6.5	3.8	58.2	2	10
17	Robbie**	M	14.0			2	10
18	Ann*	F	13.4	7.9	59.0	2	10
19	Nita	F	13.2	8.5	64.7	2	10
22	Bob	M	15.4	3.7	24.3	2	10
23	John	M	8.0	5.1	63.9	2	10
24	Mark	M	15.0	6.1	40.8	2	10
29	Sandra	F	10.7	5.9	55.0	2	10
28	Kevin*	M	13.5	7.9	58.2	2	10
33	Connie	F	11.3	4.9	43.3	2	7
Random	**Group**						
1	Frank	M	7.4	5.0	67.4	0	3
7	Francis	M	10.5	5.5	51.9	1	10~

8	Jason	M	6.5	3.2	50.0	1	8~
9	Linda	F	14.3	7.8	54.6	0	10~
10	Anthony	M	13.8	5.5	46.0	0	4
20	Lucy	F	10.6	4.9	46.0	1	3
30	Paul	M	8.0	3.7	46.3	1	10*

***Ann, Kevin, Peter, and Paul subsequently left the study after Study 5; **It was not possible to calculate the NVMA of Robbie via the BPVS**

A greater number of self-voice identifications occurred in the target group *(m* = 9.75) than in the control group (*m* = 6.85). The mean difference between conditions was 2.89, and the 95% CI for the estimated population mean difference is between 0.75 and 5.02. The effect size was (*d* = 0.680). An independent sample *t*-test showed that the difference between groups was statistically significant (*t* = 2.856, *df* = 17, *p* = .005, one-tailed). Additionally, there was no significant difference in relation to IQ between the target group (M = 50.9, SD = 8.61) and the target group (M = 50.3, SD = 12.4; t (16) = -.117, p = .90 (two-tailed).

The children in the target group, presented with slightly greater NVMA scores (*m* =63.83, SD = 28.27), scored better on this Test of voice recognition than those in the comparison group with somewhat lower NVMA scores (*m*= 61.57, SD = 17.61). However, the mean difference between conditions was 2.26, and the 95% CI for the estimated population mean difference is between -22.85 and 27.38, and the effect size was very small (*d* = 0.002). An independent t-test showed that the difference between conditions was not significant (*t* = 190, *df* = .17, *p* = .32, one-tailed).

Finally, it was shown that boys (*m* = 8.84) performed slightly better than girls (m = 8.33) on this task. The mean difference between genders was .512, and the 95% CI for the estimated population mean difference is between -2.17 and 3.19. The effect size was very small (0.009). An independent t-test showed that the difference between conditions was not significant (t = .403, *df* = 17, p = 0.57, one-tailed). Table 4-9 shows the scores of the 33 children with autism on the five empirical studies conducted thus far.

Table 4-9 Descriptive Statistics for the LFA Group on Studies 1-5

No	LFA name	Sex	CA yrs	NVMA yrs	IQ	Study 1 *Max 16*	Study 2 *Max 20*	Study 3 *Max 20*	Study 4 *Max 2*	Study 5 *Max 10*
1	**Frank**	M	7.4	5.0	67.4	15	12	11		3
2	**Jim**	M	11.4	4.8	42.3		19		2	10
3	**Peter**	M	6.5	3.8	58.2		16	12	2	10
4	**Edward**	M	9.5	3.7	39.8	10	17	16		
5	**Rachel**	F	5.0	4.2	85.0	9	10	11		
6	**Jake**	M	7.2	3.1	43.6	12	15		2	10
7	**Francis**	M	10.5	5.5	51.9	10	10	18	1	10
8	**Jason**	M	6.5	3.2	50.0	11	12	14	1	8
9	**Linda**	F	14.3	7.8	54.6	16	8	14		10
10	**Anthony**	M	13.8	5.5	40.3		7			4
11	**Tim**	M	11.5	5.3	46.0	9	20			
12	**Alan**	M	6.5	3.1	43.6	9	8	14		
13	**Brendan**	M	10.7	5.9	55.0	9	8	15		
14	**Paddy**	M	11.5	5.8	50.3	10	5	16		
15	**Ida**	F	12.4	4.2	34.2	10	4	16		

16	**Richard**	M	12.8	5.1	40.2	9	12	16	1	
17	**Robbie**	M	14.0			16	8	18	2	10
18	**Ann**	F	13.4	7.9	59.0	9	9	17	2	10
19	**Nita**	F	13.2	8.5	64.7	16		20	2	10
20	**Lucy**	F	10.6	4.9	46.0	9	8	11	1	3
21	**Maggie**	F	11.9	7.1	60.1	10	12			
22	**Bob**	M	15.4	3.7	24.3	16	16	20	2	10
23	**John**	M	8.0	5.1	63.9	12	9	20	2	10
24	**Mark**	M	15.0	6.1	40.8	16	11	18	2	10
25	**Rebecca**	F	6.3	3.1	50.0	11	9	12		
26	**Dermot**	M	6.1	3.2	52.7	9	11	12		
27	**Fiona**	F	6.6	3.1	47.5	9	16			
28	**Kevin**	M	13.5	7.9	58.2	9	10	18	2	10
29	**Sandra**	F	10.7	5.9	55.0	16	6	19	2	10
30	**Paul**	M	8.0	3.7	46.3	10	16	18	1	10
31	**David**	M	15.3	6.1	40.2	10	8	16		
32	**Ger**	M	8.1	3.7	45.9	9	2	16		
33	**Connie**	F	11.3	4.9	43.3	16	20	20	2	7
	Number	**who**	**scored**	**at maximum**		7	2	4	12	14

LFA refers to Low-Functioning Autism; DD refers to Developmental-Delay; TD refers to Typically-Developing; CA refers to chronological age; NVMA refers to non-verbal mental age; IQ is calculated via MA/CA X 100; T1-5 refers to Tests 1-5 whereby T1=Test of Familiarity; T2 =Test of Recollection; T3 =Voice-Face Matching; T4=Self Voice Recog. T5 =Pure Voice Recog.

Discussion

The ability to recognise the recorded voice as one's own, without the aid of visual cues, was explored in two groups of children with low functioning autism (LFA). The first group, referred to here as the target group, consisted of 12 children who had achieved maximum scores on a Test of Self-Voice to Self-Face Matching. The comparison group consisted of 12 children chosen randomly on the day of testing. At practice, five of the children from the comparison group showed mild distress and were excluded from the Main Test.

The task for the remaining 19 participants was to identify which one of four pre-recorded child-voice samples represented their own voice. The results indicate that the comparison group was significantly impaired, relative to the target group. In addition, boys identified their own recorded voices with slightly more accuracy than girls, and children with higher NVMA were better on this task than children with lower NVMA, although, neither of these two factors reached statistical significance.

In a somewhat unexpected turn of events, three of the seven children in the randomly chosen comparison group scored at ceiling on this task. These children, named here as Francis, Linda, and Paul, recognised their own recorded voice when it was played alongside the recorded voices of three other children at test. This was unexpected, as these three children had achieved mixed scores in the previous 4 studies. It could be that the presentation of faces and voices, presented simultaneously (as in Studies 3 and 4), inhibited rather than facilitated recognition for this small group of children (see Hughes & Nicholson, 2008), which might explain why they performed better in a task where no photographs were used. Yet one of these children (e.g., Francis) scored at ceiling in Study 4: A Test of Self-Voice-to-Self-Face Matching, which mitigates somewhat against this argument.

Alternatively, the design of Study 5: A Test of Pure-Voice Recognition, was more attractive for these three children as it contained pictures of non-social stimuli (e.g., a cow, a dog, a spoon, etc.) as opposed to photographs of people's faces (Boucher & Bowler, 2008). The findings do indicate that children in the control group had lower NVMA scores than those in the experimental group, but this difference did not reach statistical significance. In addition, there was no significant effect of gender between the two groups on this Test of Voice Recognition.

This study is useful as it clearly identifies a group of 12 children (m = 8; f = 4) with chronological ages ranging from 6;5 to 15;4 who can recognise their own recorded voices in absolute judgements. These 12 children were thus considered very suitable candidates for the allocation of a personalised AAC device as part of a semi-longitudinal study to examine preferences for natural speech outputs when communicating with others.

CHAPTER FIVE

PLACING PERSONALISED VOICE OUTPUT ON SGDS FOR THE CHILD WITH ASD

How do you find the sound of your own voice when you hear it played back to you from a wedding video, or some other form of audio or visual recording? Do you find it somewhat unfamiliar? Does it lack the usual pitch and tone that you are used to hearing when you speak ordinarily? Is it a voice you would prefer to communicate with on a speech-operated device if you lost your own voice temporarily or in the long term? These are some of the questions that form the subject matter of this chapter.

We ask if a SGD with a recording of the child's own voice will create a sense of 'owness for communication,' so that the frequency and richness of AAC use will be enhanced. We are not alone in asking this question. A number of research projects are coalescing to develop technology that performs a voice transplant of the child's natural voice onto the AAC device to explore this very concept (see van Santen & Black, 2009; Klabbers, Kain, & van Santen, 2010). In addition, a recent review of AAC use, by the child with autism, point to an increasing need for experimental research in order to examine children's preferences for different speech output options on their SGDs (van der Meer & Rispoli, 2010).

This study is an examination of children's preferences for voice type on SGDs. Twelve minimally-verbal children with low-functioning autism (LFA) were allocated SGDs programmed with a set library of 81 words and phrases (see Appendix K) for 12 weeks. These words and phrases were selected following consultation with the parents, teachers, and speech and language therapists of the 12 children, and closely reflected the typical requests and needs of this small group. Significantly, the words and phrases on the SGDs were available in three different voice types, namely, a male and a female digitised speech output and a recording of the child's own voice.

This study had three main aims: First, to measure the child's use of this new form of communication tool over the duration of the test period. Second, it was a measure of whether this form of communication device would enhance the frequency of the child's communication; and third, to assess the child's preferential use of voice-type when using the SGD over the course of 12 weeks.

What We Did and How We Did It

Participants

Twelve minimally-verbal children were initially recruited for this part of the study ($m = 8; f = 4$). These children had achieved maximum scores in Study 4: A Test of Self-Voice Recognition, which required the child to match a recording of their own voice to that of their own photograph at test. This target group of 12 children were then assessed on their ability to recognise a recording of their own voice without the aid of photographs, in Study 5: A Test of Pure Voice Recognition. Their performance on this Test was compared to that of a comparison group of children, from the original sample of 33 children with LFA, chosen randomly on the day of testing. All children in the target group scored above chance on the day, with 11 of the 12 achieving maximum scores again. It was decided, therefore, that the target group were the most suitable candidates in a study investigating children's preferences for voice-types on personalised SGDs.

Informed written consent was once again sought from parents and guardians via each child's school prior to any child being allocated a SGD. In line with Stake (1995: 58), indication was given as to why their child was selected for this part of the study and every effort was made to explain that the SGDs were not allocated to 'solve a problem or advance social well-being,' but to add to existing knowledge about the preferences children with autism may exhibit for certain features on AAC tools. A brief written description of the intended casework was offered, and plans to anonymise the identities of the children, their teachers, parents, and therapists were also clearly articulated (Stake, 1995; Yin, 2003).

The parents of three children from the target group, namely, Ann, Kevin, and Peter decided not to progress with the study (see Table 17: 197). As a result, it was decided to ask the parents and guardians of the three children from the comparison group, who had achieved maximum scores in Study 5, if they would consent to their children participating. The parents of Francis and Linda agreed, but Paul's parents did not. The child with the next highest score (i.e., 8/10) at Study 5 was a young boy called Jason, whose parents consented to him to participating in this study.

Seven of the participants were attending School A, and five were attending School D. To gather baseline data on this group of children's current form of communication (i.e., spoken words, sign language, PECs) two particularly relevant set of records held at their respective schools were accessed. One such record was the Assessment of Basic Language and Learning Skills – Revised (ABLLS-R: Partington, 2006). The ABLLS-R is a tool designed to provide a comprehensive review of more than five hundred skills from over twenty-five skills areas, including that of language and communication by the child with autism http://www.partingtonbehaviouralanalysts.com). As a result, this assessment tool provides a very comprehensive overview of a child's baseline skills before entering into a pre-school, or school. It is typically updated annually with graphs provided to the parent, teacher, and clinician, depicting a visual plot of the child's progress across several domains.

The second record consulted was the Childhood Autism Rating Scale (CARS) (Schopler, Reichier, Rochen Renner, 1988). The CARS is a 15-item behavioural rating scale, which was initially developed to identify children aged two years, and older, with autism, and to distinguish them from children with a developmental delay without autism (Morgan, 1988; Sturmey & Sevin, 1994). It is often used to evaluate young children who may have autism spectrum disorders yielding an overall composite score, ranging from mild to moderate to severe (Morgan, 1988). While it is already established that the children with autism in this study had a diagnosis of autistic disorder or LFA, the CARS report was an additional source of information as it provided these composite scores. For example, total CARS scores range from a fifteen to sixty, with a minimum score of thirty serving as the cut-off for a diagnosis of autism on the mild end of the spectrum (Morgan, 1988).

The 12 children presented with a mean chronological age (CA; m = 11.5, SD = 3.0) and non-verbal mental age (NVMA; m = 5.0, SD = 2.2). Reports on the children from the National Educational Psychologists (NEPS) confirmed that all 12 children were minimally-verbal, which is commonly defined as 'speaking fewer than 10 words' (Koegel, Shirotova, & Koegel, 2009: 282). In terms of augmentative and alternative communication (AAC) use, the children ranged in their mastery of PECS as a communication tool, from no mastery at all to level 5 (Bondy & Frost, 2001). Just six of the twelve children used sign language regularly on a daily basis, with the number of signs used ranging from 10-15 per child. Jake used no functional speech at all, while the remaining 11 children used between 2-10 words per day. Finally, the ABLLS-R reports showed that these 12 children understood between 8-34 words at the time of testing (Table 5-1).

Table 5-1 Descriptive data for the 12 children recruited for the semi-longitudinal study

Name	Sex	School	CA	NVMA	IQ	CARS	Level of PECs mastered	No. of words used per day	No of signs used per day
Jim	M	D	11.4	4.8	42.3	36	4	4	10
Jake	M	D	7.2	3.1	43.6	31	0	0	10
Robbie*	M	A	14.0			36	2	2	0
Nita	F	A	13.2	8.5	64.7	38	4	4	0
Bob	M	A	15.4	3.7	24.3	51	4	4	0
John	M	A	8.0	5.1	63.9	36	4	5	0
Mark	M	A	15.0	6.1	40.8	48	4	4	0
Sandra	F	A	10.7	5.9	55.0	42	4	4	14
Connie	F	A	11.3	4.9	43.3	34	4	4	10
Francis	M	D	10.5	5.5	51.9	36	2	2	15
Jason	M	D	6.5	3.2	50.0	31	5	5	0
Linda	F	A	14.3	7.8	54.6	36	4	10	4

***It was not possible to calculate the NVMA of this child via the BPVS**

Materials

The SGDs: The device chosen for this study was the Logan ProxTalker. This device has been defined as, 'an electronic communication aide that produces digitised or synthesised speech upon activation by individuals with little to no functional speech' (Boesch, Wendt, Subramanian, & Hsu, 2013: 481. Lloyd, Fuller, & Arvidson, 1997). Each device measured 12.9 inches x 7 inches x 3.5 inches, and, with batteries inserted, they each weighed 4.7 lbs (http://www.loganproxtalker.com). This device closely followed the principles of PECS (Boesch et al., 2013), and - as PECS was already used by 11 of the 12 participants - it was anticipated that this might enhance the children's adaptation to, and use of, this particular SGD. Few comparative efficacy studies exist when making specific AAC choices for research purposes, but there is evidence to suggest that children with autism, who can use PECS, adjust well to making requests via SGDs (Bock, Stoner, Beck, Hanley, & Prochnow, 2005; Boesch, et al., 2013; Beck, Stoner, Bock, & Parton, 2008).

Each Logan ProxTalker came equipped with three sets of 81 picture cards. Each picture card was printed in colour, and measured 1.25 inches x 1.25 inches (Fig. 14). The cards in each set corresponded to a list of 81 words and phrases stored onto the SGD. The 81 words/phrases were selected following consultation with the parents, teachers, and speech and language therapists of the participants, and closely reflected the typical items, people, and needs of the participants. When a picture card was placed on any of the five buttons, the device emitted a digitised speech output, which corresponded to the word/phrase depicted on that card.

Set 1 emitted a male digitised voice when placed on the SGD, while Set 2 emitted a female digitised voice. The cards in Set 1 had blue borders to distinguish them from Set 2, which had pink borders. Set 3 had a yellow border and they would emit the recorded voice of the child. The SGD had a number of felt storage pages to which the picture cards could be adhered to via a Velcro circle on the back of each card. The number of picture cards that were displayed could be decided by the parents or teachers of each participant. Those not in use could be stored in clear plastic bags with a zip lock, which accompanied the SGD.

Fig. 5-1 An Example of the Picture Cards Used with the SGD

The programming keys: Each SGD was equipped with a set of programming keys (see Fig. 5-2). By placing the programming keys over any of the five buttons on the SGD, a range of functions could be performed. For instance, the 'Diagnostics' key was used to diagnose any technical faults with the device. The 'Check Battery' key allowed the SGD user to know how much battery power remained on the unit. There was a key to increase the volume on the device and one to decrease the volume. Possibly the two most relevant keys to this research were the 'erase' and 'record' keys.

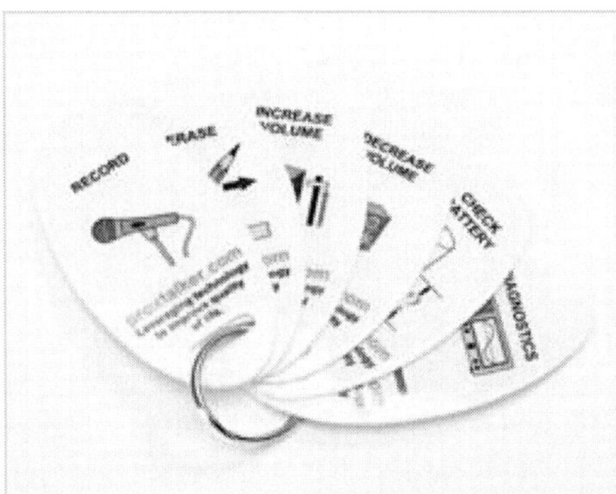

Fig. 5-2 The Programming Keys for use with the SGD

On placing the 'record' key on any of the five buttons, up to 30 seconds of the child's own voice could be recorded onto the device. This feature allowed a library of the 81 words to be recorded onto the SGD as the self-voice speech output option. To record the child's voice, a parent or teacher needed to sound out the words in order for the child to mimic them. Later the adult's voice was edited from the voice recording. If a mistake was made, placing the erase key on any of the five buttons with the relevant picture card meant that that recording could be erased and a fresh recording could occur.

As well as having coloured borders, each picture card had its own unique code. Picture cards with the male digitised voice started with the digits 0x44, while picture cards with the female digitised voice began with the digits 0x04. The code for the picture cards used for recording the child's voice was 0x00. Each of the SGDs was fitted with a language activity monitor (LAM) designed to record these codes, and other factors (http://www.aacinstitute.org).

The Language Activity Monitoring device: LAM software functions like a memory card in a typical mobile phone. It is built into the SGD/AAC device and it automatically records every utterance or 'communication event' an individual makes when using a communication device, along with the exact time the utterance occurred (Romich & Hill, 1999, 2000). Importantly, this piece of software works differently depending on which language representation model (LRM) is programmed on the speech generating device.

A LRM refers to the particular communication method, or mode, on a communication device, and typically includes *Semantic Compaction*™, *alphabetic-based methods*, and *single-meaning pictures* (SMP; Hill & Romich, 2002). Semantic Compaction™ can be defined as, 'using short sequences of symbols to represent words or phrases that follow specific rules to indicate morphology and enhance vocabulary organisation' (Todd, 2008: 11). The alphabetic-based LRM uses a keyboard (much like a keyboard used on a typical mobile phone, when texting) to spell out the word(s) (Beukelman & Mirenda, 2005; Lloyd et al., 1997; Hill & Romich, 2002). The LRM method, termed 'single meaning pictures' (SMP) uses pictures (such as PECS) to represent a single word, such as "walk," or singular phases, such as "I want," or "I see" (Hill & Romich, 2002; Todd, 2008). The LAM software records the LRM used to produce a language event in a language sample (Hill & Romich, 2002).

Hill and Romich (2002) propose that the time required to upload, edit, and analyse a two hour long sample of over 100 utterances would take between 15-20 minutes using certain software, such as the Systematic Analysis of Language Transcripts (SALT) (Miller, 1983), or the Performance Report Tool (PeRT; Hill & Romich, 2003) software. Both of these software tools calculate a range of quantitative measures, which describe the full communication performance of the individual using the device (Todd, 2008), and they are both best suited to devices using either Semantic Compaction™ or alphabetical language representation method (LRM) used.

For a SGD using *single-meaning pictures* (SMPs), the data produced can be quite extensive, and is presented as lines of codes (see Appendix J). These codes represent the picture tags placed on each of the buttons of the SGD, by the child. The first task is to convert these codes into the actual message communicated by the child. Generally, an Excel programme - called VLOOKUP (http://office.microsoft.com) - is used to organise the data. This Excel programme operates much like a word-search programme. The list of codes corresponds to the list of words and phrases stored in each SGD (see Appendix K). A code is entered into VLOOKUP as a search, and, on finding it, the code is replaced with the appropriate word or phrase. For example, the code 0x44001474 corresponds to the male digitised word saying 'afraid,' while this word uttered via the female digitised speech output is represented as 0x0400149. Working this way, each code is systematically replaced with words and phrases until the transcript is completed. This can take up to six hours per transcript per child. An example of a communication event made via a single meaning picture (SMP) LRM recorded by LAM software would look as follows:

10:46:18 SMP "I want"
10:46:23 SMP "to go"
10:46:25 SMP "home"
10:46:28 SMP "please"

The example communication event above shows the production of the utterance, *"I want to go home please."* The entire sentence was created using four single meaning pictures (SMPs) as they were placed on the voice-activating buttons on the SGD. Each communication event produce, via this LRM shows the time associated with it, making it possible to see that the entire utterance took ten seconds in total. For the purpose of this study, a number of customised SGDs using the LRM method single-meaning pictures (SMPs) were used.

Furthermore, for the purpose of recording all communication events from the SGD, each device was programmed with a 24-hour clock. These customised devices took approximately eight weeks to design and ten days to ship from the USA to Ireland. As a result, there was an approximate gap of three months between conducting the five experimental studies, and the roll out of the semi-longitudinal study.

The Parental Survey: The parents/guardians of each participant were issued a folder at the beginning of the semi-longitudinal study. Each folder contained a welcome letter thanking them for their support and assistance in this twelve-week study period; the contact details of the researcher; and those of an engineer recruited to fix any issues, which may occur with the SGD. This folder also contained instructions on how to use the SGD.

A weekly survey, comprised of 18 statements in a Likert-scale format (Appendix L), was also enclosed. This survey was designed to capture the parents' observations of the frequency and quality of communication by the child using the AAC device. It was anticipated that this information would function to triangulate the data obtained from the LAM software.

The Design of the Study

This was a semi-longitudinal study involving 12 children with LFA who were allocated a SGD over a period of 12 weeks. The longitudinal approach allowed the children time to express their continued interest in using this new form of augmentative and alternative communication (AAC) as well as their preferences for speech output options when communicating. Based on the LAM data downloaded from the devices, a preliminary quantitative analysis could be conducted followed by a case study approach. The quantitative analysis would show the duration of the child's use of the SGD over the 12 weeks, the number of their weekly communications, and the function of their communications. It would also be possible to measure the proportionate use of the self-voice speech output option, compared to their use of the equally available digitised speech output option, during the 12 weeks. The case study approach would permit a more in-depth analysis of any similarities and differences in the use of the SGD by the children (Stake, 1995; Yin, 2003).

The rationale for a longitudinal approach was based in part on the findings of previous observational research conducted on children with autism (Robins, Dautenhahn, Boekhorst, & Billiard, 2005; Stone & Caro-Martinez, 1990; Tager-Flusberg, 1999; Tager-Flusberg, Calkins, Nolin, Baumberger, Anderson, & Chadwick-Dias, et al., 1990). For instance, one observational study - designed to collect communication samples from the child with autism - video-taped the children, and subsequently analysed the data from hour-long segments (Tager-Flusberg, 1999). Agnew and Pyke (1982) suggest that this observational method is very appropriate for getting at real life issues in the real world. However, this approach often relies heavily on teachers, or SNAs, working very hard at engaging the children in social interactions (Tager-Flusberg, Calkins, Nolin, Baumberger,

Anderson, & Chadwick-Dias, et al., 1990). It is also a method that raises questions about what the children's behaviour would be like if it had not been observed (Robson, 2002).

Placing a freestanding video-recorder in the children's classrooms over the course of a week was another option in this study. Stone and Caro-Martinez (1990) chose this method to collect communication samples, from relatively able children with ASD, based on the potential of teachers and fellow pupils functioning as a possible motivation for the child with autism to communicate. The results of these methods showed that the child with autism exhibited spontaneous communicative acts at a *maximum* of two to three per hour per child (Stone & Caro-Martinez, 1990). This low-rate of spontaneous communications is not unusual in autism research, with the results of a number of studies suggesting that these children communicate less often and with a narrower range of communicative acts relative to their non-autistic peers (Landry & Loveland, 1989; Mermelstein, 1983; Tager-Flusberg et al., 1990; Tager-Flusberg, 1999). As such, relying on purely observational methods for the purpose of the current study may yield very little data. A semi-longitudinal design would allow us to avoid many of these issues, while also permitting the opportunity of evaluating the children's spontaneous use of the SGD over a given time-frame.

Hedeker, Gibbons, and Waternaux (1999) suggest that the duration of a longitudinal study is important, as are the amount of observations made by the researcher during the course of the study. As the SGDs were on loan for a maximum of sixteen weeks, this was a significant factor when calculating the *duration* of the study. Another factor under consideration was the length of the school year. Testing to date had taken part over the first half of the school year, leaving the period running from mid-January to June still available for this part of the study. This time-frame encompassed a period of no more than 16 weeks, when Easter holidays and mid-term breaks were taken into consideration (http://www.education.ie).

A study period of *longer* than two weeks was considered essential when adopting a longitudinal approach. For instance, a recent investigation of SGD use by the child with autism, indicated that a 'novelty effect' can occur in week one, whereby the frequency of children's use of the device is much greater than in week two simply, 'because the participants were genuinely excited about the device' (Emms, 2010: 40). Therefore, a longer-term study could potentially generate more 'valuable statistics' (Emms, 2010: 40).

On foot of the very practical issues associated with the length of the school year, and the proposed return date of the SGDs, a study period of no more than 12 weeks was chosen. This time-frame took into consideration the additional time required to provide parents and teachers with demonstrations on the operating systems of the SGDs, as well as factoring in an introduction period with the SGDs for the children (see Boesch, 2013; van der Meer & Rispoli, 2010).

Overall, therefore, this was a semi-longitudinal study conducted with a sample of 12 children, over a 12-week period, with one visit per school every four weeks to assess progress (Hedeker et al., 1999). Our objectives were threefold, as we were interested in (1) whether or not the child would use the device for the duration of the study. We were also interested in (2) how a personalised SGD might affect their rate, or quality, of communication. Most importantly, we want (3) to investigate the child's preference for the self-voice speech output option on the SGD for communication purposes.

General Procedural Points

All initial procedures to introduce the participant to the SGD; to train them in the use of the SGD; and to obtain baseline data on each participant's current level of communication style, occurred in the child's school during school hours.

Once every four weeks, the schools of the children were visited by the tester and the LAM was removed from each of the SGDs. This resembled a USB card and could be placed into the computer of the tester, whereby the data was uploaded into a file for later analysis. This process took no more than 5 minutes per device. Any parental surveys that were available were collected on this date also.

Finally, to address any concerns, or to deal with any queries, on these three dates across the study, the tester remained available to speak to parents, teachers or speech and language therapists for one hour after school ended.

Procedures

The SGDs were available from the manufacturers from January until the end of April. The devices were activated by the tester and checked to be in full working order. The devices were then couriered to the schools and the tester arranged a date in mid-January to go to the schools with a representative of the company loaning the devices. A demonstration of the SGDs operating procedures was delivered to staff, parents, and children in the schools. The following day, the tester allocated the devices to each child and a preference assessment was conducted.

Preference assessment: It was considered important to introduce each participant to the SGD to be used in the study. By doing so, it would be possible to see if the child was able to adapt to using this particular device and if they were happy to continue in the research. Research suggests that when introducing the child with autism to alternative and augmentative communication (AAC), such as PECS, a preference assessment is typically considered a critical step on the way to teaching the child to use the system (Boesch et al., 2013; Frost & Bondy, 2002; Schlosser, Sigafoos, Luiselli, Angermeier, Schooley, et al., 2007). This 'critical step' was recently adapted and used successfully by researchers when introducing a SGD, using the single meaning pictures (SMP) as a LRM for 3 children with autism (Boesch et al., 2013).

A training day was organised at the schools of the children and a stimulus preference assessment was conducted (see Boesch et al., 2013). The assessment of preferred stimuli refers to the identification of items, or events, for which a child will normally work to gain access (see Sigafoos & Reichle, 1992). For example, in one instance, teaching staff identified access to the playground as a strong reinforcer for a particular child; access to a segment of a favourite piece of music as a second reinforcer; with two food items identified as third and fourth preferred items for this child. These four items were then used to teach the child to make requests using the SGD.

The SGDs were placed on the desk of each participant in their respective classrooms. Only the picture cards corresponding to the four reinforcers were left on the communication device. These four picture cards were also restricted to the digitised speech output corresponding to the gender of the child using the device (e.g., a male child used an SGD with a digitised male speech output only, while a female child used a SGD with a digitised female speech output only). Male cards were highlighted with a blue outline, while a pink outline framed the female cards.

On completion of a school task, the child's special needs assistant (SNA) encouraged the child to point to the picture of the activity, or item, they wanted as their 'reward' or 'reinforcer'. The SNA prompted the child to place the tag (i.e., playground) on one of the five buttons on the SGD, and when the device generating the word "playground" operated, the child was given instant access to that reinforcer. Over the course of the morning, prompting by the SNA was faded and when the child made three consecutive unaided requests for reinforcers, it was deemed that the child understood making one-word requests via the SGD. No child failed this criterion.

For the next step, picture cards saying, '*I want*' were placed on the SGD. On this occasion, when the child had completed a school task, the SNA prompted the child to place this tag on the first button followed by the tag of their choice (i.e., computer) to create a two-part sentence, '*I want computer,*' whereby the child was given instant access to that reinforcer. Over the course of the training period, prompting was again faded. If the child 'forgot' to place the '*I want*' tag on the device, the SNA removed the card for 'computer' and showed the child how to use the two cards together to create a two-part sentence. When the child completed three consecutive requests using two picture cards, the next step was introduced.

This third step involved placing cards corresponding to the child's more typical communication needs onto the SGD. Generally, these were tags for '*mammy,*' '*daddy,*' '*toilet,*' '*stop,*' and '*home.*' Previous research indicates that children acquainted with PECS typically adapt quickly to using this type of SGD (Boesch et al., 2013. Schlosser et al., 2007), and this finding was supported during this stage of the present study. Training in the general use of the SGD therefore took no more than two hours per child.

The final step in this training day involved introducing the children to the two digitised speech output options available on the SGD. In order to complete this step the device was again limited to just four picture cards. Two of these cards emitted the words '*I see*' and the other two emitted the word '*teacher*' when placed on the buttons of the SGD, but one had a male voice and the other a female. The child was shown that placing blue edged picture cards created a male speech output, while pink edged cards created a female speech output. The blue edged cards were placed on the SGD and the tester/SNA said, '*That sounds like a boy.*' This procedure was repeated using the pink edged cards as an example of how to activate the female digitised speech output option.

The tester then pointed to the child's teacher and asked the child, "*Who do you see?*" If the child was a girl, she was prompted to place the pink-edged card for 'teacher' in a female voice output on the SGD. If the child was a boy, they were prompted to place the blue edged card for 'teacher' on the SGD. When the child chose the cards reflecting their own gender they were praised verbally and given access to a small reinforcer, such as a sweet. If the child made an incorrect choice, or chose one card in the male voice and the second in the female voice, the tester said, '*I think it must be this one,*' and showed the child which cards created the speech output that best reflected their own gender. When the children used the voice representative of their own gender on three consecutive occasions, without prompting or tangible reward (e.g., a small sweet or clapping), it was accepted that the child knew the voice output that related to their own gender. No child failed this section of training, which took less than one hour for each child.

A Trial Period with the SGD: Once it was established that the 12 participants could use the SGDs, the next step involved allocating each child the device for a trial period. The rationale for this trial period was twofold. First, it controlled for any novelty effect that might occur as a result of using a SGD for the first time, which might skew the data (Emms, 2010). Second, it allowed both parents and participants a cooling off period, during which they could withdraw from the study if they felt it might not be for them (Robson, 2002).

Over this two-week period, parents and teaching staff were encouraged to record the child's voice on to the SGD using the set of programming keys (Fig. 15). In most instances, recording the children meant an adult sounding out the words in order for the child to echo them, and then the adult's voice was subsequently edited from the voice recording. Using this method, the child could be recorded saying each of the 81 words corresponding to the picture cards, which accompanied the SGD. In this way, a library of vocabulary was set up on the SGD.

- *If the 81 Words and Phrases did not Match the Needs of the Child*

While the library of words and phrases stored on the devices had been constructed in consultation with parents and teachers, there were occasions when a parent or teacher felt a particular child might prefer to use words/phases more like those they heard at home, or at school. For instance, two of the 81 picture cards referred to the 'computer,' and the 'playground.' The parent of one child said she would not typically use those terms when addressing her son. Instead, she asked her son if he wanted to play with the 'pooter' or 'go to the swings'. As these 'replacement' words retained the meaning of the original picture cards, and thus the LAM could record their use correctly, it was considered acceptable to record these versions instead. It was made clear to parents and teachers, however, that totally novel words were not to be recorded over the library of the original 81 cards.

- *If the 81 Standard Words and Phrases was Insufficient*

There was also the finding that the 81 words provided, were not sufficient for all parents, teachers and children. For example, three parents reported that their children suffered from ear infections on a regular basis, and they wanted picture cards capable of saying 'doctor' 'pain' or 'Calpol' on their children's devices. To accommodate this, a set of thirty blank picture cards was provided with each SGD. Each of these cards could hold up to thirty seconds of recorded speech and each had a code printed clearly on the back. These codes ranged from 0x01 to 0x030. Parents and caregivers were asked to take a note of what words/phrases were recorded onto any of these blank tags, making sure to correlate the recordings with the codes on the back of each blank card. To encourage this behaviour, a predesigned table - with the codes of the blank tags clearly marked down the left hand side and spaces to log what was recorded on each tag - was included in the folder, accompanying the parental survey (see Appendix L). In addition, each parent and caregiver was allocated a pack of clear self-adhesive film so that photographs, pictures, or symbols corresponding to the recordings could be placed on the blank cards as visual markers for the child.

At the end of this two-week trial period, a young girl called Linda had completely abandoned the SGD and reverted to using PECS. It is difficult to be sure why Linda rejected the device. It could be that the device simply ceased to 'interest' her after the first few days (see Emms, 2010). Alternatively, following almost 12 years of using PECS and Lámh (www.lamh.ie), she had a learned behaviour already in place for effective communication, making it difficult for her to adapt to this new communication mode. Eleven of the twelve originally recruited children were operating the SGDs, and progressed to the semi-longitudinal phase of the study.

What We Found Out

Quantitative Analysis

The findings from the LAM data were first examined to investigate the children's individual use of the SGDs over the duration of the study. This process involved measuring each communication event made via the SGD by a child. A communication event can be defined as a child placing a single-meaning picture (SMP) on a button to create an utterance via the SGD. This measure revealed that, over 12 weeks, the 11 participants had made an average of 2923.4 communication events (SD = 5144.1), ranging from 131 to 18207 per week. The boys had made less communications (m = 1391.3, SD = 1034.2) than the girls (m = 7008.6, SD = 9702.9), and children from School A (n = 7) had exhibited more communication events (m = 3952, SD = 6331.8) than those attending School D (n = 7, m = 1122.7, SD = 1109.3). The data also revealed that five children had stopped using the SGDs by week 6. Over this time the overall communication events of these 5 children (m = 1071.0, SD = 643.1) ranged from 131 to 1716 per week.

A series of three Mann-Whitney U tests were conducted to investigate whether factors, such as the children's IQ, NVMA, or CA, influenced their decision to reject or keep the device. The first revealed no significant difference in the IQ scores of those children who left the study by week 6 (Md = 44, n =5) and those who continued (Md = 42, n = 6), U = 13, z = -.36, r = 0.1. In addition, there was no significant difference in the NVMA of those who left (Md = 4 years, n = 5) and those who remained (Md = 4 years, n =6), U = 11, z = -.73, p = .46, r = -0.2. Finally, there was no significant difference in the CA of those who rejected the devices (Md = 10years, n = 5) and those who remained (Md = 11, n =6), U = 12, z = -.54, p = .58, r = -0.1.

Next, the children's preference for communicating with the SGDs via the self-voice speech output option was measured. The data showed that the children (n = 11) used the digitised speech output option more than 60% of the time. The girls (n =3) demonstrated a greater proportional use of their own recorded voice (m = 35.6%, SD = 38.5) over that of any other voice-type available on the SGD compared to the 8 boys (m = 21%, SD = 13.5), but a Mann-Whitney U Test revealed no statistically significant difference between the use of self-voice by boys (Md = 20, n = 8) and girls (Md = 23, n = 3), U = 11, z = -.20, p = .83, r = -0.06. There was no significant difference in the use of self-voice by the 5 children who stopped using the devices in the first half of the study (Md = 190, n = 5) and those who continued for the duration (Md = 565, n = 4), U = 5.0, z = -1.8, p = .06, r = -0.5.

Finally, for this section, the 11 children had previously been assessed in relation to recognition memory and the data showed that their use of self-voice on the SGDs was significantly correlated with their performance on a Test of Familiarity (r - .57, n = 11, p = .06), with greater use of self-voice associated with children who achieved higher scores on the Test of Familiarity. There was a very small correlation between the use of self-voice and children's performance on a Test of Recollection (r = .03, n = 11, p =.91), implying a greater use of self-voice by children who not only recognised the voice as familiar, but also recognised the source as that of their own.

Table 5-2 Descriptive data for the 6 children who continued participating in the study after week 6

Id No.	Name	Sex	School	CA yrs	NVMA yrs	IQ	T1 Max16	T2 Max20	T3 Max20	T4 Max2	T5 Max10	% of use of self-voice
2	**Jim**	M	D	11.4	4.8	42.3	**	19	***	2	10	40
17	**Robbie**	M	A	14.0	*		16	8	18	2	10	22
19	**Nita**	F	A	13.2	8.5	64.7	16	****	20	2	10	24
29	**Sandra**	F	A	10.7	5.9	55.0	16	6	19	2	10	2
33	**Connie**	F	A	11.3	4.9	43.3	16	20	20	2	7	79
7	**Francis**	M	D	10.5	5.5	51.9	10	10	18	1	10	28

All names shown are pseudonyms. CA refers to chronological age. NVMA refers to non-verbal mental age. IQ is calculated via MA/CA X 100. T1-5 refers to Tests 1-5 whereby T1=Test of Familiarity. T2 =Test of Recollection. T3 =Voice-Face Matching. T4=Self Voice Recog. T5 =Pure Voice Recog. * It was not possible to calculate Robbie's NVMA via the BPVS. ** Jim was distressed on the day of testing for T1. * Jim scored below chance on T3. **** Nita was distressed on the day of testing for T2.**

Table 5-3 Descriptive Data Showing the Children's Use of the Self-Voice Speech Output Option on the SGDs

Name	Sex	School	CA	NVMA	Score from Study1**	Score from Study2***	Number of communications made via the self-voice option	The % of all communications made via the self-voice option
Connie	F	A	11.3	4.9	16	20	1334	79
Jim	M	D	11.4	4.8		19	919	40
Robbie*	M	A	14.0		16	8	681	22
Sandra	F	A	10.7	5.9	16	6	449	2
Mark	M	A	15.0	6.1	16	11	288	34
Nita**	F	A	13.2	8.5	16		264	24
John	M	A	8.0	5.1	12	9	252	27
Jason	M	D	6.5	3.2	11	12	190	11
Bob	M	A	15.4	3.7	16	16	177	11
Francis	M	D	10.5	5.5	10	10	69	28
Jake	M	D	7.2	3.1	12	15	18	16

***It was not possible to calculate Robbie's NVMA via the BPVS **The recorded voice on Nita's device was that of her aunt and not her own voice; ** refers to A Test of Familiarity where the max score was 16; ***refers to a Test of Recollection where the max score was 20**

A Case Study Approach

This was an investigation of how a SGD with a self-voice speech output option was used by 12 children with autism over a 12-week period. Specifically, we were interested in (1) the child's use of this communication device per week, (2) the frequency of the child's communications via the SGD per week, and (3) the child's preference for the self-voice speech output option when communicating over the 12 weeks.

One of the first findings from quantitative analysis was that some children's use of the SGDs stopped before the end of the first half of the study. The data could shed no light on the reasons why these children stopped using the devices, instead, it revealed no statistical differences in CA, NVMA, or IQ scores between the five children who rejected the SGD by week 6, and the six children who used the device for the duration.

The LAM data was useful in highlighting the number of communication events made by each child; for highlighting the number of communication events made by boys as opposed to girls; and between schools, as well as between the children who left the study by week 6, and those who did not. The LAM data was also a valuable means of calculating the number of times each child chose to communicate via a digitised speech output and the number of times they made utterances using their own voice recorded onto the device.

What we could not fully decipher purely via quantitative analysis was equally significant however. For instance, why did five boys stop using these devices? If not on the grounds of CA, NVMA, or IQ, what factors did form the basis of their decision? In addition, while we can see that all 11 children made communication events using the SGDs, what was the function of these communications? Furthermore, and significantly, while the data indicates that children with greater scores on the Test of Familiarity, and the Test of Recollection, used the self-voice speech output option more frequently than those with somewhat lower scores, why did the 11 children use this speech output option less than 40% of the time they communicated via the SGDs?

It is suggested that a case study approach can often provide a more in-depth analysis of a single case (Stake, 1995; Yin, 2005). Yin (2005) notes that there are six different types of case study, while Stake (1995: pp xi - xii) does not pay much attention to, 'quantitative case studies that emphasise a battery of measurements of the case,' but rather presents an approach that is more qualitative and emphasises, 'episodes of nuance, the sequentiality of happenings in context, the wholeness of the individual.'

This study will present 11 case studies, presented in two sections. Section 1 will discuss the five children who rejected the SGDs, and Section 2 will focus on the six who used the devices for the duration. Both sections will draw from observational notes on the children gathered during the collection of baseline data, and from secondary data, such as the children's ABLLS-R and CARS reports, parental surveys, and reports from teachers, parents and speech and language therapists (Yin, 2005). The central objective of this approach is to determine better a research design; data collection method; and procedures for the selection of participants for any subsequent studies that investigate preferences for speech output options on SGDs for children.

Section 1: The Children who Rejected the SGDs

JASON was a six-year old boy who had attended his current school for just over one year. He was the younger of two children and his older brother also had a diagnosis of autism. Jason communicated using a combination of eye gaze, pointing, and via a vocabulary of approximately five words (e.g., mammy, daddy, car, yes, & stop). He had been using PECS as a mode of communication since he was five years old and he was currently operating at phase 5 level, which meant he could spontaneously request a variety of items and could answer the question, 'What do you want?' (Bondy & Frost, 2001).

Jason was recruited for the longitudinal study when three of the children from the target group dropped out. He adapted well to the introduction phase of the study and he was using the device to request items prior-to, and during, the fourteen day trial. Both his parents and his teachers reported that during this period, he never used his PECS, preferring instead to use the SGD.

Jason rejected the SGD at week 4. During this time he made a total of 1717 communication events (defined here as a child placing a single-meaning picture (SMP) on a button to create an utterance via the SGD) ranging from 1-1357 per week. The majority of his communications (80%) occurred in the first two weeks of the study and he used the male digitised speech output for 89% of his communications.

Both the speech and language therapist (SLT) and his parents reported that, after the trial period, Jason began to use the SGD very much 'like a toy.' For example, a note made on the parental survey confirmed that Jason liked to place a card on the device to hear the same word emitted in a repeated fashion. Similarly, the LAM data indicated that on three separate occasions, the word 'yellow' was uttered up to 46 times in succession.

When the school was visited by the researcher at week 4, Jason had reverted to using PECS and was not interested in the SGD. The device was left in his classroom for the remainder of the study in case he changed his mind, but he did not. During the second visit at week 8, his mother described Jason's rejection of the SGD as 'understandable' as it was 'very heavy to carry around,' and that he often appeared 'confused' by the number of picture cards made available to him on the storage pages of the device. His mother also felt that because Jason's older brother did not have a SGD, but instead communicated via PECS, that it was 'easier for Jason to stick with what he saw at home.'

Analysis: It is interesting that Jason was reported to have used the SGD as a toy rather than as a means of functional communication, but it is not very surprising. Autism is a spectrum disorder that implies huge differences among these children (Waterhouse, 2013). Previous case study evaluations of therapeutic/educational interventions, for the child with LFA, suggest that - for some children - the simple cause and effect of certain technologies, such as the AIBO dog or robotic dolls, serve to encourage, 'tactile and playful explorations,' which in turn lead to, 'the development of basic imitation,' and, 'communication with other people' (Robins, Dautenhahn, & Dickerson, 2009: e1). For other children, however, it is sometimes noted that these technologies are distracting and serve only as cause-and-effect toys (Robins, Dautenhahn, & Dickerson, 2009). This latter observation appears to have been the case for Jason.

Another element underpinning Jason's acceptance, or rejection, of the device so quickly may have been its physical size and weight. The SGD, used in this study, measures 12.9 inches x 7 inches x 3.5 inches and with its batteries it weighs 4.7 lbs (http://www.loganproxtalker.com). A recent review of different SGDs, and their design, suggests that children often reject ones that are considered 'cumbersome' (Shane et al., 2011). It is further suggested that the larger devices (as opposed to the *iPhone* or the *Android* phones with speech-activated features) often serve to 'stigmatise' the user (Shane et al., 2011: e2). These barriers may have led Jason to revert back to the more discreet AAC model, such as sign language or PECS (see Ogletree & Harn, 2001).

Finally, the child with autism can show difficulty in generalising behaviours learned in one domain (i.e., school) to another (i.e., home; Keenan et al., 2007; Wing, 1999). Because the introduction, training, and trial periods, with the SGDs were conducted in the school domain, a schedule of reinforcements for using the device at home would likely have been useful to encourage Jason's use of the device in the home.

All in all, a 'bottom-up' approach to introducing AAC interventions would potentially have been best here. In other words, it would have been more advantageous for this child had the communication device, allocated to him, been better matched to his current level of needs and abilities. Something smaller, more portable, and easier to use across several domains, such as the *iPhone* with a 'Grace app' (http://www.graceapp.com) may have worked better here. A 'clinical feature matching' approach is one also endorsed by Blischak and Ho (2000), and Shane et al., (2011). In addition, it is well established that when the preferences of the child are not taken into account during AAC decision-making, partial or complete rejection of the allocated AAC can occur (van der Meer & Rispoli, 2010; Shane et al., 2011). This appears to be the reason Jason abandoned this SGD.

JAKE was seven years old at the time of testing, and had attended a school that operated with an autism-specific educational focus since the age of five years. He did not talk and refused all eye contact. Reports held at his school indicated that he did not understand social interactions, he often secluded himself from other people, and even his mother found it difficult to interact with him. He had not adapted to PECS and while he used up to ten signs a day to make himself understood, most of these comprised tugging at an adult's sleeve or using eye gaze to communicate his needs.

Prior to conducting the semi-longitudinal study, Jake's mother described the situation as 'very difficult' and said that all attempts to get Jake to communicate via PECS had failed to date. His mother was somewhat sceptical about the SGD as a communication tool for her son, and although she consented to his participation, she said she doubted he would 'go anywhere near it.'

Teaching staff indicated that, while often appearing 'lost in his own world,' when engaged with directly and given clear instructions, Jake was very cooperative and 'compliant.' This was certainly the case when Jake was invited to participate in the five empirical tests conducted during this study. The only study Jake did not participate in was the Test of Voice-Face Matching, and he achieved maximum scores on the Test of Self-Voice-to-Self-Face Matching, and on the Test of Pure Voice Recognition. During testing he always had his SNA present and she reinforced his positive behaviours (i.e., listening, sitting quietly, looking) very regularly. Accompanied by his SNA, Jake participated in the introduction period with the SGD. He also used the device over the 14-day-trial period, however during this time he only made 9 single-word communication events.

Jake rejected the device at week 5. In this period, his communication events, ranged from 4-80 per week, and totalled 131, with 87% of these made during school day. The LAM data revealed that 84% of all his communicative events were made in the first two weeks, and these were conducted via the male digitised speech output option. During this period, Jake used the device primarily to request food and snacks by placing one single-meaning picture card on a button at a time. The parental survey confirmed that Jake had reverted to using pre-linguistic communications, such as pulling at adult's sleeves and pointing by week 5.

Analysis: Firstly, it is informative that for a child who had not adopted to using PECS, or more conventional sign language, that he could and did communicate functionally via the SGD. He used it to make requests, and for a child who does not appear to be very socially interactive, either in the home or school, this is an encouraging finding. Secondly, it is interesting to note that almost 90% of these communications occurred within the hours he attended school (Appendix N; p. 442). It is possible to infer that this child, who apparently could, and would, engage with others when asked to, only used the SGD when he was asked/prompted to. Like all young children—the child with autism, learning a new skill, will benefit from frequent practice and immediate reinforcing feedback (Keenan, Dillenberger, & Kerr, 1999; Wing, 1989). However, while the TD child may take their cues about learning a new skill (i.e., tying their shoelace) from watching others demonstrate the task or via spoken instructions, the child with autism may need a prompt, or an extra stimulus introduced to a situation (e.g., a hand-over-hand instruction on tying laces) that elicits the desired response from the child (Keenan et al., 2007; Wing, 1989). For many children with autism, prompts need to be continual and only faded out over time. In a few instances, a child with autism can become what is known as 'prompt-dependent' (Taylor & Fischer, 2002).

Jake appears to have required a certain amount of prompting to encourage his participation in class and to engage with testing. This suggests that he may possibly have benefited from greater instructional procedures throughout the first few weeks of his use of the SGD, rather than adapting the more ecological approach adapted here. Further support for this argument comes from a recent review of SGD use by children with autism, which found that these devices were often abandoned if the instructional approach incorporated at the start of the intervention was insufficient, or when generalisation and maintenance strategies were not taught to the child using the device (van der Meer & Rispoli, 2010). Future research would benefit from not assuming a naturalistic approach, such as the one adopted here, will work for all children with LFA.

MARK was fifteen years old and had been attending school since he was eight. Prior to this, he was home-educated via Applied Behaviour Analysis (ABA) methods. Mark engaged in echolalia (e.g., the immediate or delayed repetition of words or phrases he had heard), with a verbal repertoire of approximately five words. He was communicating with PECS at level 4, which meant that he could build two-part sentences to communicate his needs.

The speech and language therapist (SLT) at Mark's school felt that this adolescent was a 'prime example of a prompt-dependent child.' The SLT indicated that Mark was so reliant on a schedule of prompts and reinforcers that he never acted or communicated spontaneously. He also remarked that Mark was capable of much more than one might imagine on first meeting him.

Support for the latter remark rests in the finding that Mark was happy to participate in all five tests conducted during this study, achieving maximum scores on the Test of Familiarity, the Test of Self-Voice-To-Self-Face Recognition, and the Test of Pure Voice Recognition. He scored above chance on the Test of Recollection and the Test of Familiar Voice-to-Face Matching. He appeared to enjoy the verbal praise and the interaction with the tester during these tasks. Mark participated in the introduction to the SGD and over the 14-day trial period, he made 192 communications. All of these communications were two-part messages, such as *'I want—chocolate,'* or, *'I like—crisps,'* suggesting he could use this form of AAC as functionally as he used PECS.

Mark abandoned the device after week 5 after a total of 699 communication events, ranging from 1-248 per week. The LAM data shows that 40% of these communications took place in the first two weeks after the trial period and that Mark used the digitised speech output on his device 88% of the time. The device was used primarily to request food items.

Analysis: Mark was one of the older participants in this study. His CARS report indicated a rather severe form of autism, and his SLT suggested that he never initiated behaviours or communication events with others, preferring instead to respond only to requests that were always reinforced. Yet, his performance on the five tests conducted here suggest that he could stay on task, understand what was expected of him, and score well above chance on tasks that assessed the declarative memory system. Moreover, his use of the device over the five weeks was relatively consistent.

This study was one where adults such as teachers and parents were specifically asked *not* to prompt the child to use the device. The goal was to consider whether a recording of self-voice on the device would *naturally* reinforce the child's desire to communicate more often. As a result, it is possible to speculate that Mark could and did use the device naturally and independently over the five weeks.

So why was it rejected at week 5? One possible reason is that over the course of the study, just 39 of the 81 words and phrases, stored on the SGD, were recorded in Mark's own voice. Teachers reported a lack of time to record the full library of words, and an incomplete parental report suggests time was also an issue in the home. The hypothesis of van Santen and Black (2009) is that a SGD that sounds more like the child will enhance the frequency and quality of communication. In addition, it is suggested that when the user's preferences are not valued during AAC decision making, partial or complete abandonment of AAC in the home, and school, settings may result (VanBiervliet & Parette, 1999). Given that this child could recognise his own voice at test, he may have valued the device more if the library of words recorded in his own voice had been extended. Future research would benefit from providing teachers and caregivers more support around creating the library of words recorded in the child's voice.

JOHN was an eight year old who had attended school since the age of five, but was only in his current school for the past eight months. He was building two-part sentences using PECS and was using up to five functional words a day (e.g., yes, no, want, home, and Game-Boy). His teachers reported that over the past six months, his focus and attention only lasted a very short time (i.e., a maximum of five minutes), and that he could be aggressive to others and cause self-injury. His parental survey informed us that John was a foster-child who was only with his foster family for the past 8 months and that they were concerned he was unhappy in his new school. Every attempt was made to make his involvement in this study fun and enjoyable, and it was rewarding to see him achieve maximum scores on the Test of Familiar-Voice-Face Matching, the Test of Self-Voice-to-Self-Face Matching, and the Test of Pure-Voice Recognition. He had scored well above chance on both the Test of Familiarity and Recollection.

Unfortunately, John abandoned the device after week 5. However, his communication events totalled at 5987 and ranged from 111-260 per week. The LAM data showed that 43% of his communications were conducted in the first two weeks of the study. He used the digitised voice for 73% of all his communications and he used the device primarily to request items, such as books, games, and puzzles.

The parental report at week 4 indicated that John became unwell in early March and that he did not return to school (where the device was left) until the last week in March. This time-frame corresponds with John's initial abandonment of the device. It is very likely that the 'break' of almost three weeks irreparably interrupted his focus and attention toward the device. Children with autism frequently require routine for slow, incremental learning (Keenan et al., 1999, 2007; Wing, 1999). If this routine is broken, the child may take a while to re-adjust. This may be a factor in why this child abandoned the device. Alternatively, given the degree of change in his personal life, the introduction of a new AAC may just have occurred at the wrong time.

BOB was 15 years old at the time of this study. He was close in age to Mark; they came from the same village, and had attended the same home-tutor before they both began school at the age of eight years. This child rarely interacted on his own initiative and generally ignored other children around him in the classroom and the playground.

It was possible to record all 81 words comprising the SGD vocabulary in Bob's voice in less than two hours, as he would repeat any word, if asked. His parents commented that, over the 14-day-trial period with the device, Bob reached out to his father as if to request him to 'join in' placing SMP cards on the buttons of the SGD. His mother commented that this type of behaviour was 'remarkable' as he was typically a very withdrawn child. Despite the enthusiasm of his parents, and Bob's own initial excitement about the SGD, he rejected the device by week 6. He had made a total of 1633 communication events ranging from 76-707 per week. Bob conducted up to 47% of his communications with this device in the first two weeks, and he used the male digitised speech output option for 89% of the time.

Analysis: Of the 11 children recruited for this study, Bob had the lowest NVMA and the lowest IQ scores. Furthermore, Bob, like many children with autism, had a preference for a predictable, structured, and safe environment. He seemed to like being 'in control' of situations, only interacting on his terms and with whom he chose. He was very used to an Applied Behaviour Analysis approach up to the age of five years, and within school, he was using a system called TEACCH (Treatment and Education of Autistic and related Communication handicapped Children; Watson, Lord, Schaffer, & Schopler, 1989). Both these approaches emphasise structure, and use prompts and rewards to elicit appropriate behaviours (Keenan et al., 2007). Possibly, as a consequence of such structured teaching, it should come as no surprise to realise that this child was the only child to achieve maximum scores on all five empirical studies. He worked well, stayed on task, and completed all tests in a timely fashion. Accordingly, the SGD should have worked well for Bob on two fronts. First, he should have engaged well with a piece of technology that functioned in a constant and predictable manner. Second, he should have had the ability to recognise the voice on the SGD on the basis of both familiarity and recollection (Atkinson & Juola, 1974; Jacoby, 1991; Mandler, 1980; Tulving, 1985; Yonelinas, 1994). This finding can only imply that he did not 'prefer' to use this voice-type on his SGD when communicating.

Summary

Combined, these findings suggest that these five children exhibited an initial interest in, and ability to use, a speech generated device. This finding is consistent with previous research investigating AAC and the child with autism (Boesch et al., 2013; Emms, 2010; Sigafoos & Drasgow, 2001; van der Meer & Rispoli, 2010). However, the results also suggest that after a relatively short time-frame, the 'dazzle' of this new communication tool may wear off, a finding which resonates with the work of Shane, Laubscher, Schlosser, Flynn, Sorce, & Abramson (2011). Significantly, the data demonstrates a clear preference for a digitised speech output option by these five children. This important finding is consistent with previous studies showing a lack of preference for the sounds of natural speech as opposed to electronically produced speech in young children with autism spectrum disorder (Klin, 1991; Kuhl et al., 2005).

Section 2: The Children who Continued to Use the SGD

This meant that six children continued to use the SGD between week 6 and week 12. Each of the six children will be discussed individually, beginning with Sandra - who communicated via the self-voice speech output option the least amount of all participants - and ending with Connie - the child who chose to use this speech output on her SGD the most during this study. A brief synopsis of their performance on the five empirical tests, conducted thus far, will be outlined followed by the findings from the LAM data and sources, such as the parental reports or discussions with their teachers or clinicians. A general discussion of these findings will be provided in the Discussion, which follows this section.

SANDRA

SANDRA was an only child with a diagnosis of moderate to severe autism. She communicated primarily through nonverbal means and used communication solely for behavioural regulation. She initiated requests by reaching for the hand of her communication partner (e.g., parent or teacher) and placing it on the desired object. When cued, she used an approximation of the 'more' sign when holding the hand of the communication partner along with a verbal production of the sound 'm'. She had approximately six functional words (i.e., mamma, papa, no, yes, go away, and doggie) but was inclined to use any of these words less than four times in any given day.

Sandra knew about 10 approximate signs when asked to label objects or people in the classrooms, but these were not used in a communicative fashion. Protests were demonstrated most often through pushing hands. She played functionally with cause-and-effect toys when seated, and used eye gaze appropriately during this type of play, but, otherwise, eye gaze was absent. Sandra often appeared to be non-engaged and responded inconsistently to her name.

This child used the SGD over the full twelve weeks of this study. Over this time her communication events totalled at 18, 173, ranging from 175-5498 per week, making her the most avid SGD user of the 11 children. We can also see that 2942 (16%) of this participant's communications related to requests for food (e.g., apple, cereal, chocolate), 2148 (12%) for items (e.g., computer, trampolines, playground), and 1667 (9%) for access to places (e.g., outside, home). Sandra used the SGD more in the evenings (42.45%) than in the afternoons (29%) or mornings (27%), implying she liked to communicate with the SGD at home. In addition, Sandra used the SGD most during weeks 9 and 10. She used the self-voice speech output option for less than 3% of all her communications over the 12 weeks.

Analysis: The first point of analysis here has to be the reason why self-voice was used so little by the child who made the highest number of communication events via the SGD, over the course of this study. Was it that she did not prefer this voice type; was it that the voice was unrecognisable to her; or was there another factor at play in this scenario?

Table 5-4 A Report from the LAM Data on the Use of Voice Type by Sandra

Child:	Sandra	**Gender:**	Female	**Age:**	129 months
School:		**School Terms:**	3	**NVMA:**	71 months
Time of Day:	**Mornings**	**Afternoons**	**Evenings**		**Total**
Number of uses:	5066	5413	7728		18207**
Percentage:	27.82%	29.73%	42.45%		100.00%
Voice type:	**Male (1)**	**Female (2)**	**Self (3)**	***Self over PreR (4)**	**Total**
Times used:	1	17193	449	530	18173**
Percentage:	0.01%	94.61%	2.47%	2.92%	100.00%

***Self over PreR refers to original picture cards that were recorded over with a replacement word (e.g., 'pooter' for computer). **The sum 18207 differs from the sum of 18173, as the former includes data from the introductory period.**

In terms of recognition, we have argued throughout that this cognitive capacity is accomplished on the basis of both familiarity and recollection. It may be that an event sparks recognition on the grounds of pure familiarity (Mandler, 1980), but, in the absence of contextual information and relaying the more meaningful aspect of that event to mind, full recognition will not be achieved (Jacoby, 1991; Mandler, 1980; Tulving, 1985). This is often the case in natural aging, or in Alzheimer's: Was this the case for Sandra?

Findings from the five studies, conducted within, suggest that recollection may be an issue for Sandra. The immediate testing of her ability to match a familiar voice to a face - even her own voice - resulted in maximum scores for this child. She also recognised the sound of her own voice when presented alongside three others when no visual prompts were provided, but she recalled just six of the sixteen items presented during a TSM task. Taken as a whole, these findings imply that Sandra relied more heavily on familiarity than recollection when making recognition judgements.

Previous studies using the RK procedure have also found that individuals with autism often exhibit far more 'know' than 'remember' responses, suggesting a greater reliance of familiarity than recollection (Bowler et al., 2000a, 2000b). Perhaps therefore, Sandra recognised the self-voice speech output option in the SGD as familiar, but, unable to recollect the source of the voice as that of her own, she failed to identify fully with it and chose instead the female digitised voice.

Alternatively, Sandra simply preferred the digitised female voice over that of the natural voice recording. Support for this inference would come from Kuhl et al., (2005) and Klin (1991), who both found a lack of preference by children with autism for the sounds of natural speech, as opposed to electronically produced speech, when the studies were experimental in their design. Sandra did use the SGD for the full 12 weeks of the study however, with a clear peak in this usage between weeks 8 -11 (see Fig. 16).

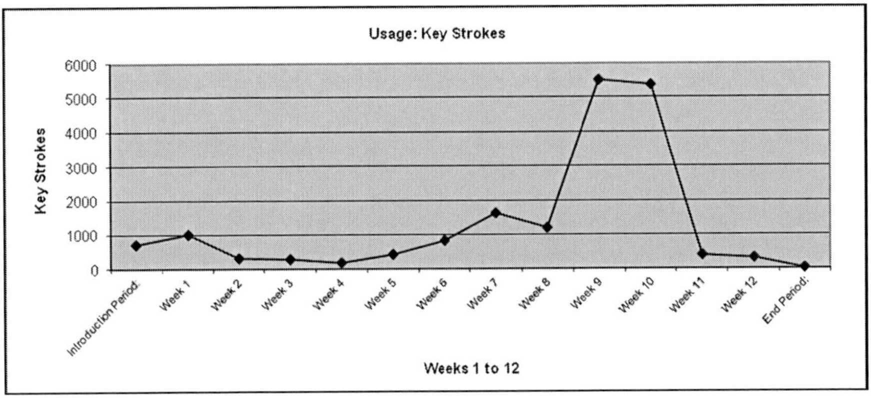

Fig. 5-3 A Graph Depicting Sandra's Use of the SGD Over the 12-Week Study

The LAM data showed that, during this time, the bulk of these communication events not only occurred in the late evening, but that they comprised single-word events that made very little meaning.

Table 5-5 A Report from the LAM Data on Sandra's Use of the SGD

Date	Time	Button	Code	Words
31/03/2012	19:25:29	SM2	0x04001449	Afraid
31/03/2012	19:25:30	SM3	0x04001A30	Angry
31/03/2012	19:26:21	SM4	0x04003B63	Animal
31/03/2012	19:26:22	SM1	0x04001E16	Apple
31/03/2012	19:26:23	SM2	0x0400351A	Arm
01/04/2012	20:33:04	SM1	0x04004C28	Dad
01/04/2012	20:33:06	SM2	0x04003AB3	Dog
01/04/2012	20:33:09	SM3	0x04004DF8	Friend
01/04/2012	20:33:11	SM4	0x04004464	Game

The SLT at Sandra's school was contacted, and confirmed that in school, the device 'had not worked' for Sandra in that she rarely - if ever - created a sentence with the device, preferring instead to 'play' with it repeatedly to, 'hear the voice.'

Of interest, the parental report indicated that, in the evenings, Sandra would remove every picture card from her device and replace them one-by-one after pressing them on any of the five buttons to hear the digitised 'voice.' Sandra would repeat this procedure often in a two-hour period before bedtime, which explains, at least in part, the high number of single-word events.

On completion of the study, the SLT at Sandra's school made contact to say that Sandra had increased her verbal repertoire from 6 words to 24 words, since using the SGD. Furthermore, the 'new' vocabulary reflected words that were programmed on the SGD, such as *'shoes,' 'pain,'* and *'sorry,'* The SLT, and Sandra's mother, deduced that she must have been using the SGD to familiarise herself with new words when she was activating the device each night. This finding would be in line with previous findings from a small number of empirical studies, which also reported improvement in speech skills after interventions via augmentative and alternative communication devices (see Beukelman & Mirenda, 1998; Romski & Sevcik, 1996; Romski & Sevcik, 2005 for reviews).

The findings lend support to the suggestion that familiarity increases with stimulus repetition, as it builds on perceptual representations that may initially have been implicit, and is important for slow, incremental learning (see Aggleton & Brown, 2006; Boucher et al., 2012; Montaldi, Spencer, Roberts, & Mayes, 2006).

Overall, therefore, while the self-voice option does not seem to have been preferred by Sandra when using the SGD, and while it seemed that she was utilising the device more as a cause-and-effect toy than a communication tool, future research would benefit from testing the hypothesis that this mode of voice-operated communication device can enhance the communicative ability of certain children with autism (Beukelman & Mirenda, 1998; Romski & Sevcik, 1996; van Santen & Black, 2009).

ROBBIE

ROBBIE was fourteen at the time of this study. He presented with a CARS score of 36 (moderate-severe) and his performance on the BPVS failed to produce a score. He had attended an autism-specific school for over six years, and, prior to this, he was tutored at home via Applied Behaviour Analysis (ABA) methods. Robbie could repeat almost any word that he heard, but had no functional speech. The SLT reported that this child used a combination of manual signs and PECS to make himself understood. Robbie would go to his communication board, remove a single picture, then go to an adult and place the picture in their hand, indicating he was communicating with PECS at phase 2 level (Bondy & Frost, 1994). Robbie never communicated spontaneously using PECS at home, preferring instead to rely on pre-linguistic gestures, such as pointing or tugging on the sleeve of an adult. His use of PECS in school hours was at a rate of no more than 10 per day.

Robbie used the SGD for 11 of the 12 weeks of the study. His communicative events ranged from 0 to 580 per week with an overall total of 3133. It was shown that 35% (1056) of his communications related to requests for items (e.g., T.V., computer, puzzle, ball), 548 (18%) for food (e.g., ice-cream, sandwich, apple), and 370 (12%) for people (e.g., mum, dad, teacher).

The data revealed that while Robbie made a number of unrelated one-word events (Robbie repeated the word '*computer*' over 120 times in a twenty-minute period), he also used the device to build a number of two-and-three-part sentences. Finally, it was possible to see that Robbie communicated via the male digitised speech output option 77% of the time.

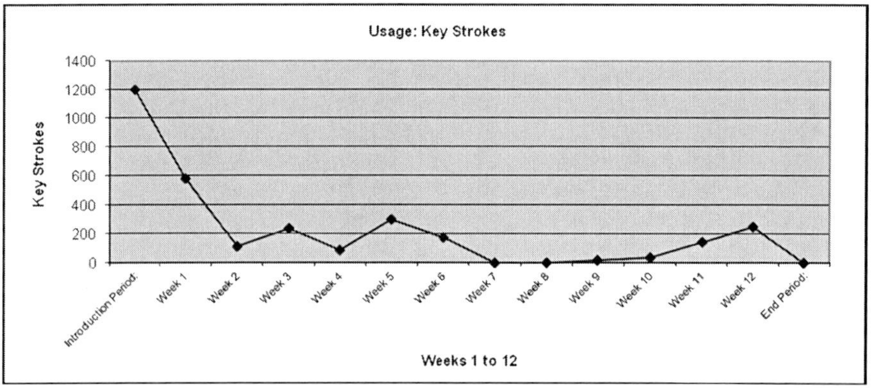

Fig. 5-4 A Graph Depicting the Use of the SGD over the 12 week Study by Robbie

Table 5-6 An Example of Sentence Building on the SGD: Robbie

Date	Time	Button	Code		Voice
27/01/2012	09:25:27	SM1	0x4400011a		I want
27/01/2012	09:25:29	SM2	0x440004ec		To eat
27/01/2012	09:25:30	SM3	0x44002199		Cereal
27/01/2012	09:26:21	SM1	0x44000886		I like
27/01/2012	09:26:22	SM2	0x440049e3		More
27/01/2012	09:26:23	SM3	0x4400479a		Thank you
14/03/2012	09:33:04	SM1	0x440017b7		Too loud
14/03/2012	09:33:06	SM2	0x0000128b		doctor
14/03/2012	09:33:09	SM3	0x0000084c		Calpol
14/03/2012	09:33:11	SM4	0x000007e5		ear

0x44 = male digitised voice. 0x00 = self-voice

Analysis: Robbie should have been able to recognise the voice on the device as that of his own, as he had achieved maximum scores on the Test of Familiarity, Self-Voice Recognition, and the Test of Pure-Voice Recognition - with an almost perfect score (e.g., 18/20) on a Voice-Face Matching Test. He scored 16/20 on the Test of Recollection.

There was a three-month gap between conducting these five studies and the allocation of the personalised SGDs however, which could mean that any recognition of self-voice at testing was simply not maintained over that time (Norbury, Griffiths, & Nation, 2010). In other words, the findings from Studies 4 & 5 may only have focused on Robbie's ability to 'fast map' (or the ability to map the sound of his own recorded voice to memory after one or two exposures), which was then assessed immediately via a Recognition Test. We did not consider the effect of a child's ability to remember the sound of his/her own recorded voice over an extended time period.

It was recently suggested, that while the child with autism may initially recognise the phonological forms of new words or sounds, these initial representations are fragile and may not be consolidated in memory in the long term (Norbury et al., 2010). When tested immediately following exposure to new words, 'the ease at which children with ASD,' learn and recognise the new words - relative to age and ability matched TD children - was noted (Norbury et al., 2010: 4017). However, despite a poorer performance on this task by age and ability matched TD children, when assessed after a time delay, the TD children demonstrated greater recall, 'despite having no further exposure to the novel words' (Norbury et al., 2010: 4017). It was suggested that the TD child had assimilated and encoded the novel words into memory, transferring the newly formed memories, 'from medial temporal lobe structures, including the hippocampus, to neocortical structures,' making the new memories robust over time (Norbury et al., 2010: 4013). However, the children with autism did not show any such consolidation effect. It was suggested that that there is, 'considerable evidence that neural connectivity is disrupted in ASD, which may interfere with the transfer and integration of newly learned information with existing knowledge' (Norbury et al., 2010: 4017). While investigating the recognition of self-voice, rather than new word learning, the results of the study by Norbury might imply that Robbie may not have maintained the auditory representations of self-voice in the three-month gap between testing and SGD allocation.

As such, while highly speculative, it is possible to infer that in the absence of - or with only poorly consolidated - memory for self-voice over time, Robbie may have failed to 'recollect' the natural voice on the SGD as that of his own, which in turn may have affected his preference for that voice-type. This would prove an interesting topic for future research.

NITA

Nita was thirteen years old at the time of testing and she presented with a CARS rating of 38 (moderate-severe) and an IQ of 64, and was the only non-Irish child in the study - having moved from India with her family six years previously. Her parents spoke a mixture of English and Urdu, and, while Nita could say 3-4 words in English, she preferred to utter these words in her native tongue.

Nita's father described his daughter as 'very rigid' in her behaviours. He said she, *'had to sit in exactly the same spot on the couch,'* every evening and she had to stir her tea, '*exactly seven times,'* prior to drinking it. Her father described all her communication as '*sporadic*' and '*sparse*' and wrote that Nita veered between sign language and PECS in the home. Nita had had access to a Go Talk 4+ (www.assistireland.ie) voice operated communication aid (VOCA) in the past, but her parents and teachers reported that this had not worked for Nita and that she preferred to use sign and/or PECS to make herself understood.

Nita used the SGD over 10 of the 12 weeks (missing weeks 9 & 10). She used her device most (56.3%) during the first two weeks of the study, thereafter tapering off to between 1-57 communication events per week. Most of Nita's communications related to requests for items (19%) and for access to places (15%), such as 'home,' the 'car,' and 'outside.' Over this time her communication events totalled at 1,101, ranging from 0- 332 per week with a mean average of 1.5 utterances per hour, which is relatively consistent with previous research collecting communications samples from children with ASD (Stone & Caro-Martinez, 1990).

This child had achieved maximum scores on four of the five studies conducted prior to partaking in the semi-longitudinal study, but was unwilling to participate on the Test of Recollection on the day of testing.

***Analysis**:* Before surmising that recollection was impaired in this child - making self-voice less recognisable and thus not preferred as the main speech output option - it is necessary to state that the voice recorded onto the SGD was not Nita's, but that of her aunt. Nita was unwilling to echo any of the 81 words to be recorded, and, while content to use the SGD, did not wish to cooperate with this part of the proceedings. It was not possible to find a child of similar age, gender, and ethnicity, at the time, so Nita's aunt (who was ten years her senior) agreed to provide her voice for recording purposes.

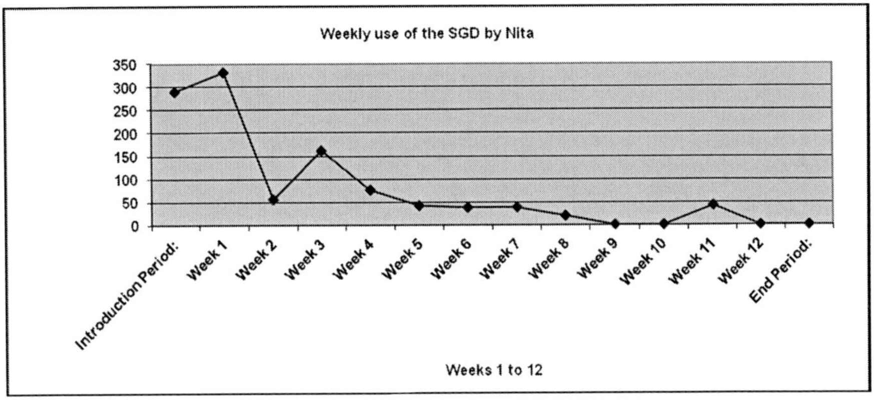

Fig. 5-5 A Graph Depicting the Use of the SGD over the 12 week Study by Nita

Obviously, using the voice of an adult, as opposed to an adolescent, is problematic when it comes to discussing the child's preference for self-voice on her SGD. However, it could be argued that, in line with the hypothesis of van Santen and Black (2009: e1), rather than digitised speech - using a personalised natural voice as opposed to either digitised or synthesised speech - 'will psychologically reinforce powerful motivational factors and a sense of owness for communication so that the frequency and richness of AAC use, and its acceptance by family members and friends, will be enhanced.' In any event, this was not the case here. Nita maintained a communication style that was relatively 'sparse' and 'sporadic' and one that veered between PECS and sign during her time with the SGD.

Despite showing no overt preference for a natural recorded voice on the SGD, Nita did use the device to communicate for the duration of the study. It is difficult to ascertain any preference for using the SGD over that of any other AAC available to her, as the parental report indicated that she, 'veered between PECS, sign and the SGD.' It is clear that her use of the SGD was fairly minimal however, with approximately one-to-two utterances per hour.

There are two possible ways of analysing Nita's use of the SGD as a communication tool. We could conceptualise her low communication rate as a function of her cognitive level and her degree of autism (e.g., Stone & Caro-Martinez, 1990). From this, we could infer that, because of her diagnosis and its associated impairment of social interaction, Nita will always display a lack of spontaneity when seeking to communicate with others (Forde, Holloway, Healy, & Brosnan, 2011). Via this lens, allocating any form of AAC will certainly provide the child with a means of expressing oneself, but, rather than serving as a gateway to more frequent and richer AAC use, the SGD would potentially only ever be used, 'to request something or to attract attention to oneself' (Forde, Holloway, Healy, & Brosnan, 2011: 1472).

Alternatively, we could look beyond the diagnosis and consider the child's social world.

For instance, it has been suggested that from the moment a child receives a diagnosis a change in their environment, in which the child develops (Karmiloff-Smith, D'Souza, Dekker, Van Herwegen, XU, Rodic, & Ansari, 2012), takes place. People in the child's life are often more cautious of allowing their diagnosed infant to explore objects with their mouths, or to crawl or walk freely - most likely because of a natural fear of accidents in vulnerable children. Nonetheless, this results in a less richly explored environment by the developing child (Karmiloff-Smith et al., 2012).

In terms of communication, it is noted that when TD toddlers begin to name things, their parents allow them to make grammatical errors and overgeneralisations, but not so when the child has a diagnosis. Karmiloff-Smith et al., (2012) suggest that parents are often afraid that their child with lower intelligence will never learn the correct term if the child is allowed to over-generalise in the first instance. However, initial over-generalisations by the TD child are said to encourage category formation; for instance, by calling different animals 'cats,' the child started to create an implicit animal category (e.g., Quine, 1960, 1969; Rosch, 1978). It is well established that category formation is impaired in several neurodevelopment disorders, and Karmiloff-Smith et al., (2012: e2) suggests that the often, 'unconscious assumptions about what atypical children can and cannot learn may unwittingly lead parents to provide less variation in linguistic input and in general, a less varied environment to explore.'

Nita shows evidence of recognition, at least on the basis of familiarity (e.g., Mandler, 1980; Yonelinas, 2002). She successfully matched the voices of people from her school to their corresponding photographs at tests, and was able to recognise a recording of her own voice with and without visual prompts, which suggests some form of intact ability to retrieve contextual information from memory. What is being suggested here is that Nita may not communicate very much via any form of AAC, but this may be less as a result of her cognitive capacity or the severity of her disorder *per se*, and more to do with the ways we all contribute to her environment, often unwittingly. Perhaps greater interaction with the child with autism in general, and Nita in particular, would encourage her to reciprocate.

FRANCIS

Francis was ten years old at time of testing and he presented with a CARS score of 36 (moderate-severe), with an IQ of 52. The teacher reported that Francis would go to his communication board, remove a single picture, then return to a caregiver and place the picture in the caregiver's hand, but that he preferred to use gestures and manual signs to gain attention. Data from the parental report confirmed the teachers report, and added that, *'Francis will tug at sleeves or grab my hand to point it in the direction of what he wants.'* Accordingly, Francis could communicate using single-meaning pictures, but he primarily relied on pre-linguistic behaviours, such as pointing, reaching, eye-gazing and other facial expressions (Rapin & Dunn, 2003). Francis used a maximum of two words per day to communicate (i.e., yes and no) and this child had no previous experience with a speech generated communication device.

The LAM data shows that Francis used the SGD unevenly over the 12 weeks of the study (see Fig. 5-6), with his lowest usage indicated during the first four weeks. Over this time his communications totalled 255 events, ranging from 0- 80 per week. This result suggests that, of the six children who continued to use the device after week 6, Francis was the least frequent user of the SGD as a communication tool.

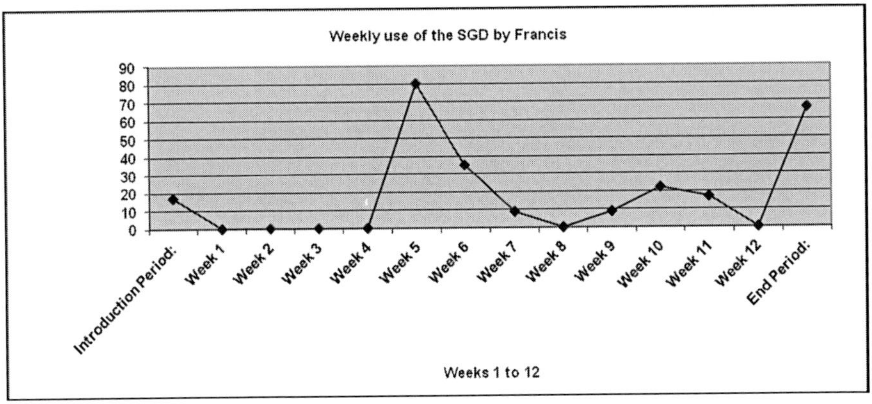

Fig. 5-6 A Graph Depicting the Use of the SGD over the 12-Week Study by Francis

During this time most of his communications (19%) were requests for items, such as the computer and games, and for access to places (8%). Francis was unusual insofar as he used the digitised *female* voice for 70% of his total communications via the SGD.

Analysis: There are three main points to discuss here, the first relates to the low rate of SGD usage by Francis, the second to the function of his communications, and the third to his choice of voice-type. In relation to the first point, prior to allocating the personalised SGD to Francis, baseline data of his current rate and mode of communication was obtained. It was noted that Francis could echo words after a speaker, but that he uttered no more than two words spontaneously most days, preferring instead to use pre-linguistic gestures, such as gesturing, pointing, facial expressions, and tugging at the sleeves of others to make his needs understood. Francis was at phase-two level in his use of PECS, and both his teachers and his parents stated that his communications via this mode was also less than three events a day. Accordingly, an average of 80 communications per week (or 11 communications per day) is neither an increase nor a decrease in his typical rate of communication, nor is it out of line with the findings of Stone and Caro-Martinez (1990) who found an average communication rate of 1.5 per day in children with autism, during school hours.

In terms of the function of his communication, which was the second point under discussion, baseline data suggest that when Francis made contact with others prior to having the SGD, most of his requests were for access to activities or items - for instance, access to the school yard or to a favourite DVD. The findings from the LAM data suggest little change in the function of his communication as a result of using a voice-operated communication aid (VOCA). Both these observations imply that while Francis accepted the SGD as a communication tool, and while he was very capable of operating it, having a VOCA did not enhance the frequency or richness of his AAC use (van Santen & Black, 2009).

The third point relates to his use of the female voice as his preferred speech output option when using this SGD. One possible reason for this is that the SGD was damaged in some way, leaving him no option but to use this voice. This was checked, however, and it was possible to see that he did use the other two speech output options over the 12 weeks, just not to the same extent as he used the female voice.

Table 5-7 A Report From the LAM Data on the Use of Voice-Type by Francis

Time of Day:	**Mornings (1)**	**Afternoons (2)**	**Evenings (3)**		**Total**
Number of uses:	174	58	23		**255***
Percentage:	68.24%	22.75%	9.02%		**100.00 %**
Voice type:	**Male (1)**	**Female (2)**	**Self (3)**	**Self over PreR (4)**	**Total**
Times used:	1	169	69	0	**239***
Percentage:	0.42%	70.71%	28.87%	0.00%	**100.00 %**

***The totals reported here differ, as the first includes data from the introductory period while the latter does not.**

There was no parental report for this child, and neither his teacher nor the SLT could offer any reason for his choice of voice type, so his performance on the five empirical studies was re-examined for some clues to his behaviour.

This ten-year old boy performed well on a Test of Familiarity and less well on a Test of Recollection, implying some impairment at the point of retrieval from memory at the point of making a recognition judgement (e.g., Jacoby, 1991; Mandler, 1980; Tulving, 1985). In line with Mandler, this could be reflective of the child's ability to recognise well via familiarity, but less well when a search of contextual information was required. Jacoby, by contrast, might suggest that the issue with the child's recollection is a reflection of how deeply Francis may have processed the information to-be-remembered at the time of encoding. Moreover, given that children with autism are characterised by a low level of social interest, it is likely that impaired recognition of faces and voices is a result of an initial lack of attention to people in the first instance (Burack, Enns, Stauder, Mottron, & Randolph, 1997).

His ability to match the voices of familiar people to their corresponding photographs at test was very good, however, and he managed to match a recording of his own voice to a photograph of himself on one of two occasions. Both these results suggest that when visual cues or prompts are given to support retrieval, recognition is then accomplished. This finding resonates with the task-support hypothesis - according to which, 'procedures that provide cues to the remembered material at test attenuate the memory difficulties experienced by individuals with ASD' (Bowler, Matthews, & Gardiner, 1997; Gaigg, Gardiner, & Bowler, 2007: 983). In the future, it would be advantageous to test the hypothesis that Francis used the female voice on the SGD primarily because - while all three voices on the SGD were somewhat familiar to him - without some form of prompt or memory cue he was unable to recollect which voice-type was his own.

Alternatively, Francis simply preferred the sound of the female digitised voice. I suggest this because he recognised his own voice on ten occasions in Study 5: A Test of Self-Voice Recognition in LFA where no photographs were used as prompts, implying this child could recognise self-voice, but chose not to use it when communicating via the SGD.

Perhaps self-voice 'vexed' him, as there was too great a discrepancy between what he thought it should sound like versus how it actually sounded (Holzman & Rousey, 1966; Hughes & Nicholson, 2010), or, perhaps it was simply too difficult to recognise a voice that was hardly ever used by the child in the first instance. Either way, the data suggests that the use of a personalised SGD did not enhance the frequency or richness of his AAC use, and that he did not prefer to communicate via the self-voice speech output option.

JIM

Jim was eleven years old and presented with a CARS score of 36 (moderate-severe), with an IQ below 50. The ABLLS-R report from Jim's school indicated that Jim was at level 4 in his use of PECS, which meant he could build sentences, such as, '*I want crisps'* by placing two single-meaning PECS cards '*I want'* and '*crisps*' on a sentence strip. Jim's teachers and parents indicated that Jim used PECS or signs less than ten times a day and primarily for requesting access to reinforcers, such as access to a trampoline or the DVD player. Jim could repeat a wide range of words, but his teacher suggested that he used a maximum of four functional words in any given school day and that these were almost always restricted to access to home, his mother, and use of the words 'yes' and 'no.'

Jim used the SGD for 9 of the 12 weeks to a maximum of 2,389 communication events that ranged from 15 - 88 per week. 19% of this child's communications were expressions of emotion (e.g., *'I want—*

happy' and 'I don't like—pain'), while 12% were requests for items (e.g., ball, book, computer) with 6% related to items of clothing (e.g., '*I want—coat'*). In addition, 55% of Jim's communications comprised two-part messages, such as *'I want—toilet'* and '*I want—toy,'* while 11% constituted three-part messages, such as *'I want—computer—please,'* while 34% of this child's communications comprised of single word events. Of interest, the LAM data indicated Jim used the self-voice speech output option for 40% (919) of all his communications. Of these 919 communication events, over half (462) were expressions of emotions (see Table 5-8).

Table 5-8 An Extract From the LAM Data Showing a Child's Use of Digitised and Self-Voice to Communicate.

DATE	TIME	BUTTON	CODE	WORD
14/02/2012	09:30:23	SM1	0x4400011a	I want
14/02/2012	09:30:25	SM2	0x00000b8f	happy
14/02/2012	09:31:37	SM1	0x4400011a	I want
14/02/2012	09:31:43	SM2	0x00000b8f	happy
14/02/2012	09:31:44	SM1	0x4400011a	I want
14/02/2012	09:31:47	SM2	0x00000b8f	happy
14/02/2012	09:32:34	SM1	0x4400011a	I want
14/02/2012	09:32:38	SM2	0x00000b8f	Happy
DATE	TIME	BUTTON	CODE	WORD
20/02/2012	09:26:07	SM2	0x00000fa9	I don't like
20/02/2012	09:26:12	SM3	0x00000426	pain
20/02/2012	09:26:28	SM3	0x00000a5f	home

0x44 = male digitised voice. 0x00 = self-voice

Analysis: Let us examine the amount of communications made by Jim via the SGD first (see Table 5-9). On average, Jim made 12 communications per day via the SGD, which amounts to 1.5 per hour over an eight-hour day. This finding correlates with that of Stone and Caro-Martinez (1990) whose observational study found that, over a ten-day period, school children with autism exhibited communicative acts in class at a *maximum* of two to three per hour per child. Prior to using a VOCA, Jim used AAC less than ten times a day on average, which suggests that use of a personalised voice operated communication device did not enhance the amount of communications made by this child (see van Santen & Black, 2009).

Table 5-9 A Weekly Analysis of Jim's Communications Via the SGD over the 12 Weeks of the Study

Total Usage:				
	Date From:	**Date To:**	**Key Strokes**	**% by Week**
Introduction Period:		03/02/2012	33	1.38%
Week 1	04/02/2012	10/02/2012	166	6.95%
Week 2	11/02/2012	17/02/2012	303	12.68%
Week 3	18/02/2012	24/02/2012	120	5.02%
Week 4	25/02/2012	02/03/2012	279	11.68%
Week 5	03/03/2012	09/03/2012	71	2.97%
Week 6	10/03/2012	16/03/2012	0	0.00%
Week 7	17/03/2012	23/03/2012	0	0.00%
Week 8	24/03/2012	30/03/2012	15	0.63%
Week 9	31/03/2012	06/04/2012	883	36.96%
Week 10	07/04/2012	13/04/2012	89	3.73%
Week 11	14/04/2012	20/04/2012	0	0.00%
Week 12	21/04/2012	27/04/2012	291	12.18%
End Period:	28/04/2012		139	5.82%
Total:			**2389**	**100.00%**

Usage outside Trial period:			
Introduction Period:		Up to: 03/02/2011	33
End Period:		From: 28/04/2012	139

Jim was building sentences with PECS before the allocation of the SGD, some of which were two-part in their composition. The LAM data suggest that - when using the SGD - the majority of his communications were two-part events, which further suggests a lack of significant enhancement to the 'richness' of his AAC communications.

What is interesting is that he chose to communicate via the self-voice speech output option very regularly (Table 5-10). Indeed, an examination of Table 5-10 suggests he veered between his own male voice and the digitised male voice in a rather yo-yoing fashion. Did he recognise the voice as that of his own and just not prefer to communicate consistently with the male digitised speech output, or, were all the voices familiar, but not distinct to him resulting in a non-discriminatory use of voice-type?

Table 5-10 A Report from the LAM Data on the Use of Voice Type by Jim

Voice type:	Male (1)	Female (2)	Self (3)	Self over PreR (4)	Total
Times used:	1226	181	919	0	**2326***
Percentage:	52.71%	7.78%	39.51%	0.00%	**100.00%**

***The sum 2326 differs from the sum of 2389 reported earlier, as the latter includes data from the introductory period.**

Jim did not participate on the Test of Familiarity because he was distressed. He did score 19/20 on the Test of Recollection however. In line with Tulving (1985), it is impossible for information to be stored in episodic memory without having been stored in semantic memory first. This implies that one cannot recollect someone, or something, that was not first made familiar to a person. Using this argument it might be suggested that had Jim participated on the Test of Familiarity that he would have performed at least as well as he did on the Test of Recollection.

However, Bowler (2011) suggests we should be aware that declarative memory, which comprises episodic and semantic memory, is mediated by the MTL, and that part of the structure of the MTL is the hippocampus. According to Bowler, the hippocampus works 'like a neural switchboard in memory, relaying information from sensory inputs to different parts of the brain' (Bowler, 2011: e1). He claims that recognition depends, in part, on how the information received from sensory inputs is organised in memory, and that, if it is stored atypically—not necessarily because of hippocampal dysfunction, but because some other connections are functioning atypically—then the hippocampus will be, 'doing different things' (Bowler, 2011: e1). One of these different things may be that recollection is not impaired in some instances, but familiarity is (e.g., Bowles et al., 2007). In Jim's case, therefore, it would be of interest to design a study to examine whether some abnormality occurs in the 'connectivity' of the hippocampal-frontal-cortical system - required for achieving typical recognition in the child with autism - when using a personalised SGD (e.g., Bowler, 2011).

CONNIE

Connie was eleven years of age at time of testing, with a CARS score of 36 (moderate-severe). The ABLLS-R reports from her school indicated that she was at level 4 in her use of PECS, and that she could use up to 10 signs to make herself understood during the school day. Her teacher and parents agreed that Connie rarely initiated communications with adults or children, and that, when she did so, it was mainly in the form of requests for her parents, food, or a toy.

Connie used the SGD for the full 12 weeks of the study with a total of 1,718 events recorded, ranging from 8-222 per week. The data indicated her greatest use of the device related to requests for food (36%), followed by requests for access to items (15%), and places (13%). The LAM data further indicated that Connie rarely built two-or-three word sentences, such as 'I want—chocolate' preferring instead to just use the word 'chocolate.' In fact, 88% of Connie's communications were single word events. Significantly, Connie showed the greatest use of the self-voice speech output option (79%) when communicating via the SGD than any of the children who participated in the semi-longitudinal study.

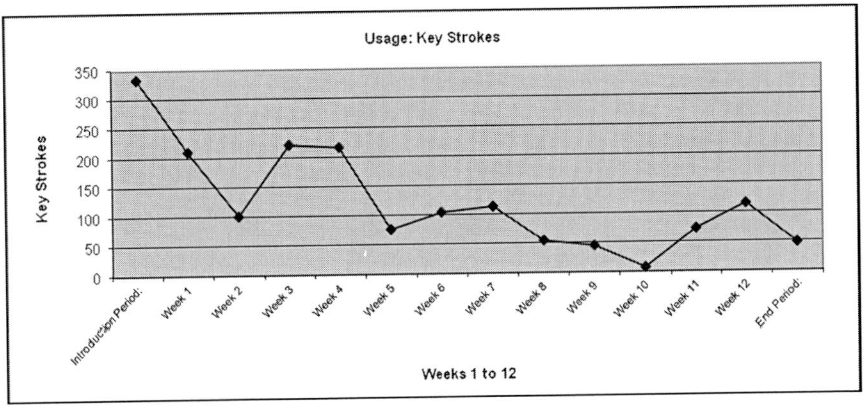

Fig. 5-7 A Graph Depicting the Usage of the SGD over the 12 - week Study by Connie

Analysis: At first glance, it appears that Connie was *the* success story of the present study. This child achieved maximum scores on the first two experimental studies, suggesting recognition could be accomplished on the basis of two memory retrieval processes: Familiarity and recollection. To support this finding, despite a diagnosis of moderate to severe autism and an IQ below 50, this child successfully matched the voices of staff and pupils from her school to their corresponding photographs at test, and also managed to match a recording of her own voice to her own image in Study 4. Taken together, these findings strongly suggest that Connie's use of self-voice, for most of her communications when using the SGD, were based firmly on her ability to recognise the voice and because she preferred that voice-type to any of the alternatives.

However, Connie did not do quite as well in Study 5 where she was required to identify her own voice when presented alongside the recordings of three other children without any photographs to prompt memory. This finding might suggest impairment at the point of recollection when no support (e.g., cues or prompts) is provided (e.g., Bowler et al., 1997; Gardiner et al., 2007). This finding could further imply that Connie failed to use the self-voice speech output option, for all her communications, because her recollection of whose voice it was actually faltered on occasions - but on which occasions?

An initial examination of the LAM data shows that Connie used the device mostly in the mornings and afternoons, and least in the evenings (Table 5-11). Future research should examine whether Connie used the SGD primarily during school times in response to questions asked of her by teachers or pupils. It may be, therefore, that - because the SGD was introduced in the school, her voice was recorded in the school, and training occurred in the school - Connie failed to generalise her use of the SGD to other environs, such as the home. This would not be an unusual finding amongst individuals with autism who often demonstrate poor generalisation of learning (Dautenhahn, 1999, 2010; Tager-Flusberg, 1991; Wing, 1999).

Table 5-11 A Report from the LAM Data on the Use of the SGD by Connie

Time of Day:	**Mornings (1)**	**Afternoons (2)**	**Evenings (3)**		**Total**
Number of uses:	842	699	177		**1718**
Percentage:	49.01%	40.69%	10.30%		**100.00 %**
Voice type:	**Male (1)**	**Female (2)**	**Self (3)**	**Self over PreR (4)**	**Total**
Times used:	0	356	1334	0	**1690**
Percentage:	0.00%	21.07%	78.93%	0.00%	**100.00 %**

Did the frequency and quality of her AAC use improve as a result of using a VOCA? At first glance, it might appear so, as Connie's rate of communication prior to having the SGD was reported as no more than four spontaneous communications per day, via sign, spoken words, or PECS. She was progressing from building two-to-three part sentences with PECS, however, and - according to her ABLLS-R report - this improvement had occurred in the previous twelve months, since the allocation of a special needs assistant (SNA) who was working with Connie on a one-to-one basis.

An average of 222 communication events per week would indicate an average of 31 communications per day, which would suggest a significant increase in her previous rate of 4 daily communications. Of course, it is possible that the new SNA was a factor in this, as a one-to-one teaching environment likely heralded an increase in responses from Connie over the course of her school day. On a related note, it is also likely that the increase in single word communication events - visible from the LAM data - reflect Connie's answers to requests from her SNA, rather than spontaneous communication events.

Significantly, if we look at the 177 communication events from after 3pm on any given day, or at weekends, or during week 10 - when Connie was on Easter holidays - a very different communication landscape appears. Over these time-frames, while the actual number of communications dips dramatically, this is when she demonstrates most use of self-voice on the device. This finding merits further research.

In addition, the parental report informs us that during her time using the SGD, Connie did not revert back to using PECS, suggesting a preference for this form of AAC, over that of another (van der Meer & Rispoli, 2010). However, during this 12-week period, Connie lapsed from sentence building to communicating primarily via single word communications, when using the SGD.

Overall, it is possible to suggest that Connie's performance on the five studies - combined with her use of the self-voice speech output option on the SGD - is somewhat in line with the hypothesis of van Santen and Black (2009). Support for this hypothesis is qualified, because while the 'frequency and richness' of her communications did not improve dramatically as a result of using a personalised SGD, she did appear to 'identify' with this communication tool and this is possibly on foot of it sounding more like her. It is also possible that her family and other communicative partners increased their interaction with her on foot of their preference for that particular voice, which in turn enhanced her use of self-voice on the SGD.

Most importantly, however, because Connie performed so well on four of the five studies, it is possible to hypothesise that she, more than any of the children allocated the device, recognised the sound of her own voice most reliably (e.g., Jacoby, 1991; Mandler, 1980). If so, this recognition possibly formed the basis for her preference of this speech output option more than any alternative. Future studies would benefit from providing the child with a longer period of time with the device, to examine whether the number of her communications might increase and whether the child may also have begun to build sentences that are more complex.

Summary

This chapter presented the findings of a semi-longitudinal study conducted with children diagnosed with LFA to examine their preferences for speech output options on speech generating devices. It described the processes undertaken to select these children for the study, the design of the devices, and the procedures used throughout. Some statistical analyses were reported, mainly in an attempt to ascertain the individual usage of the devices as communication tools over the course of the study, and to examine the children's preferences for voice types on the SGDs over this period of time. This analysis showed that five children had rejected the devices half way through the study and six continued to sue them for the duration. In addition, it was found that while factors, such as chronological age, non-verbal mental age, or IQ, did not influence the children's decisions to reject or continue with the devices. The girls showed a greater preference for using self-voice than the boys, and children who had performed well on the Tests of Familiarity and Recollection used this voice type more than those who had not.

CONCLUSION

So, we have reached the end of our journey. We began with the child with low functioning autism (LFA) and we asked two very simple questions: Can this child recognise their own recorded voice and, if so, is this the voice-type they would like most on their speech generating device (SGD) as they communicate with others in their social worlds?

Initially, answering those two questions appears deceptively straightforward. Why not simply record the child with LFA saying a few words, play that recording back to them - alongside the recordings of other children of the same age and gender - and measure the target child's responses. Simple! Moreover, given modern advances in technology, it should be relatively easy to download that voice recording onto a SGD, and thereafter assess the child's preference for communicating via that voice over that of the default speech output typically found on such devices. Again, simple! However, the apparent straightforwardness of these approaches was more complicated than imagined.

For instance, accurate voice recognition is dependent on numerous variables, such as the age and stage of development of the child (Bartholomeus, 1973; Mann et al., 1980; Spence et al., 2002; Strömbergsson, 2009); the length of the speech segment played (Bricker & Pruzansky, 1976); and the listener's familiarity with the speaker (Hollien, Majewski, & Doherty, 1982; Spence et al., 2002).

In addition, when the voice to be recognised is that of self-voice, accurate recognition is also influenced by the person's age and stage of development (Shuster, 1991; Strömbergsson, 2009); the quality of the recording (Shuster, 1991); and potentially, is made more difficult because the recorded self-voice lacks air and bone conduction filtering, rendering it less familiar to the listener than before (Maurer & Landis, 1990). Moreover, on hearing a recording of self-voice, people are often defensive or vexed by the aspects of personality (e.g., accent, ethnicity, age, health, and attitude), which can be carried on voice, but is not realised by the speaker (Belin, et al., 2001, 2011; Holzman et al., 1967; Hughes & Nicholson, 2010; Rosa et al., 2008).

There is also some debate as to whether memory in autism is best discussed in relation to memory systems, such as long-term or short-term memory systems, which differ in terms of the information they process, their rules of operation and the conscious states they may give rise to (Gardiner, 2008; Tulving, 1985; Sherry & Schacter, 1987), or, in relation to memory processes. Memory processes refer more to the ways information is encoded, organised, stored, and retrieved from memory. While it makes sense to consider memory as a function of interplay between memory systems and memory processes, it is true to say that, for decades, theory of memory has been divided between theories based exclusively on one or the other approach (see Gardiner, 2008).

One consequence of this division is that the findings of most studies of memory in autism have been interpreted via a systems perspective (see Bigham et al., 2010; Boucher et al., 2012). The most common model used to discuss memory in autism is Tulving's (1985) taxonomy of memory systems. This model distinguishes between memory for personally experienced events (episodic memory) and memory for decontextualised facts (semantic memory), in the declarative memory system (Tulving, 1985). Based on this assumption, a number of tests have been developed to assess declarative memory - the most popular of which is the Remember Know (RK) procedure (Gardiner & Java, 1993; Tulving, 1985). What people 'remember' is said to reflect their recollection of information in the episodic memory, while what they 'know' is more reflective of the retrieval of information from semantic memory. Using this distinction, the findings of several studies, conducted with individuals with Asperger Syndrome or high -functioning (HF) autism, suggests that memory in HF autism reflects a combination of mildly impaired episodic memory and spared semantic memory.

Recently, however, individuals have begun to discuss their own and others' findings on memory in autism in terms of a dual process model, which cuts across the episodic-semantic contents-based distinction (see Joseph et al., 2005). According to this model, declarative memory is underpinned by at least two distinct, but interactive and mutually supportive processes, namely recollection and familiarity (Aggleton & Brown, 2006; Jacoby, 1991; Mandler, 1980; Mayes, Montaldi, & Migo, 2007; Yonelinas, 2001, 2002). Recollection is defined as a kind of recall in which a recognised stimulus (e.g., a voice on the phone) cues recall of assorted kinds of contextual information experienced within the episode in which the stimulus was first encountered (e.g., the voice is that of Mary, a lady from my children's school, whom I met at a school meeting October of 2010). This model assumes that recollection is heavily dependent on intact functioning of the hippocampus and connectivity, and also potentially on intact connectivity and functioning of other regions of the pre-frontal cortex (Aggleton & Brown, 2006; Kirwan et al., 2008; Mayes et al., 2007). Familiarity, on the other hand, can be defined as a feeling that a stimulus has been encountered before without recalling any other information, including any episodic contextual detail (see Boucher et al., 2012). Familiarity is sometimes associated with 'recognition memory.' However, this association is erroneous because recognition is believed to depend on recollection as well as familiarity (Boucher et al., 2012; Jacoby, 1991; Mandler, 1980; Yonelinas, 2001, 2002). Familiarity certainly contributes to recognition of people, places, and events - possibly as a result of stimulus repetition. For example, the process of becoming familiar with faces and voices is one that likely builds on perceptual representations, which were initially implicit (e.g., Atkinson & Juola, 1974; Mandler, 1980). It also underpins slow and incremental learning (Boucher et al., 2012) and is considered to be heavily dependent on intact function and connectivity of the perirhinal and entorhinal MTL cortex (Aggleton & Brown, 2006; Montaldi, Spencer, Roberts, & Mayes, 2006). As with systems theorists, process theorists have developed a number of procedures for assessing recognition memory. Most importantly, two paradigms had been recently developed to investigate familiarity and recollection separately in LFA (Bigham et al., 2010). Assessing recognition via a dual-process approach would lead to a further distinction in the literature on declarative memory. In particular, it would allow us to see whether overall performance on tests of recognition were more reflective of familiarity (or what the child might know about a stimulus, such as voice) or recollection (for instance, what a child might remember about the source of that voice).

Using a Shape Recognition Test we firstly assessed familiarity in children with LFA and compared their performance to that of children with developmental-delay (DD) of the same non-verbal mental age (NVMA) and chronological age (CA). This allowed us to say that any findings from the children with autism could not be as a result of their age or stage of development, but must be reflective of having a diagnosis of autism. We also compared their performance with that of young typically-developing (TD) children matched with the LFA group for NVMA. This allowed us to conclude whether any findings from the children with autism were in line with typical performance or not (Burack et al., 2002; Charman, 2004).

The children with autism did well on this Test, which tasked them with recognising one of four abstract shapes as the shape they had encountered previously at study. However, they did not do as well as children with DD, or the TD children, with just seven of the thirty-three children achieving perfect scores on this test.

We then assessed recollection using a temporal source memory task, which required the children to recollect which one of sixteen items they saw presented directly before a target item, and which one was presented directly after this target item. Once again, their performance was compared to that of DD and TD groups. Just two children with autism achieved perfect scores on this Test, one of which was Connie, a child who had also achieved full scores in the Shape Recognition Test.

The studies reported in this thesis demonstrate the ability of the child with autism to experience familiarity and recollection - two processes that underpin recognition - but to a much lesser extent than either the child with DD or the very young TD child. Children with LFA may 'know' that they have heard a voice presented on a SGD as familiar. Several children with autism with non-verbal mental ages of four years and older achieved full scores on this Test, which compares with the age when most TD children in their ability to recognise familiar people by voice (Bartholomeus, 1973), and to recognise self-voice (Strömbergsson, 2009). However, by four years of age most TD children are also able to recollect more person-specific details, such as the name, social role, and place they may have met that person before - albeit not reliably (Spence et al., 2002) - and can do so at adult-level capacity by the age of fourteen (Mann et al., 1979). That recognition is more seriously impaired in the child with LFA is shown by the participant's inability to recollect the location of two items from a set at test, which should have been possible if they had intact recollection.

Overall, these two studies have added to the research literature on the ways children with autism process information. The findings have added to previous models of memory systems insofar as a further distinction can be made to the distinction in declarative memory - namely familiarity and recollection. Now rather than stating episodic memory is mildly impaired in HFA leaving semantic memory intact, it may be possible to suggest that this group of individuals may 'know' a substantial amount about what they are asked to recognise, but may not 'remember' how they learned this information. In other words, recollection is mildly impaired, leaving familiarity intact.

For the child with LFA, however, it appears that both familiarity and recollection may be impaired, and this has serious implications for the way these children experience and respond to their social worlds, and, most significantly, for this study, how they may recognise voice.

Based on this information, it was decided not to immediately assess their ability to recognise self-voice, but - in an incremental fashion – to examine first their ability to match the voices of people they were used to seeing on a daily basis at school with their corresponding photographs at test. This paradigm was one previously used with TD nursery school children (Bartholomeus, 1973), and slightly older TD school-aged children (Spence et al., 2002) as well as with school-aged children with autism (Boucher et al., 1998, 2000). Given that their processing strengths involved 'knowing' people, rather than 'recollecting' specific details about how and why they knew them, the use of visual prompts - such as photographs - should serve as memory retrieval prompts to aid recollection.

Once again, while the child with LFA showed some ability to master this task, they did not display the same level of mastery as either children with DD or young TD children. This was a disappointing outcome, especially as the children with autism had spent the longest time in school on average than either the DD or TD children, and thus had significantly more time to familiarise themselves with the people whose voices and faces were used as stimuli. This might imply that the child with autism simply did not pay as much attention to person-specific details - such as faces and voices - at the point of encounter, making any subsequent ability to recognise them on the basis of recollection very weak. This finding would be in line with both the levels-of-processing theory proposed by Craik and Lockhart (1972) and the dual-process theory of recognition set down by Jacoby (1991). Using this model of recognition memory, children may have correctly identified some of the staff and pupils from their school on the basis of pure familiarity, but others did so on foot of a particular meaning associated with that person at the point of encoding (i.e., she is my teacher, her voice is deep, she wears glasses). This model is one that assumes familiarity is not simply the activation of a process distinct from recollection - nor might it always rely on the activation of an existing perceptual representation in memory -, rather, both processes can be assumed to rely on detailed memory for prior events. As such, the findings from the study in this thesis resonate with Jacoby's model of recognition memory. In other words, recollection and familiarity operate differently in LFA as a result of intentional control at the point of recognition. Just four children, with autism, matched voices to faces successfully in this study - one of whom was once again, Connie.

There was hope however that the children with LFA would show more confidence and accuracy on this type of Forced-Choice Test, when the voice and face provided as stimuli was that of their own. After all, information to do with the 'self' (e.g., one's name, address, birthday, face, and voice) often creates a very reliable stamp, known as the self-reference effect (SRE) in memory (Rogers et al., 1977). Furthermore, children with autism, just like TD children, show a reliable ability to recognise themselves in a mirror from the developmental age of eighteen months (see Lind, 2010). Based on these observations, a Test of Self-Voice to Self-Face Matching was carried out with the three groups of children.

Twelve children with autism managed to match a recording of self-voice to a photograph of themselves on this Test. What was intriguing at this point was the lack of consistency between the children who were achieving maximum scores on each of these studies. Apart from Connie, no other one child with autism maintained a consistent score or performed consistently across tests. Happé, Ronald, and Plomin (2006: 1220) cautioned that, 'the biggest single obstacle to research at all levels' is the variation in performance amongst children with autism, and, while this was becoming apparent here, it was also curious that neither age, mental age, or gender provide any clues as to the degree of variation noted across tests. What was glaringly obvious was almost two-thirds of the children with autism in this study demonstrated no familiarity for self-voice, even when a visual prompt was used to cue memory at the point of recollection. This is a significant finding, given that the average person shows greater recall for information that is related to the 'self' (Rosa et al., 2008), with larger brain responses for images of self-face over other face (Ninomiya, Onitsuka, Chen, Sato, & Tashiro, 1998) and greater emotional response for the sound of self-voice than that of any other presented (Hughes & Nicholson, 2010).

The central aim of this study was to assess incrementally the child's ability to recognise voice. Using a dual-process approach, we investigated the potential of the child to recognise stimuli by firstly administering a Test of Familiarity and a Test of Recollection. Knowing that recollection posed a greater struggle for the child with LFA, we assessed their ability to recognise the voices of familiar people using photographs of these individuals as prompts for recollection. The children did well on this task, but not as well as either DD or very young TD children, which was cause for concern. Given that the recognition of people - whose voices they were exposed to almost daily - was impoverished, rather than remove visual prompts immediately when testing self-voice recognition, instead, we introduced a recording of the child's own voice and a photograph of the child to this Test and measured the child's ability to match these two stimuli. Twelve children with LFA succeeded on this task, and, based on this, we invited them to participate in one last study. The children were asked to listen to recordings of their own voice played alongside the voices of three other children, but, this time, no photographs were used. All children achieved either perfect, or very close to perfect, scores on this task.

It is possible that these children - who were listening to recordings of familiar voices and self-voice, over three studies in a short space of time - were building familiarity with self-voice over this time (Boucher et al., 2012). It is also possible that given the one-to-one instruction during practice periods, that the children were paying more attention to the stimuli to be remembered than they would normally. If this was the case, and the child was processing the sounds and images more deeply, this could potentially have led to better recall over time (see Craik & Lockhart, 1972; Jacoby, 1991). They did demonstrate recognition of self-voice with, and without, visual prompts however, making them the most suitable candidates for participating in a twelve-week study investigating the child's preference for voice-types on speech generating devices (SGDs).

Three months after the five studies had been conducted, twelve specially designed SGDs arrived from America and were allocated to the children. During these weeks, the parents and guardians of three of the twelve children withdrew from the study, and children with the next highest scores, on the Test of Voice Recognition without photographs, were invited to participate in their stead. The children were trained in the use of these devices during school hours, and, like most children with autism, they adapted well to this type of communication technology (Dautenhahn, 1999; Kee, 2012). A library of 81 words accompanied each device in a digitised male child voice and a digitised female child voice. Over a two-week period, the child was recorded saying these same 81 words, and this library was programmed onto the device. The intention was to give the children these devices for three months to track their use of self-voice during this time-frame.

One child left the study after two weeks, and five had completely rejected the devices midway through the study. Of these six children, two were those who had been invited to participate when three of the originally chosen children had withdrawn. None of these six children had preferentially used the self-voice speech output option over the duration of the study.

Six children did use the SGDs for the majority of the study period however, one of whom was Connie. Of these six children, there was no clear preference for self-voice made by any of the children, except Connie. She was also the only child who achieved perfect scores on the Test of Familiarity and the Test of Recollection. This strongly suggests a link between the child's ability to recognise a voice on the device as that of their own, and an ability to identify with that voice (see van Santen & Black, 2009). It was proposed that a device that sounded more like the child using it would create a sense of owness for communication, and it was further proposed that, on foot of this preference for natural voice over digitised voice, the child's communications via the SGD would increase in frequency and improve in terms of how sentences were built and conversations were initiated (Klabbers et al., 2010; van Santen & Black, 2009).

Curiously, the availability of a personalised SGD did not manifest in any dramatic improvements in how often Connie communicated during the study, as opposed to before the study. Rather, a young girl called Sandra showed the most striking change in her communicative abilities following the study. This child began to speak more, using words she had listened to on her device nightly. This was an exciting outcome and one that resonates with a small number of other studies also reporting enhanced speech following interventions with SGDs (see Beukelman & Mirenda, 1998; Romski & Sevcik, 1996; Romski & Sevcik, 2005 for reviews).

Most of the children - whether they had rejected the devices or continued with them for the duration - did not increase their rate of communication much past two-to-three per-hour per-child. This is a finding, which echoes that of Stone and Caro-Martinez (1990) who studied the spontaneous communications of school-aged children with autism during the school day. This might suggest that voice operated communication aids, while more popular than traditional AAC, are not offering a communicative panacea for the child with autism (see also Shane et al., 2011). This finding also suggests that having a more natural sounding voice on SGDs does not enhance the rate or style of the child's typical communicative events, as proposed by van Santen and Black and also Klabbers.

While the number of children participating in this study is small - making generalisation to wider populations difficult - the semi-longitudinal study, described in this thesis, has added to the literature related to AAC and autism. For instance, the study has added to previous studies of AAC use by individuals with autism by attempting to explain the speed at which these children learned to use all the features and functions on the Logan Prox-Talker, and has also contributed to the debate on which AAC is best for the child with autism thereby providing support for a clinical feature matching approach that considers the very individual needs and abilities of each child at the point of decision making (see also Blischak and Ho, 2000; Shane et al., 2011). The findings with children who rejected the device, before the halfway mark of the study, extend our knowledge of design issues in AAC (Shane et al., 2011); novelty effects, which may occur on the introduction of a new communication tool (Emms, 2010); and the need for ensuring that the child is sufficiently inducted on the use of the device across people, places, and times, before leaving them to their own devices (Sigafoos & Drasgow, 2001; van der Meer & Rispoli, 2010).

The findings with children who used the device for the duration of the study lend support to previous studies showing a lack of preference for natural speech sounds as opposed to electronically produced speech, in the child with autism (Klin, 1991; Kuhl et al., 2005). There is also tentative support for the suggestion that the child with autism may prefer digitised speech over that of speech rich in pitch, tone and accent, because the former is more predictable than the latter (Gergely, 1999). As far back as 1943, it was noted that the child with autism often displays an insistence on sameness (Kanner, 1943), and this desire for perfectly predictable responses from the environment also underpins their attraction to computers, robotic toys, and electronic devices (Dautenhahn, 1999; Gergely, 1999; Kee, 2012; Robins et al., 2005). Unfortunately, this lifelong devotion for perfection-seeking possibly underpins the child with autism's lack of interest in faces and voices whose expressions are never the same on any two occasions (see Ambridge & Lieven, 2011). Perhaps this is one reason why they do not 'tag' these person-specific details as emotionally relevant in memory in the first instance, making the recognition of same, at a later date, difficult - if not impossible.

Several limitations must be considered when interpreting these findings. First, most of the tests conducted here were modifications of previous paradigms, some of which had only ever been designed for use with young typically-developing children, and, as such, require replication before generalising the results to other children with LFA. Second, only a small number of children participated in the semi-longitudinal study making the results difficult to generalise. In addition, this study only focused on one type of SGD. It would be instructive to consider the use of a natural voice option on the Apple iPad or the Google Android for instance, given their current popularity with typical adolescents and those with a diagnosis of LFA (Kee, 2012, Prensky, 2012). Third, future research should examine time-related factors that might influence a child's preference for using a personalised SGD. This is particularly relevant, considering that our findings suggest that the child with autism may demonstrate signs of normal learning and memory function when tested immediately, but that this effect may not be maintained over time - a finding also noted by Norbury et al., (2010).

In sum, our results lend support to previous findings suggesting certain impairments of memory are present in all individuals with autism, with potentially more pervasive impairments of recognition memory in LFA than in HFA (Boucher et al., 2012). The results extend the work of Boucher et al., (1998, 2000) by showing that - while the child with autism finds it difficult to recognise the voices of people well known to them - this may be as a result of impaired familiarity, recollection, or both, in the child with LFA. In addition, the present results provide evidence to suggest that - while the child with autism may show recognition of voices immediately after testing - this effect may not be maintained over time (Norbury et al., 2010). It would appear that children with LFA showed an initial preference for a personalised SGD. However, over time, it became clear that any sustained preferences related to the device itself rather than the actual 'voice' of the device. This finding was also noted in a similar study conducted by van der Meer & Rispoli (2012).

Importantly, the high level of individual variation in the scores of children with LFA finds resonance in the recent words of Boucher (2011: 473) who said that, 'the concept of autism as a unitary disorder resulting from a single common cause….may be at the point of being abandoned.' That is not to say that we no longer seek answers to understanding the needs and abilities of individuals with autism, rather, it requires an open mind where we no longer consider a one-size-fits-all rule for the very unique needs of this population. Robert Schulz is correct, 'If you have seen one child with autism, you've seen one child with autism. Autism's like a snowflake' (Schultz as cited by Scott, 2011).

References

Aggleton, J., & Brown, M. (2006). Interleaving brain systems for episodic and recognition memory. *Trends in Cognitive Sciences, 10,* 455-463.

Alegria, J., & Pignot, E. (1979). Genetic aspects of verbal mediation in memory. *Journal of Child Development, 50* (1), 253–258.

Ambery, F., Russell, A., Perry, K., Morris, R., & Murphy, D. (2006). Neuropsychological functioning in adults with Asperger syndrome. *Autism, 10,* 551-564.

American Psychiatric Association (2013). *Diagnostic and statistical manual of mental disorders* (5th Edition) (DSM-V). Washington DC: APA.

Ambridge, B., & Lieven, E. (2011). *Child Language Acquisition: Contrasting Theoretical Approaches*. Cambridge: CUP.

Assist Ireland Information on daily living aids. http://www.assistireland.ie

Atkinson, D., (2002). Toward a Sociocognitive Approach to Second Language Acquisition. *Modern Language Journal, 86* (4), 525-545.

Atkinson, R. C., Hertmann, D. J., & Wescourt, K. T. (1974). Search processes in recognition memory. In R. L. Solso (Ed.), *Theories in cognitive psychology: The Loyola symposium* (pp. 101–146). Potomac, MD: Erlbaum.

Atkinson, R. C., & Juola, J. F. (1973). Factors influencing speed and accuracy of word recognition. In S. Kornblum (Ed.), *Fourth international symposium on attention and performance* (pp. 583–611). New York: Academic Press.

Atkinson, R. C., & Juola, J. F. (1974). Search and decision processes in recognition memory. In D. H. Krantz, R. C. Atkinson, R. D. Luce, & P. Suppes (Eds.), *Contemporary developments in mathematical psychology: Vol. 1. Learning, memory & thinking.* San Francisco: Freeman.

Atkinson, R.C. & Shiffrin, R.M. (1968). Human memory: A proposed system and its control processes. In K.W. Spence & J.T. Spence (Eds.), *The psychology of learning and motivation: Advances in research and theory*. (Vol. 2). (pp. 742-775). New York: Academic Press.

Atkinson, R. C. & Wescourt, K. T. (1975). 'Some Remarks on a Theory of Memory', in P. M.A. Rabbitt and S. Dornic (eds.), *Attention and Performance V*, Academic Press, London.

Attwater, D. (2010). Is Natural Language Right For You? *Speech Technology Magazine* (2010). Retrieved Monday 2nd September 2013 from http://www.speechtechmag.com

Baddeley, A. D. (2000) Working memory: The interface between memory and cognition. In: M. Gazzaniga (Ed.), *Cognitive Neuroscience: A Reader* (pp. 292-304). Oxford, UK: Blackwell Publishers Ltd.

Baddeley, A. D. (2002). Is working memory still working? *European Psychologist, 7,* 85-97.

Baddeley, A.D. (2006). Working memory: An overview. In S.L. Pickering (Ed.), *Working memory and education* (pp. 3-26). Burlington, MA: Elsevier Inc.

Baddeley, A. D., & Hitch, G. (1974). Working memory. In G.H. Bower (Ed.), *The psychology of learning and motivation: Advances in research and theory* (Vol. 8, pp. 47–89). New York: Academic Press

Bahrick, L. E., & Watson, J. S. (1985). Detection of intermodal proprioceptive-visual contingency as a potential basis of self-perception in infancy. *Developmental Psychology, 21*, 963-973.

Bailey, R. L., Parette, H. P., Stoner, J. B., Angell, M. E., & Carroll, K. (2006). Family members' perceptions of augmentative and alternative communication device use. *Language, Speech and Hearing Services for Schools, 37* (1), 50-60.

Baker-Ward, L., Hess, T. M., & Flannagan, D. A. (1990). The effects of involvement on children's memory for events. *Cognitive Development, 5,* 55–69.

Barresi, J. (2007). The origins of autism: A commentary on Muratori & Maestro's "Autism as a downstream effect of primary difficulties in intersubjectivity interacting with abnormal development of brain connectivity." *International Journal for Dialogical Science, 2*, 119-124.

Bartholomeus, B. (1973). Voice identification by nursery school children. *Canadian Journal of Psychology, 27*, 464-472.

Bastin, C., & Van der Linden, M. (2003). The contribution of recollection and familiarity to recognition memory: A study of the effects of test format and aging. *Neuropsychology, 17*, 14–24.

Batki, A., Baron-Cohen, S., Wheelwright, S., Connellan, J., & Ahluwalia, J. (2000). Is there an innate gaze module? Evidence from human neonates. *Infant Behavior and Development*, *23*, 223–229.

Bayley, P.J., Wixted, J.T., Hopkins, R.O., Squire, L.R. Yes/No recognition, forced–choice recognition, and the human hippocampus, *Journal of Cognitive Neuroscience, 20*, 505-512, 2008.

Beck, A. R., Stoner, J. B., Bock, S. J., & Parton, T. (2008). Comparison of PECS and the use of VOCA: A replication. *Education and Training in Developmental Disabilities, 43*, 198–216.

Bedford, R., Elsabbagh, M., Gliga, T., Pickles, A., Senju, A., Charman, T., Johnson, M. H, BASIS Team (2012). Precursors to social and communication difficulties in infants at-risk for autism: Gaze following and attentional engagement. *Journal of Autism and Developmental Disorders, 10*, 2208-2218.

Belin, P., Bestelmeyer, P. E. G., Latinus, M., & Watson, R. (2011). Understanding Voice Perception. *British Journal of Psychology, 102*, 711-725.

Belin, P., Fecteau, S., & Bédard, C. (2004). Thinking the voice: neural correlates of voice perception. *Trends in Cognitive Science, 3*, 129-135.

Bennetto, L., Pennington, B., & Rogers, S. (1996). Intact and impaired memory functions in autism. *Child Development, 67,* 1816-1835.

Beukelman, D. R., & Mirenda, P. (1998). *Augmentative and Alternative Communication: Management of Severe Communication Disorders in Children and Adults.* Baltimore, MD: Paul H. Brookes Publishing Co.

Beukelman, D. R., & Mirenda, P. (2005). *Augmentative and Alternative Communication: Supporting Children and Adults with Complex Communication Needs.* Baltimore, MD: Paul H. Brookes Publishing Co.

Beukelman, D. R., & Mirenda, P. (2012). *Augmentative and Alternative Communication: Supporting Children and Adults with Complex Communication Needs.* Baltimore, MD: Paul H. Brookes Publishing Co.

Bigham, S., Boucher, J., Mayes, A., & Anns, S. (2010). Assessing recollection and familiarity in autistic spectrum disorders: methods and findings. *Journal of Autism and Developmental Disorders, 40*, 878-889.

Billard, A., Robins, B., Nadel, J., & Dautenhahn, K. (2006). Building Roberta, a mini-humanoid robot for the rehabilitation of children with autism. *RESNA Assistive Technology Journal, 19 (1)* pp. 27-49.

Bock, M.A. (1994). Acquisition, maintenance, and generalisation of a categorisation strategy by children with autism. *Journal of Autism and Developmental Disorders, 24*, 39-51.

Bock, S., Stoner, J., Beck, A., Hanley, L., & Prochnow, J. (2005). Increasing functional communication in non-speaking preschool children: Comparison of PECS and VOCA. *Education and Training in Developmental Disabilities, 40*, 264–278.

Boddaert, N., Chabane, N., Belin, P., Bourgeois, M., Royer, V., Barthélémy, C., Mouren-Simeoni, M. C., & Zilbovicius, M. (2004). Perception of complex sounds: abnormal auditory cortical processing in children. *American Journal of Psychiatry, 161*, 2117–2120.

Boesch, M., Wendt, O., Subramanian, A., & Hsu, N. (2013). Comparative efficacy of the Picture Exchange Communication System (PECS) versus a speech-generating device: Effects on requesting skills. *Research in Autism Spectrum Disorders, 7*, 480-493.

Bondy, A., & Frost, L. (1994). The Picture Exchange Communication System. *Focus on Autistic Behavior, 9,* 1–19.

Bortfeld, H., Morgan, J., Golinkoff, R., & Rathbun, K. (2005). Mommy and me: Familiar names help launch babies into speech stream segmentation. *Psychological Science, 16,* 298-304.

Boucher, J. (1978). Echoic memory capacity in autistic children. *Journal of Child Psychology and Psychiatry, 19,* 161–166.

Boucher, J. (1981). Immediate free recall in early childhood autism: Another point of behavioural similarity with the amnesic syndrome. *British Journal of Psychology, 72,* 211-215.

Boucher, J., Bigham, S., Mayes, A., & Muskett, T. (2008). Recognition and language in lower-functioning autism. *Journal of Autism and Developmental Disorders, 38,* 1259-1269.

Boucher, J., & Bowler, D. (2010). *Memory in Autism: Theory and Evidence*. Cambridge: CUP

Boucher, J., Cowell, P., Howard, M., Broks, P., Mayes, A., & Roberts, N. (2005). A combined clinical neuropsychological and neuroanatomical study of adults with high-functioning autism. *Cognitive Neuropsychiatry,* 10, 165-214.

Boucher, J., & Lewis, V. (1989). Memory impairments and communication in relatively able autistic children. *Journal of Child Psychology and Psychiatry, 30*, 99-122.

Boucher, J., & Lewis, V. (1992). Unfamiliar face recognition in relatively able autistic children. *Journal of Child Psychology and Psychiatry, 33,* 843-860.

Boucher, J., Lewis, V., & Collis, G.M. (1998). Familiar face and voice matching and recognition in children with autism. *Journal of Child Psychology and Psychiatry, 39*, 171-181.

Boucher, J., Lewis, V., & Collis, G.M. (2000). Voice processing abilities in children with autism, children with specific language impairments, and young typically developing children. *Journal of Child Psychology and Psychiatry, 41,* 847-857.

Boucher, J., Mayes, A., & Bigham, S. (2008). Memory, language, and intellectual ability in low functioning autism. In J. Boucher & D. M. Bowler (Eds.), *Memory in Autism: Theories and Evidence* (pp. 268-290). Cambridge: CUP.

Boucher, J., Mayes, A., & Bigham, S. (2012). Memory in Autistic Spectrum Disorder. *Psychological Bulletin, 138(3),* 458-496.

Boucher, J., Pons, F., Lind, S., & Williams, D. (2007). Temporal cognition in children with autistic spectrum disorders: tests of diachronic thinking. *Journal of Autism and Developmental Disorders, 37 (*8), 1413-1429.

Boucher, J., & Warrington, E. (1976). Memory deficits in early infantile autism: Some similarities to the amnesic syndrome. *British Journal of Psychology, 67*, 73-87.

Bourguignon, N., Nadig, A., & Valois, D. (2012). The Biolinguistics of Autism: Emergent Perspectives. *Biolinguistics, 6* (2), 124-165.

Bowler, D.M. (2011). *Memory in autism: Interview with Dermot Bowler.* By James Brooks. http://jimbrux.wordpress.com

Bowler, D. M., Gaigg, S. B. & Gardiner, J. M. (2008). Effects of related and unrelated context on recall and recognition by adults with high-functioning autism spectrum disorder. *Neuropsychologia, 46*, 993-999.

Bowler, D. M., Gardiner, J., & Berthollier, N. (2004). Source memory in adolescents and adults with Asperger syndrome. *Journal of Autism and Developmental Disorders, 34,* 533-542.

Bowler, D. M., Gardiner, J. M., Grice S., & Saavalainen, P. (2000). Memory illusions: false recall and recognition in high functioning adults with autism. *Journal of Abnormal Psychology, 109*, 663-672.

Bowler, D. M., Matthews, N. J., & Gardiner, J. M. (1997). Asperger's syndrome and memory: Similarity to autism but not amnesia. *Neuropsychologia, 35*, 65-70.

Bowles, B., Crupi, C., Mirsattari, S.M., Pigott, S. E., Parrent, A.G., Pruessner, J.C., Yonelinas, A.P., Köhler, S. (2007). Impaired familiarity with preserved recollection after anterior temporal-lobe resection that spares the hippocampus. *Proceedings of the National Academy of Sciences of the USA*; 104:16382–16387.

Brazelton, T. B., Tronick, E., Adamson, L., Als, H., & Wise, S. (1975). Early mother-infant reciprocity. In, *Parent-infant interaction*, Amsterdam: Elsevier.

Bricker, P. D., & Pruzansky, S. (1976). Speaker recognition. In, Lass, N.J. *Contemporary Issues in Experimental Phonetics.* Academic, New York, pp. 295–326.

Bruce, V., & Young, A. (1986). Understanding face recognition. *British Journal of Psychology, 77,* 305-327.

Bryson, S. E., Wainwright-Sharp, J. A., & Smith, I. M. (1990). Autism: A developmental spatial neglect syndrome? In J. Enns (Ed.), *The development of attention: Research and theory (*pp. 405-427). Amsterdam: Elsevier.

Burack, J. A., Enns, J. T., Stauder, J. E. A., Mottron, L., & Randolph, B. (1997). Attention and autism: Behavioural and electrophysiological evidence. In D. J. Cohen & F. R. Volkmar (Eds.), *Autism and pervasive developmental disorders: A handbook.* New York: Wiley.

Burack, J.A., Iarocci, G., Bowler, D., & Mottron L. (2002). Benefits and pitfalls in merging disciplines: *Development and Psychopathology, 14*, 225-237.

Butterfield, E. C., & Siperstein, G. N. (1970). Influence of contingent auditory stimulation upon non-nutritional suckle. In J. F. Bosma (Ed.), *Third symposium on oral sensation and perception: The mouth of the infant* (pp. 313–334).Springfield, IL: Charles C. Thomas.

Carey, S., & Diamond, R. (1977). From piecemeal to configurational representation of faces. *Science, 195*, 312-314.

Carey, S., Diamond, R., & Woods, B. (1980). The development of face recognition-a maturational component? *Developmental Psychology, 16* (4), 257-269.

Casanova, M. F., Buxhoeveden, D., & Gomez, J. (2003). Disruption in the inhibitory architecture of the cell minicolumns: implications for autism. *Neuroscientist, 9* (6), 496-507.

Casey, B. J., Gordon, C. T., Mannheim, G. B., & Rumsey, J.M. (1993). Dysfunctional attention in autistic savants. *Journal of Clinical and Experimental Neuropsychology, 15*, 933-946.

Cavarero, A. (2005). *For More Than One Voice: Toward a Philosophy of Vocal Expression.* Stanford University Press.

Ceponiene, E, R., Lepistö, T., Shestakova, A., Vanhala, R., Alku, P., Näätänen, R., & Yaguchi, K. (2003). Speech–sound selective auditory impairment in children with autism: they can perceive but not attend. *Proceedings of the National Academy of Sciences, 100*, 5567–5572.

Charman, T. (2004). Matching pre-school children with autism spectrum disorders and comparison children for language ability: Methodological challenges. *Journal of Autism and Developmental Disorders, 34*, 59-64.

Cheslack-Postava, K., & Jordan-Young, M. (2011). Autism Spectrum Disorder: toward a gendered embodiment model. *Social Science & Medicine, 74*, 1667-1674.

Children First—National Guidelines for the Protection and Welfare of Children (2004). Retrieved Monday 2nd September 2013 from http://www.dcya.gov.ie

Chun, M. M., & Turk-Browne, N. B. (2007). Interactions between attention and memory. *Current Opinion in Neurobiology, 17*, 177-184.

Clearfield, M. W., & Nelson, N. M. (2006). Sex differences in mother's speech and play behaviours with 6-, 9-, and 14-month-old infants. *Sex Roles, 54*, 127-137.

Cohen, J. (1992). A power primer. *Psychological Bulletin, 112* (1), 155-159.

Collins, A. M., & Quillian, M. R. (1969). Retrieval time from semantic memory. *Journal of Learning and Verbal Behavior, 8,* 240-247.

Condon, W. S., & Sander, L. W. (1974). Neonate movement is synchronised with adult speech: interactional participation and language acquisition. *Child Development, 45* (2), 99-101.

Condry, J., & Condry, S. (1976). Sex differences: A study of the eye of the beholder. *Child Development, 47, 812*-819.

Cooper, R. P., Abraham, J., Berman, S., & Staska, M. (1997). The development of infant preference for motherese. *Infant Behavior and Development, 20*, 477-488.

Costanzo, F., Vicari, S., & Carlesimo, G.A. (2013). Familiarity and recollection in Williams syndrome. *Cortex, 49*, 232-242.

Courchesne, E., Kilman, B. A., Galambos, R., & Lincoln, A. L. (1984). Autism: Processing of novel auditory information assessed by event-related potentials. *Electroencephalography and Clinical Neurophysiology. 59,* 238-248.

Courchesne, E., Lincoln, A. J., Kilman, B.A., & Galambos, R. (1985). Event-related potential correlates of the processing of novel visual and auditory information in autism. *Journal of Autism and Developmental Disorders, 15,* 55-76.

Craik, F. I. M., & Lockhart, R. S. (1972). Levels of processing: A framework for memory research. *Journal of Verbal Learning and Verbal behavior,* 11, 671-684.

Craik, F.I.M., & Tulving, E. (1975). Depth of processing and the retention of words in episodic memory. *Journal of Experimental Psychology: General*, 104, 268-294.

Craik, F.I.M. (1971). Primary Memory. *British Medical Bulletin, 27*, 232-236.

Cutler, A., & Butterfield, S. (1992). Rhythmic cues to speech segmentation: Evidence from juncture misperception. *Journal of Memory and Language, 31*, 218–236

Culp, R. E., Cook, A. S., & Housley, P. C. (1983). A comparison of observed and reported adult-infant interactions: Effects of perceived sex. *Sex Roles, 9,* 475-479.

Cunningham, S. J., van den Bos, M., & Turk, D. J. (2011). Exploring the effects of ownership and choice on self-memory biases. *Memory, 19* (5), 449-461.

Dahlgren, S. O., & Gillberg, C. (1989). Symptoms in the first two years of life. A preliminary population study of infantile autism. *European Archives of Psychiatry and Neurological Sciences, 238,*169–174.

Darwin, C. (1859). *On the Origin of Species*. London: John Murray.

Dautenhahn, K. (1999). Robots as social actors: aurora and the case of autism. In *Proceedings CT99, The Third International Cognitive Technology Conference,* August, San-Francisco, pp. 359–374.

Dautenhahn, K. (2003). Roles and Functions of Robots in Human Society - Implications from Research in Autism Therapy. *Robotica, 21* (4), pp. 443-452.

Dawson, G., & Lewy, A. (1989). Arousal, attention, and the social impairments of individuals with autism. In G. Dawson (Ed.), *Autism: Nature, diagnosis, and treatment* (pp. 49-74). New York: Guilford.

Dawson, G., Meltzoff, A. N., Osterling, J., Rinaldi, J., & Brown, E. (1998). Children with autism fail to orient to naturally occurring social stimuli. *Journal of Autism and Developmental Disorders, 28,* 479-485.

Dawson, G., Toth, K., Abbott, R., Osterling, J., Munson, J., Estes, A., & Liaw, J. (2004). Early social impairments in autism: social orienting, joint attention, and attention to distress. *Developmental Psychology, 40* (2), 271-288.

DeCasper, A. J., & Fifer, W. P. (1980). Of human bonding: Newborns prefer their mother's voice. *Science, 208,* 1174-1176.

DeCasper, A. J., & Spence, M. J. (1986). Prenatal maternal speech influences newborns' perception of speech sounds. *Infant Behaviour and Development 9*, 133-150.

De Giacomo, A., Fombonne, E. (1998). Parental recognition of developmental abnormalities in autism. *European Journal of Child and Adolescent Psychiatry, 7,* 31–136

Dobbins, I.G., Kroll, N.E.A., Yonelinas, A.P., & Liu, Q. (1998). Distinctiveness in recognition and free recall: The role of recollection in the rejection of the familiar. *Journal of Memory and Language*, 38 (1), 381-400.

Donaldson, W. (1996). The role of decision processes in remembering and knowing. *Memory & Cognition, 24*, 523-533.

Drager, K. D. R., Postal, V. J., Carrolus, L., Castellano, M., Gagliano, C., & Glynn, J. (2006). The effect of aided language modeling on symbol comprehension and production in two preschoolers with autism. *American Journal of Speech-Language Pathology, 15,* 112-125.

Dunn, J. C. (2004). Remember-Know: A matter of confidence. *Psychological Review, 111*, 524-542.

Dunn, L. M., Dunn, L. M., Whetton, C., & Burley, J. (1997). *The British picture vocabulary scale (BPVS) (2nd Ed.).* Windsor: National Foundation for Educational Research.

Dunphy-Lelii, S., & Wellman, H. M., (2012). Delayed self-recognition in autism: A unique difficulty? *Research in Autism Spectrum Disorders, 6* (2), 212-223.

Dyer, C. (1999). *Research in Psychology: A Practical Guide to Methods and Statistics*. London: Wiley-Blackwell.

Dykens, E. M., Hodapp, R. M. & Finucane, B. M. (2000). *Genetics and Mental Retardation Syndromes: A New Look at Behavior and Interventions.* Baltimore: Brookes.

Ebbinghaus, H. (1913). *Memory: A contribution to experimental psychology.* New York: Teachers College, Columbia University. (Original work published 1885).

Education and Classroom Staffing in Autism Units. Retrieved Thursday 5th September 2013 from http://www.education.ie/en/AdvancedSearch/?q=autism&pageNumber=2#sthash.4nLC06Ab.dpuf

Eigsti, I. M., de Marchena, A. B., Schuh, J. M., & Kelley, E. (2011). Language acquisition in autism spectrum disorders: A developmental review. *Research in Autism Spectrum Disorders, 5* (2), 681-691.

Eimas, P. D., Siqueland, E. R., Jusczyk, P. W., & Vigorito, J. (1971). Speech perception in infants. *Science, 171,* 303–306.

Eisenberg, R. (1976). *Auditory competence in early life: The roots of communicative behavior*. Baltimore, MD: University Park Press.

Ellis, K. (1990). *Autism: Professional Perspectives and Practice*. London: Chapmen and Hall.

Farrant, A., Boucher, J., & Blades, M. (1999). Metamemory in children with autism. *Child Development, 70,* 107-131.

Farroni, T., Csibra, G., Simion, F., & Johnson, M. H. (2002). Eye contact detection in humans from birth. *Proceedings of the National Academy of Sciences, 99*, 9602–9605.

Farroni, T., Johnson, M. H., Menon, E., Zulian, L., Faraguna, D., & Csibra, G. (2005). Newborns' preferences for face-relevant stimuli:

effects of contrast polarity. *Proceedings of the National Academy of Sciences of the United States of America, 102*, 17245-17250.

Farroni, T., Massaccesi, S., Pividori, D., & Johnson, M. H. (2004). Gaze following in newborns. *Infancy, 5,* 39-60.

Fantz, R. L. (1963). Pattern vision in newborn infants. *Science, 140* (3564), 296-297.

Fein, D., Dunn M., Allen, D. A., Aram, D. M., Hall, N. Morris, R., & Wilson, B. C. (1996). Neuropsychological and language data. In Rapin, I. (Ed.), *Preschool Children with Inadequate Communication: Developmental Language Disorder, Autism, Low IQ* (pp123-154). London: Mac Keith Press.

Fernald, A., & Simon, T. (1984). Expanded intonation contours in mothers' speech to newborns. *Developmental Psychology, 20,* 104–13.

Fernald, A. (1985). Four-month-old infants prefer to listen to motherese. *Infant Behaviour and Development, 8,* 181-195.

Fisher, C., & Tokura, H. (1996). Acoustic cues to grammatical structure in infant-directed speech: Cross-linguistic evidence. *Child Development, 67*, 3192-3218.

Fitch, W. T. (2000). The evolution of speech: a comparative review. *Trends in Cognitive Science, 4,* 258 – 267.

Fivush, R., & Hammond, N. (1990). Autobiographical memory across the preschool years: toward reconceptualising childhood amnesia. In R. Fivush and J. Hudson (Eds.), *Knowing and Remembering in Young Children.* New York: Cambridge University Press.

Fountain, C., Winter, A. S., & Bearman, P. S. (2012). Six developmental trajectories characterise children with autism. *Paediatrics, 129* (5), 1112- 11120.

Frith, U. (1970). Studies in pattern detection in normal and autistic children: Immediate recall of auditory sequences. *Journal of Abnormal Psychology, 76*, 413-420.

Frost, L. A., & Bondy, A. (2002). *The Picture Exchange Communication System training manual* (2nd ed.). Newark, DE: Pyramid Educational Products.

Fyffe, C., & Prior, M. (1978). Evidence for language recoding in autistic, retarded and normal children. *British Journal of Psychology, 69,* 393–402

Gardiner, J. M. (1988). Functional aspects of recollective experience. *Memory & Cognition, 16*(4), 309–313.

Gardiner, J. M. (2008). Introduction: Concepts and theories of memory. *Journal of Autism and Developmental Disorders, 33,* 3-20.

Gardiner, J. M., Java, R. I., & Richardson-Klavehn, A. (1996). How level of processing really influences awareness in recognition memory. *Canadian Journal of Experimental Psychology, 50*(1), 114–122.

Gardiner, J. M., Ramponi, C., & Richardson-Klavehn, A. (1999). Response deadline and subjective awareness in recognition memory. *Consciousness and Cognition, 8*(4), 484–496.

Gastgeb, H. Z., Wilkinson, D., Minshew, N. J., & Strauss, M. S. (2011). Can individuals with autism abstract prototypes of natural faces? *Journal of Autism and Developmental Disorders, 41*, 1609-1618.

Gazzaniga, M.S., & Hillyard, S.A. (1971). Language and speech capacity of the right hemisphere. *Neuropsychologia 9,* 273-280.

Gergely, G. (2001). The obscure object of desire. 'Nearly but clearly not like me.' Contingency preference in normal children versus children with autism. *Cognitive and interactional foundations of attachment, 65* (3), 411-426.

Gervais, H., Belin, P., Boddaert, N., Leboyer, M., Coez, A., Sfaello, I., Barthelemy, C., Brunelle, F., Samson, Y., Zilbovicius, M. (2004). Abnormal cortical voice processing in autism. *Nature Neuroscience, 7,* 801– 802.

Gogate, L., Bahrick, L. E., & Watson, J. D. (2000). A study of multimodal motherese: The role of temporal synchrony between verbal labels and gestures. *Child Development, 71*, 878-894.

Goldsmith, T. R., & LeBlanc, L. A. (2004). Use of technology for children with autism. *Journal of early and Intensive Behavioural Intervention, 1*, 166-178.

Goldstein, H. (2002). Communication intervention for children with autism: A review of treatment efficacy. *Journal of Autism and Developmental Disorders, 32*, 373–39.

Goldstein, A. G. (1975). Recognition of inverted photographs of faces by children and adults. *Journal of Genetic Psychology, 127*,109-123.

Goldstein, H. (2011). *Cognitive psychology.* (3rd ed.) Belmont, CA: Wadsworth, Cengage Learning.

Graf, P., & Mandler, G. (1984). Activation makes words more accessible, but not necessarily more retrievable. *Journal of Verbal Learning and Verbal Behavior, 23*(5), 553–568.

Graf, P., Squire, L. R., & Mandler, G. (1984). The information that amnesic patients do not forget. *Journal of Experimental Psychology: Learning, Memory, and Cognition, 10*(1), 164–178.

Gregg, V. H., & Gardiner, J. M. (1994). Recognition memory and awareness: A large effect of study-test modalities on "know" responses following a highly perceptual orienting task. *European Journal of Cognitive Psychology, 6*(2), 131–147.

Grieser, D. L., & Kuhl, P. K. (1988). Maternal speech to infants in a tonal language: Support for universal prosodic feature in motherese. *Developmental Psychology, 24,* 14–20.

Grossman, T., Oberecker, R., Koch, S. P., & Friederici, A. D. (2010). The developmental origins of voice processing in the human brain. *Neuron, 65* (6), 852-858.

Happé, F., Ronald, A., & Plomin, R. (2006). Time to give up on a single explanation for autism. *Nature Neuroscience, 9* (10), 1218-1220.

Hauck, M., Fein, D., Maltby, N., Waterhouse, L., & Feinstein, C. (1998). Memory for faces in children with autism. *Clinical Neuropsychology, 4,* 187–198.

Hauser, M. (1996). *The Evolution of Communication*. MIT Press.

Hawking, Stephen, (2014). Read a review from my brief history. http://www.hawking.org.uk

Heaton, P. (2003). Pitch memory, labelling and disembedding in autism. *Journal of Child Psychology and Psychiatry, 44*, 543– 551.

Hepper, P.G. (1991). *Kin Recognition.* Cambridge: CUP.

Hepper, P. G., Scott, D., & Shahidullah, S. (1993). Newborn and fetal response to maternal voice. *Journal of Reproductive and Infant Psychology 11,* 147–153.

Hermelin, B., & O'Connor, N. (1967). Remembering of words by psychotic and subnormal children, *British Journal of Psychology, 58*, 213-218.

Hill, K., & Romich, B. (2002). A rate index for augmentative and alternative communication. *International Journal of Speech Technology 5*, 57-64.

Hillier, A., Campbell, H., Keillor, J., Phillips, N., & Beversdorf, D.Q. (2007). Decreased false memory for visually presented shapes and symbols among adults on the autism spectrum. *Journal of Clinical and Experimental Neuropsychology, 29*, 610-616.

Hobson, R.P. (1991). Methodologic issues for experiments on autistic individuals' perception of emotion. *Journal of Child Psychology and Psychiatry, 32*, 1135-1158.

Hobson, R. P., Ouston, J., & Lee, T. (1988). Emotion recognition in autism: Coordinating faces and voices. *Psychological Medicine, 18,* 911-923.

Holdstock, J., Mayes, A., Isaac, C., Gong, Q., & Roberts, N. (2002). Differential involvement of the hippocampus and temporal lobe cortices in rapid and slow learning of new semantic information. *Neuropsychologia, 40,* 748-768.

Holzman, P. S., Berger, A., & Rousey, C. (1967). Voice confrontation: A bilingual study. *Journal of Personality and Social Psychology, 7* (4), 423-428.

Howe, M. L., & Courage, M. L. (1997). The emergence and early development of autobiographical memory. *Psychological Review, 104,* 499–523.

Howlin, P., Goode, S., Hutton, J., & Rutter, M. (2004). Adult outcome for children with autism. *Journal of Child Psychology and Psychiatry, 45* (2), 212-229.

Hughes, S. M., & Nicholson, S. E. (2010). The processing of auditory and visual recognition of self-stimuli. *Consciousness and Cognition, 19*(4), 1124-1134.

Hunter, P. (2010). Is Natural Language Right For You? *Speech Technology Magazine* (2010). Retrieved Monday 2nd September 2013 from http://www.speechtechmag.com.

Irish Autism Action (IAA) Raising Standards: http://www.autismireland.ie

Jacoby, L. L. (1991). A process dissociation framework: Separating automatic from intentional uses of memory. *Journal of Memory and Language, 30*(5), 513–541.

Jacoby, L. L. (1998). Invariance in automatic influences of memory: Toward a user's guide for the process-dissociation procedure. *Journal of Experimental Psychology: Learning, Memory, and Cognition, 24*(1), 3–26.

Jacoby, L. L. (1999). Ironic effects of repetition: Measuring age-related differences in memory. *Journal of Experimental Psychology: Learning, Memory, and Cognition, 25*(1), 3–22.

Jacoby, L. L., Begg, I. M., & Toth, J. P. (1997). In defence of functional independence: Violations of assumptions underlying the process-dissociation procedure? *Journal of Experimental Psychology: Learning, Memory, and Cognition, 23*(2), 484–495.

Jacoby, L. L., & Dallas, M. (1981). On the relationship between autobiographical memory and perceptual learning. *Journal of Experimental Psychology: General, 110*(3), 306–340.

Jacoby, L. L., Jones, T. C., & Dolan, P. O. (1998). Two effects of repetition: Support for a dual-process model of knowledge judgments and exclusion errors. *Psychonomic Bulletin and Review, 5*(4), 705–709.

Jacoby, L. L., & Kelley, C. M. (1992). Unconscious influences of memory: Dissociations and automaticity. In E. A. D. Milner, & E. M.

D. Rugg (Eds.), *The neuropsychology of consciousness* (pp. 201–233). San Diego, CA: Academic Press.

Jacoby, L. L., Kelley, C. M., & Dywan, J. (1989). Memory attributions. In E. Henry, L. Roediger III, E. Fergus, & I. M. Craik (Eds.), *Varieties of memory and consciousness: Essays in honour of Endel Tulving* (pp. 391–422). Hillsdale, NJ: Erlbaum.

Jacoby, L. L., & Shrout, P. E. (1997). Toward a psychometric analysis of violations of the independence assumption in process dissociation. *Journal of Experimental Psychology: Learning, Memory, and Cognition, 23*(2), 505–510.

Jacoby, L. L., Toth, J. P., & Yonelinas, A. P. (1993). Separating conscious and unconscious influences of memory: Measuring recollection. *Journal of Experimental Psychology: General, 122*(2), 139–154.

Jacoby, L. L., & Whitehouse, K. (1989). An illusion of memory: False recognition influenced by unconscious perception. *Journal of Experimental Psychology: General, 118*(2), 126–135.

Jacoby, L. L., & Witherspoon, D. (1982). Remembering without awareness. *Canadian Journal of Psychology, 36*(2), 300–324.

Jacoby, L. L., Yonelinas, A. P., & Jennings, J. M. (1997). The relation between conscious and unconscious (automatic) influences: A declaration of independence. In E. Jonathan, D. Cohen, & W. Schooler (Eds.), *Scientific approaches to consciousness* (pp. 13–47). Hillsdale, NJ: Erlbaum.

Jarrold, C., & Brock, J. (2004). To match or not to match? Methodological issues in autism-related research. *Journal of Autism and Developmental Disorders, 34*, 81-86.

Java, R. I., Gregg, V. H., & Gardiner, J. M. (1997). What do people actually remember (and know) in "remember/ know" experiments? *European Journal of Cognitive Psychology, 9*(2), 187–197.

Johnson, M. H., Dziurawei, S., Ellis, H., & Morton, J. (1991). Newborn's preferential tracking of face-like stimuli and its subsequent decline. *Cognition, 90*, 1-19.

Johnson, M. K., Hashtroudi, S., & Lindsay, D. (1993). Reality monitoring. *Psychological Bulletin, 114*, 3–28.

Johnson, M. H., Posner, M.I., & Rothbart, M.K. (2007). Components of Visual Orienting in Early Infancy: Contingency Learning, Anticipatory Looking, and Disengaging. *Journal of Cognitive Neuroscience, 3* (4), 335-344.

Joseph, R. M., & Tanaka, J. (2002). Holistic and part-based face recognition in children with autism. *Journal of Child Psychology and Psychiatry, 44* (4), 529-542.

Joseph, R., Steele, S., Meyer, E. & Tager-Flusberg, H. (2005). Self-ordered pointing in children with autism: Failure to use verbal mediation in the service of working memory? *Neuropsychologia, 43,* 1400-1411.

Jusczyk, P. (1999). Infant speech perception. *Journal of Communication Disorders, 32,* 4–20.

Jusczyk, P., Houston, D., & Newsome, M. (1999). The beginnings of word segmentation in English-learning infants. *Cognitive Psychology, 39,* 159–207

Kanner, L. (1943). Autistic disturbances of affective contact. *Nervous Child, 2,* 217-250.

Karmiloff, K., & Karmiloff-Smith, A. (2001). *Pathways to Language: From Fetus to Adolescent.* Harvard University Press: Cambridge Massachusetts

Karmiloff-Smith, A., D'Souza, D., Dekker, T. M., Van Herwegen, J., Xu, F., Rodic, M. & Ansari, D. (2012). Genetic and environmental vulnerabilities in children with neurodevelopmental disorders. *Proceedings of the National Academy of Sciences 109* (2), 17261-17265.

Kee, N.K.N. (2012). *Notes on Digital Wisdom in the 21st Century.* Retrieved Tuesday 3rd September 2013 from http://www.keefamily.org/announcement/Norman_Submission.pdf

Keenan, M., Dillenburger, K., Doherty, A., Byrne, T., & Gallagher, S. (2007). *Meeting the needs of families with children diagnosed with autism spectrum disorders.* Children and Adolescents Service, 1096. Retrieved Thursday 5th September 2013 from http://www.peatni.org/uploads/27122007215234_AUTISMREPORT.pdf

Keenan, M., Kerr, K., & Dillenburger, K. (1999). *Parent's Education as Autism Therapists: Applied Behaviour Analysis in Context.* London: Jessica Kingsley Publishers.

Kelley, C. M., & Jacoby, L. L. (2000). Recollection and familiarity: Process-dissociation. In E. E. Tulving, E. Fergus, & I. M. Craik (Eds.), *The Oxford handbook of memory* (pp. 215–228). New York, NY: Oxford Univ. Press.

Kemner, C., Verbaten, M.N., Cuperus, J.M., Camfferman, G., & Van England, H. (1995). Abnormal saccadic eye movements in autistic children. *Journal of Autism and Developmental Disorders, 28* (1), 61-67.

Kennedy, C. H., Meyer, K. A., Knowles, T., & Shukla, S. (2000). Analyzing the multiple functions of stereotypical behavior for students with autism: Implications for assessment and treatment. *Journal of Applied Behavior Analysis, 33,* 559–572.

Khoe, W., Kroll, N. E. A., Yonelinas, A. P., Dobbins, I. G., & Knight, R. T. (2000). The contribution of recollection and familiarity to yes-no and forced-choice recognition tests in healthy subjects and amnesics. *Neuropsychologia, 38*(10), 1333–1341.

Kirwan, C. B., Wixted, J. T., & Squire, L. R. (2008). Activity in the medial temporal lobe predicts memory strength, whereas activity in the prefrontal cortex predicts recollection. *Journal of Neuroscience, 28,* 10541–10548.

Klabbers, E., Kain, A., & van Santen, J. (2010), Evaluation of Speaker Mimic Technology for Personalizing SGD Voices, *Proceedings Interspeech 2010, Makuhari, Japan*, pp. 2154-2157.

Klin, A. (1991). Young autistic children's listening preferences in regard to speech: A possible characterisation of the symptom of social withdrawal. *Journal of Autism and Developmental Disorders, 21*, 29-42.

Klin, A., Jones, W., Schultz, R., & Volkmar, F. (2003). The enactive mind, or from actions to cognition: lessons from autism. *Philosophical Transactions of the Royal Society of London, B Biological Sciences, 358,* 345– 360.

Klin, A., Jones, W., Schultz, R., Volkmar, R., & Cohen, D. (2002). Visual fixation patterns during viewing of naturalistic social situations as predictors of social competence in individuals with autism. *Archives of General Psychiatry, 59* (9), 809-816.

Klin, A., Sparrow, S., de Bildt, A., Cicchetti, D.V., Cohen, D., & Volkmar, F. (1999). A normed study of face recognition in autism and related disorders. *Journal of Autism and Developmental Disorders, 29,* 499-508.

Koegel, R.L., Shirotova, L., & Koegel, L.K. (2009). Antecedent Stimulus Control: Using Orienting Cues to Facilitate First-Word Acquisition for Nonresponders with Autism. *Behavioural Analyst, 32*, (2), 281-284.

Koul, R. K., & Allen, G. D. (1993). Segmental intelligibility and speech interference thresholds of high quality synthetic speech in the presence of noise. *Journal of Speech and Hearing Research, 36,* 790-798.

Koul, R. K., & Hanners, J. (1997). Word identification and sentence verification of two synthetic speech systems by individuals with intellectual disabilities. *Augmentative and Alternative Communication, 13,* 99-107.

Koul, R. K. (2003). Perception of synthetic speech in individuals with and without disabilities. *Augmentative and Alternative Communication, 19,* 49-58.

Krejcie, R. V., & Morgan, D. W. (2007). Determining sample sizes for research activities. *Educational and Psychological Measurement, 30,* 607-610.

Konstantinou, I., & Gardiner, J. (2005). Conscious control and memory awareness when recognising famous faces. *Memory 13* (5), pp. 449-457. London: Psychology Press.

Kuhl, P. K. (2004). Early language acquisition: Cracking the speech code. *Nature Reviews Neuroscience, 5*, 831-843.

Kuhl, P. K. (2007). Is speech learning 'gated' by the social brain? *Developmental Science, 10*, 110-120.

Kuhl, P. K. (2011). Who's Talking? *Science, 333,* 529-530.

Kuhl, P. K., & Rivera-Gaxiola, M. (2008). Neural substrates of language acquisition. *Annual Review of Neuroscience, 31,* 511-553.

Kuhl, P. K., Tsao, F. M., & Liu, H. M. (2003). Foreign-language experience in infancy: Effects of short-term exposure and social interaction on phonetic learning. *Proceedings of the National Academy of Sciences, 100,* 9096-9101.

Kuhl, P. K., Coffey-Corina, S., Padden, D., & Dawson, G. (2005). Links between social and linguistic processing of speech in preschool children with autism: behavioral and electrophysiological measures. *Developmental Science, 8*, F1-F12.

Kuhl, P. K., Conboy, B. T., Padden, D., Nelson, T., & Pruitt, J. (2005). Early speech perception and later language development: Implications for the critical period. *Language Learning and Development, 1*, 237-264.

Lámh Communication Augmentation Sign System Ltd. (2014). *A manual sign system for people with intellectual disabilities and communication needs in Ireland.* http://www.lamh.org

Landry, R., & Bryson, S. E. (2004). Impaired disengagement of attention in young children with autism. *Journal of Child Psychology and Psychiatry, 45*, 1115–1122.

Landry, S.H., & Loveland, K.A. (1989). The effect of social context on the functional communication skills of autistic children. *Journal of Autism and Developmental Disorders, 19,* 283-299.

Laznik, M. C., Maestro, S., Muratori, F., & Parlato, E. (2005). Les interactions sonores entre les bébés devenus autistes et leurs parents. In Castarede M.F., Konopczynski G. (eds.). *Au commencement était la voix*, pp171–181, Paris, Erès.

Leehey, S. C. (1977). *A developmental change in right hemispheric specialisation*. Paper presented at the meetings of the Society for Research in Child Development, New Orleans.

Lepistö, T., Kujala, T., Vanhala, R., Alku, P., Houtilainen, M., & Näätänen, R. (2005). The discrimination of and orienting to speech and non-speech sounds in children with autism. *Brain Research, 1066*, 147-157.

Lepistö, T., Kujala, M., Vanhala, R., Alku, P., Houtilainen, M., Näätänen, R., & Kujala, T. (2008). The perception of invariant speech features in children with autism. *Biological Psychology, 77* (1), 25-31.

Lind, S. (2010). Memory and the self in autism spectrum disorder: A review and theoretical framework. *Autism, 14,* 430-456.

Lind, S., & Bowler, D. M. (2009a). Recognition memory, self-other source memory, and theory-of-mind in children with autism spectrum disorder. *Journal of Autism and Developmental Disorders, 39,* 1231-1239.

Lind, S., & Bowler, D.M. (2009b). Delayed self-recognition in children with autism spectrum disorder. *Journal of Autism and Developmental Disorders, 39*, 643-650.

Lloyd, L. L., Fuller, D. R., & Arvidson, H. H. (1997). *Augmentative and Alternative Communication: A Handbook of Principles and Practices.* Boston: Allyn and Bacon.

Lord, C. & Paul, R. (1997). Language and communication in autism. In D. J. Cohen & F. R. Volkmar (Eds.), *Handbook of autism and pervasive development disorders*, 2nd edition. New York: John Wiley.

Lowell, M. (1972). Audiological assessment. In E. R. Ritvo (Ed.), *Autism: Diagnosis, current research and management*. New York: Spectrum.

Macchi Cassia, V., Turati, C., & Simion, F. (2004). Can a non specific bias toward top-heavy patterns explain newborns' face preference? *Psychological Science, 15*, 379–383.

Mahdhaoui, A., Chetouani, M., Cassel, R.S., Saint-Georges, C., Parlato, E., Laznik, M. C., Apicella, F., Muratori, F., Maestro, S., & Cohen, D. (2011). Computerized home video detection for motherese may help to study impaired interaction between infants who become autistic and their parents. *International Journal of Methods in Psychiatric Research, 20,* e6-e18.

Mandler, G. (1979). Organization and repetition: Organizational principles with special reference to rote learning. In L. G. Nilsson (Ed.), *Perspectives on memory research* (pp. 293–327). Hillsdale, NJ: Erlbaum.

Mandler, G. (1980). Recognizing: The judgment of previous occurrence. *Psychological Review, 87*(3), 252–271.

Mandler, G. (1991). Your face looks familiar but I can't remember your name: A review of dual process theory. In E. William, E. Hockley, & E. S. Lewandowsky (Eds.), *Relating theory and data: Essays on human memory in honor of Bennet B. Murdock* (pp. 207–225). Hillsdale, NJ: Erlbaum.

Mandler, G., & Boeck, W. (1974). Retrieval processes in recognition. *Memory & Cognition, 2*, 613-615.

Mandler, G., Graf, P., & Kraft, D. (1986). Activation and elaboration effects in recognition and word priming. *Quarterly Journal of Experimental Psychology: Human Experimental Psychology, 38*(4-A), 645–662.

Mandler, G., Pearlstone, Z., & Koopmans, H. S. (1969). Effects of organization and semantic similarity on recall and recognition. *Journal of Verbal Learning and Verbal Behavior, 8*(3), 410–423.

Mann, V. A., Diamond, R., & Carey, S. 1979. Development of voice recognition: Parallels with face recognition. *Journal of Experimental Psychology, 27,* 153-165.

Maurer, D., & Landis, T. (1990). Role of bone conduction in the self-perception of speech. *Folia Phoniatrica, 42,* 226-229.

Mayes, A., & Boucher, J. (2008). Acquired memory disorders in adults: implications for autism. In. j. Boucher & D.M. Bowler (Eds.), *Memory in Autism: Theories and Evidence* (pp. 43-62). Cambridge: CUP.

Mayes, A.R., Montaldi, D., & Migo, E. (2007). Associative memory and the medial temporal lobes. *Trends in Cognitive Sciences, 11,* 126-135.

Mehler, J., Bertoncini, J., Barriere, M., & Jassik-Gerschenfeld, D. (1978). Infant recognition of mother's voice. *Perception, 7* (5), 491-497.

Mermelstein, R. (1983). *The relationship between syntactic and pragmatic development in autistic, retarded, and normal children*. Paper presented at the Eighth Annual Boston University Conference on Language Development, Boston.

Migo, E.M., Mayes, A. R., & Montaldi, D. (2012). Measuring recollection and familiarity: Improving the remember/know procedure. *Consciousness and Cognition, 21* (3), 1435-1455.

Migo, E.M., Montaldi, D., Norman, K.A., Quamme, J., & Mayes, A.R. (2009). The contribution of familiarity to recognition memory is a function of test format when using similar foils. *Quarterly Journal of Experimental Psychology, 62*(6), 1198-1215.

Miller, J. (1983). The History of SALT software. Retrieved Tuesday 3rd September 2013 from http://www.saltsoftware.com/company/history/

Mills, M., & Melhuish, E. (1974). Recognition of mother's voice in early infancy. *Nature, 252*, 123-124.

Millward, C., Powell, S., Messer, D., & Jordan, R. (2000). Recall for self and other in autism: children's memory for events experienced by themselves and their peers. *Journal of Autism and Developmental Disorders, 30,* 25-28.

Milner, B. (1966) Amnesia following operation on the temporal lobes. In C.W.M. Whitty and O. L. Zangwill, (Eds.), *Amnesia*. pp. 109-133, Butterworths: London.

Minshew, N.J., & Goldstein, G. (2001). The pattern of intact and impaired memory functions in autism. *Journal of Child Psychology and Psychiatry, 42*, 1095–1101.

Minshew, N., Goldstein, G., Muenz, L. R., & Payton, J. (1992). Neuropsychological functioning in nonmentally retarded autistic individuals. *Journal of Clinical and Experimental Neuropsychology, 14*, 749–761.

Mirenda, P. (2001). Augmentative communication. In A. Bondy & L. Frost (Eds.), *A picture's worth: PECS and other visual communication strategies in autism* (pp. 43-66). Bethesda, MD: Woodbine House.

Mirenda, P., & Schuler, A. L. (1998). Augmenting communication for individuals with autism: Issues and strategies. *Topics in Language Disorders, 9*(1), 24-43.

Montaldi, D, Spencer, T.J., Roberts, N., & Mayes, A.R. (2006). The neural system that mediates familiarity memory. *Hippocampus, 16,* 504-520.

Moon, C., Pennton-Cooper, R., & Fifer, W. (1993). Two-day-olds prefer their native language. *Infant Behaviour & Development, 16,* 495–500.

Morgan, S. (1988). Diagnostic assessment of autism: a review of objective scales. *Journal of Psychoeducational Assessment, 6, 139*-151.

Morton, J., & Johnson, M. H. (1991). Conspecifics and Con-learning: a two-process theory of infant face recognition. *Psychological Review, 98*, 164–181.

Mottron, L., Morasse, K., & Belleville, S. (2001). A study of memory functioning in individuals with autism. *Journal of Child Psychology and Psychiatry, 42*, 253-260.

Mundy, P., & Gomes, A. (1998). Individual differences in joint attention skill development in the second year. *Infant Behavior and Development, 21*, 469–482.

Mundy, P., & Neal, R. (2001). Neural plasticity, joint attention and a transactional social-orienting model of autism. *International Review of Mental Retardation, 23*, 139–168.

Murdock, B. B. (1965). Signal-Detection Theory and short term memory. *Journal of Experimental Psychology, 70*(5), 443–447.

National Educational Psychological Services (NEPS). Retrieved Wednesday 4th September 2013 from http://www.education.ie/en/The-Department/Management-Organisation/National-Educational-Psychological-Service-NEPS-.html

Nazzi, T., Kemler Nelson, D. G., Jusczyk, P. W., & Jusczyk, A. (2000). Six-month-olds' detection of clauses embedded in continuous speech: Effects of prosodic well-formedness. *Infancy, 1*, 123–147

Neisser, U. (1988). Five kinds of self-knowledge. *Philosophical Psychology, 1,* 35-59.

Ni Chuileann, S., & Quigley, J. (2012). Assessing recollection and familiarity in low-functioning autism. *Journal of Autism and Developmental Disorders, 43* (6), 1406-1422.

Ninomiya, H., Onitsuka, T., Chen, C, H., Sato, E., & Tashiro, N. (1998). P300 in response to the subject's own face. *Psychiatry and Clinical Neuroscience,* 52 (5), 519-522.

Norbury, C. F., Griffiths, H., & Nation, K. (2010) Sound before meaning: word learning in autistic disorders. *Neuropsychologia, 48* (14) 4012–4019.

Norman, D.A. & Shallice, T. (1986). Attention to action: willed and automatic control of behaviour. In R.J. Davidson, G.E. Schwartz and D. Shapiro (Eds.) *Consciousness and Self Regulation: Advances in Research, Vol. IV* pp1-18, New York: Plenum.

Nyberg, L., Cabeza, R., & Tulving, E. (1996). PET studies of encoding and retrieval: The HERA model. *Psychonomic Bulletin & Review, 3*(2), 135–148.

Nygaard, L.C. & Pisoni, D.B. (1998). Talker-specific learning in speech perception. Perception & Psychophysics, 60, 335-376

O'Connor, N., & Hermelin, B. (1967). The selective visual attention of psychotic children. *Journal of Child Psychology and Psychiatry, 8,* 167-179.

O'Shea, A., Fein, D., Cillessen, A., Klin, A., & Schultz. R. (2005). Source memory in children with autism spectrum disorders. *Developmental Neuropsychology, 27,* 337-360.

Ogletree, B., & Harn, W. (2001). Augmentative and alternative communication for persons with autism: history, issues, and unanswered questions. *Focus on Autism and Other Developmental Disabilities, 16* (3), 138-140.

Ozonoff, S., Pennington, B.F., & Rogers, S.J. (1990). Are there emotion perception deficits in young autistic children? *Journal of Child Psychology and Psychiatry, 31*, 343-361.

Page, M., Wilhelm, M. S., Gamble, W. C., & Card, N. A. (2010). Comparison of maternal sensitivity and verbal stimulation as unique predictors of infant social-emotional and cognitive development. *Infant Behavior and Development, 33*(1), 101-110.

Palmeri, T.J., Goldinger, S. D., & Pisoni, D.B. (1993). Episodic encoding of voice attributes and recognition memory for spoken words. *Journal of Experimental Psychology: Learning, Memory, & Cognition, 19*, 309–328.

Panneton, R. K. (1985). *Prenatal experience with melodies: Effect on postnatal auditory preference in human new-borns.* Unpublished doctoral dissertation, University of North Carolina, Greensboro.

Partington, J.W. (2006). *The Assessment of Basic Language and Learning Skills - Revised* (ABLLS®-R). Retrieved Wednesday 4th September 2013 from http://www.partingtonbehavioranalysts.com/page/ablls-r-25.html

Paul, R. (2008). Interventions to improve communication in autism. *Child and Adolescent Psychiatric Clinics of North America, 17*(4), 835–856.

Paul, R., Augustyn, A., Klin, A., & Volkmar, F. (2008). Perception and production of prosody by speakers with autism spectrum disorders. *Journal of Autism and Developmental Disorders, 35* (2), 205-220.

Paul, R., Chawarska, K., Fowler, C., Cicchetti, D., & Volkmar, F. (2007). "Listen my children and you shall hear": Auditory preferences in toddlers with autism spectrum disorders. *Journal of Speech, Language, and Hearing Research, 50,* 1350-1364.

Perfect, T. J., Williams, R. B., & Anderton-Brown, C. (1995). Age differences in reported recollective experience are due to encoding effects, not response bias. *Memory, 3*(2), 169–86.

Peña, M., Bonatti, L., Nespor, M., & Mehler J. (2002). Signal-Driven Computations in Speech Processing, *Science,* 298, 604-607.

Perner, J., & Ruffman, T. (1995). Episodic memory and autonoetic consciousness: Developmental evidence and a theory of childhood amnesia. *Journal of Experimental Child Psychology, 59* (3), 516-548.

Perrachione, T.K., Del Tufo, S.N., & Gabrieli, J.D.E. (2011). Human voice-recognition depends on language ability. *Science, 333,* 595.

Piaget, J. (1952). *The origins of intelligence in children.* New York. International Universities Press.

Pollack, I., Pickett, J. M., & Sumby, W. H. (1954). On the identification of speakers by voice. *Journal of the Acoustic Society of America, 26*, 403–406.

Pons, F., & Montangero, J. (1999). Is diachronic thought a specific ability? *Swiss Journal of Psychology, 58* (3), 191-200.

Posner, M. I. (1988). Structures and functions of selective attention. In T. Boll & B. Bryant (Eds.), *Master lectures in clinical neuropsychology and brain function: Research, measurement and practice.* Washington, DC: American Psychological Association.

Posner, M.I., & Warren, R.E. (1972). Traces, Concepts, and conscious constructions. In *Coding processes in human memory,* (Eds.). A.W. Melton & E. Martin. pp. 25-43.

Prensky, M. (2012). *From Digital Natives to Digital Wisdom.* Retrieved Wednesday 4th September 2013 from http://marcprensky.com/writing/Prensky-Intro_to_From_DN_to_DW.pdf

Rabinowitz, J. C., Mandler, G., & Patterson, K. E. (1977). Determinants of recognition and recall: accessibility and generation. *Journal of Experimental Psychology, General, 106*, 3022-329.

Renner, P., Klinger, L.G., & Klinger, M.R. (2000). Implicit and explicit memory in autism: Is autism an amnesic disorder? *Journal of Autism and Developmental Disorders, 30*, 3-14.

Rice, K., Moriuchi, J. M., Jones, W., & Klin, A. (2012). Parsing heterogeneity in autism spectrum disorders: visual scanning of dynamic social scenes in school-aged children. *Journal of the American Academy of Child and Adolescent Psychiatry, 51* (3), 238-248.

Rimland, B. (1964). *Infantile autism.* New York, New York: Appleton–Century–Crofts.

Rincover, A., & Ducharme, J.M. (1987). Variables influencing stimulus overselectivity and "tunnel vision" in developmentally delayed children. *American Journal of Mental Deficiency, 91*, 422-430.

Robins, B., Dautenhahn, K., Boekhorst, R. T., & Billard, A. (2004). *Robots as Assistive Technology–Does Appearance Matter?* Paper presented at the 13th IEEE International Workshop on Robot and Human Interactive Communication, ROMAN 2004, Kurashiki, Japan, 20-22 September

Robins, B., Dautenhahn, K. & Dickerson, P. 2009 *Proceedings of 2nd International Conference on Advances in Computer-Human Interaction: ACHI'09.* IEEE, Vol. 2009, p. 205-211.

Robson, C. (2002). *Real World Research* (2nd Ed.). Malden, Oxford, Victoria: Blackwell Publishing

Rochat, P., & Striano, T. (1999). Social cognitive development in the first year. In P. Rochat (Ed.), *Early Social Cognition*, (pp. 3-34). Hillsdale, NJ: Erlbaum.

Roediger, H. L., & McDermott, K. B. (1995). Creating false memories: Remembering words not presented in lists. *Journal of Experimental Psychology: Learning, Memory, & Cognition. 19*, 21, 803–814.

Rogers, S. J., & DiLalla, D.L. (1990). Age of symptom onset in young children with pervasive developmental disorders. *Journal of the American Academy of Child and Adolescent Psychiatry,* 29, 863–872.

Rogers, T.B., Kuiper, N.A., & Kirker, W.S. (1977). Self-reference and the encoding of personal information. *Journal of Personality and Social Psychology, 35*, 677-688.

Romich, B., & Hill, K. (1999). A language activity monitor for AAC and writing systems: clinical intervention, outcomes measurement, and research. *In Proceedings of the RESNA 1999 annual conference*. pp. 19-21. Atlanta, GA: RESNA Press.

Romich, B. A., & Hill, K. (2000). Language activity monitor feasibility study. National Institute for Deafness and other Communication Disorders of the National Institutes of Health (NIH No. 1 R43 DC 4246-01).

Romich, B. A., & Hill, K. J. (2000, June). AAC core vocabulary analysis: Tools for clinical use. In Proceedings of the RESNA 1999 Annual Conference (pp. 67-69). Arlington, VA: RESNA Press.

Romski, M. A., & Sevcik, R. A. (1996). *Breaking the speech barrier: Language development through augmented means.* Baltimore: Brookes.

Rosch, E. (1973). On the internal structure of perceptual and semantic categories. In T. E. Moore (Ed.), *Cognitive development and the acquisition of language*. New York: Academic Press.

Rosch, E. (1978). Principle of Categorization. In E. Rosch, & B. B. Lloyd (Eds.), *Cognition and Categorization* (pp. 27-48). Hillsdale, NJ: Lawrence Erlbaum

Rosa C., Lassonde M., Pinard C., Keenan J.P., & Belin P. (2008) Investigations of hemispheric specialization of self-voice recognition *Brain & Cognition, 68*, 204-214.

Rotello, C. M., MacMillan, N. A., Reeder, J. A., & Wong, M. (2005). The remember response: Subject to bias, graded, and not a process-pure indicator of recollection. *Psychonomic Bulletin & Review, 12,* 865-873.

Rothbart, M. K., & Posner, M. I. (2001). Mechanism and variation in the development of attentional networks. In C. A. Nelson & M. Luciana (Eds.), *Handbook of Developmental Cognitive Neuroscience.* Cambridge, MA: MIT Press.

Ruff, H. A., & Rothbart, M. K. (1996). *Attention in early development: Themes and variations.* New York: Oxford University Press.

Russell, J., & Jarrold, C. (1999). Memory for actions in children with autism: self versus other. *Cognitive Neuropsychiatry, 4*, 303-331.

Rutter, M., Mawhood, L., & Howlin, P. (1992). Language delay and social development. In P. Fletcher & D. Hall (Eds.), Specific speech and language disorders in children: Correlates, characteristics, & outcomes (pp. 63-78). London, England: Whurr.

Saint-Georges, C., Mahdhaoui, A., Chetouani, M., Laznik, M.C., Apicella, F., Muratori, P., Maestro, S., & Cohen, D. (2011). Do parents recognize autistic deviant behavior long before diagnosis? Taking into account interaction using computational methods. *PLOS ONE, 6* (7), e22393.

Salmond, C., Ashburner, J., Connelly, A., Friston, K., Gadian, D., & Vargha-Khadem, F. (2005). The role of the medial temporal lobe in autistic spectrum disorders. *European Journal of Neuroscience, 22,* 764-772.

Satt, B. J. (1984). *An investigation into the acoustical induction of intra-uterine learning.* PhD Dissertation, California School of Professional Psychology, Los Angeles

Schacter, D., & Tulving, E. (1994). What are the memory systems of 1994? In D. Schacter & E. Tulving (eds.), *Memory Systems 1994* (pp. 1-38). Cambridge, MA: MIT Press.

Schlosser, R. W., Sigafoos, J., Luiselli, J., Angermeier, K., Schooley, K., Harasymowyz, U., et al. (2007). Effects of synthetic speech output on requesting and natural speech production in children with autism. *Research in Autism Spectrum Disorders, 1*, 139–163.

Schopler, E., Reichler, R., & Rochen Renner, B. (1988). *The Childhood Autism Rating Scale.* Western Psychological Services.

Schuler, A. L., & Baldwin, M. (1981). *Non-speech communication and childhood autism. Language, Speech, and Hearing Services in the Schools, 12*, 246-257.

Schultz, S., & Vouloumanos, A. (2010). Three-month-olds prefer speech to other naturally occurring signals. *Language and Learning Development, 6*, 241-257.

Schuster, L.I. (1998). The perception of correctly and incorrectly produced /r/. *Journal of Speech, Language, and Hearing Research, 41*, 941-950.

Scott, R. (2011). "Autism's like a snowflake"—doctors study symptoms, possible causes of autism with hopes of learning more. August 28. Retrieved Friday 5th September 2013 from *Gloucester County Times*. http://www.nj.com/gloucester-county/index.ssf/2011/08/autisms_like_a_snowflake_-_doc.html

Seal, B. C., & Bonvillian, J. D. (1997). Sign language and motor functioning in students with autistic disorder. *Journal of Autism and Developmental Disorders, 27*, 437-466.

Seltzer, M.M., Shattuck, P., Abbeduto, L., & Greenberg, J.S. (2004). The trajectory of development in adolescents and adults with autism. *Mental Retardation Developmental Disabilities Research Reviews, 10,* 234-247.

Shaked, M., & Yirmiya, N. (2004). Matching procedures in autism research: Evidence from meta-analytic studies. *Journal of Autism and Developmental Disorders, 34,* 35-40.

Shane, H.C., Laubscher, E.H., Schlosser, R.W., Flynn, S., Sorce, J.F., & Abramson, J. (2011). Applying technology to visually support language and communication in individuals with autism spectrum disorders. *Journal of Autism and Developmental Disorders, 42 (*6), 1228-1235.

Sheese, B. E., Rothbart, M. K., Posner, M. I., White, L. K., & Fraundorf, S. H. (2008). Executive attention and self-regulation in infancy. *Infant Behaviour & Development, 31*, 501 -510.

Sherry, D. F., & Schacter, D. L. (1987). The evolution of multiple memory systems. *Psychological Review, 94,* 439-454.

Sigafoos, J., & Drasgow, E. (2001). Conditional use of aided and unaided AAC: A review and clinical case demonstration. *Focus on Autism and Other Developmental Disabilities, 16,* 152-161.

Sigafoos, J., & Reichle, J. (1992). Comparing explicit to generalized requesting in an augmentative communication mode. *Journal of Developmental and Physical Disabilities, 4*,167–188.

Sigafoos, J., O'Reilly, M., Ganz, J., Lancioni, G., & Schlosser, R., (2005). Supporting self-determination in AAC interventions by assessing preference for communication devices. *Technology and Disability, 17,* 143-153.

Sigman, M., & McGovern, C.W. (2005).Improvement in cognitive and language skills from preschool to adolescence in autism. *Journal of Autism and Developmental Disorders, 35*, 15–23.

Smith, B., Gardiner, J., & Bowler, D. M. (2007). Deficits in free recall persist in Asperger syndrome despite training in the use of list appropriate learning strategies. *Journal of Autism and Developmental Disorders, 37*, 445–454.

Soderstrom, M., & Morgan, J.L. (2007). Twenty-two-month-olds discriminate fluent from disfluent adult-directed speech. *Developmental Science, 10*, 641-653.

Solso, R. L., Maclin, K., & Maclin, O. H. (2005). *Cognitive Psychology.* New York: Pearson.

Spence, M. J., Rollins, P. R., & Jerger, S. (2002). Children's recognition of cartoon voices. *Journal of Speech, Language, and Hearing Research, 45,* 214-222.

Standley, J.M., & Madsen, C.K. (1990). Comparison of infant preferences and responses to auditory stimuli: Music, mother, and other female voice. *Journal of Music Therapy, 27*(2), 54-97.

Stone, W., & Cam-Martinez. L. M. (1990). Naturalistic observations of spontaneous communication in autistic children. Journal of Autism and Developmental Disorders, 20, 437-453.

Stone, W., Lee, E., Ashford, L., Brissie, J., Hepburn, S., Coonrod, E., & Weiss, B. (1999). Can autism be diagnosed accurately in children under 3 years? *Journal of Child Psychology and Psychiatry, 40*, 219-226.

Straight, H. S. S. (1980). Auditory versus articulatory phonological processes and their development in children. In G. H. Yeni-Komshian, J. F. Kavanagh, & C. A. Ferguson (Eds.), *Child phonology*: Vol. 1. Production (pp. 43-71). New York: Academic Press.

Stake, R. E. (1995). *The art of case study research.* London: Sage.

Streeter, L. A. (1976). Kikuyu labial and apical stop discrimination. *Journal of Phonetics, 9*, 43-49.

Strömbergsson, S. (2009). Self-voice recognition in 4 to 5 year-old children. Department of Speech, Music and Hearing. Proceedings, FONETIK, 2009. Retrieved Wednesday 4th September 2013 from http://www.speech.kth.se/prod/publications/files/3385.pdf

Sturmey, P., & Sevin, J.A. (1994). Defining and assessing autism. In J.L. Matson (Ed.), *Autism in children and adults: Etiology, assessment, and intervention* (pp. 13-36). Pacific Grove, CA: Brooks/Cole.

Summers, J., & Craik, F. (1994). The effect of subject-performed tasks on the memory performance of verbal autistic children. *Journal of Autism and Developmental Disorders, 24,* 773-783.

Swettenham, J., Baron-Cohen, S., Charman, T., Cox, A., Baird, G., Drew, A., Rees, L., & Wheelwright, S. (1998). The frequency and distribution of spontaneous attention shifts between social and non-social stimuli in autistic, typically developing, and non-autistic developmentally delayed infants. *Journal of Child Psychology and Psychiatry, 9*, 747–753.

Symons, L.A., Hains, S.M.J., & Muir, D.W. (1998). Look at me: Five-month-old infants' sensitivity to very small deviations in eye-gaze during social interactions. *Infant Behavior and Development, 21,* 531–536.

Tager-Flusberg, H., & Calkins. S. (1990). Does imitation facilitate the acquisition of grammar? Evidence from a study of autistic, Down syndrome, and normal children. *Journal of Child Development, 17,* 591-606.

Tager-Flusberg, H. (1991). Semantic processing in the free recall of autistic children. *British Journal of Developmental Psychology, 9,* 417–430.

Tager–Flusberg, H. (1999). A psychological approach to understanding the social and language impairments in autism. *International Review of Psychiatry, 11*, 325–334.

Tager-Flusberg, H. (1999). The Challenge of Studying Language Development in Children with Autism. Retrieved Wednesday 4th September 2013 from http://www.abiliko.co.il/Media/Uploads/challenge_lang_dev_autism.pdf

Tager-Flusberg, H., Calkins, S., Nolin, T., Baumberger, T., Anderson, M., & Chadwick-Dias, A. (1990). A longitudinal study of language acquisition in autistic and Down syndrome children. *Journal of Autism and Developmental Disorders, 20*, 1-21.

Tantam, D., Monaghan, L., Nicholson, H., & Stirling, J. (1989). Autistic children's ability to interpret faces: A research note. *Journal of Child Psychology and Psychiatry, 30* (4), 623–630.

Todd, J. L., (2008). *Gender differences in performance measures of individuals who use augmentative and alternative communication.* Master's Thesis, University of Pittsburgh.

Toichi, M. (2008). Episodic memory, semantic memory, and self awareness in high-functioning autism. In J. Boucher & D. Bowler (Eds.), *Memory in autism: Theory and evidence* (pp. 143–165). Cambridge, England: Cambridge University Press.

Toichi, M., & Kamio, Y. (2003). Long term memory in high functioning autism: Controversy on episodic memory reconsidered. *Journal of Autism and Developmental Disorders, 33,* 151-161.

Toth, J. P. (1996). Conceptual automaticity in recognition memory: Levels-of-processing effects on familiarity. *Canadian Journal of Experimental Psychology, 50*(1), 123–138.

Townsend, J., Courchesne, E., & Egaas, B. (1996). Slowed orienting of covert visual-spatial attention in autism: Specific deficits associated with cerebellar and parietal abnormality. *Development and Psychopathology, 8, 563*-584.

Tulving, E. (1982). Synergistic ecphory in recall and recognition. *Canadian Journal of Psychology, 36*(2), 130–147.

Tulving, E. (1985). How many memory systems are there? *American Psychologist, 40,* 385-398.

Tulving, E. (1990). Episodic memory. In M.W. Eysenck (Ed.), *The Blackwell Dictionary of Cognitive Psychology,* (pp. 137-139). Oxford: Blackwell.

Tulving E. (1999). On the uniqueness of episodic memory. In *Cognitive Neuroscience of Memory*, (Eds.). L-G Nilsson, HJ Markowitsch, pp.11–42. Gottingen: Hogrefe & Huber.

Tulving, E. (2001). Episodic memory and common sense: how far apart? *Philosophical Transactions of the Royal Society of London, 356,* 1505-1515.

Tulving, E., & Markowitsch, H. J. (1998). Episodic and declarative memory: Role of the hippocampus. *Hippocampus, 8*(3), 198–204.

Tulving, E., & Patterson, R. D. (1968). Functional units and retrieval processes in free recall. *Journal of Experimental Psychology, 77*, 239-248.

Tulving, E., & Schacter, D.L. (1990). Priming and human memory systems. *Science 247*, 301-306.

Valenza, E., Simion, F., Cassia, V. M., & Umilta, C. (1996). Face preference at birth. *Journal of Experimental Psychology: Human Perception and Performance, 22*(4), 892-903.

Vallar, G. & Baddeley, A.D. (1984a). Fractionation of working memory. Neuropsychological evidence for a phonological short-term store. *Journal of Verbal Learning and Verbal Behaviour, 23*, 151-162.

Van-Biervliet, A., & Parette, H. P. (1999). *Families, cultures, and AAC* [CD-ROM].Little Rock, AR: Southeast Missouri State University and University of Arkansas for Medical Sciences

van der Meer, L. A., & Rispoli, M. (2010). Communication interventions involving speech-generating devices for children with autism: A review of the literature. *Developmental Neurorehabilitation, 13* (4), 294-306.

van Santen, J., & Black, L. (2009). In your own voice: Personal augmentative and alternative communication voices for minimally verbal children with autism spectrum disorders. *Proceedings Interspeech 2010*, Makuhari, Japan.

Wagner, A. D., Gabrieli, J. D. E., & Verfaellie, M. (1997). Dissociations between familiarity processes in explicit recognition and implicit perceptual memory. *Journal of Experimental Psychology: Learning, Memory, and Cognition, 23*(2).

Ward, C. D., & Cooper, R. P. (1999). A lack of evidence in 4-month-old human infants for paternal voice preference. *Developmental Psychobiology, 35*, 49–59.

Waterhouse, L. (2013). *Rethinking Autism: Variation and Complexity* (1st Edition). San Diego: Elsevier: Academic Press.

Watson, J. S. (1994).Detection of self: The maximum algorithm. In S. T. Parker, R. W. Mitchell, & M. L. Boccia (Eds.), *Self-awareness in animals and humans: Developmental perspectives* (pp.131-148). New York: Cambridge University Press.

Webb, S. (2008). Impairments in social memory in autism? Evidence from behavior and neuroimaging. In J. Boucher & D. M. Bowler (Eds.), *Memory in Autism: Theories and Evidence* (pp. 188-209). Cambridge: CUP.

Wechsler, D. (1999). *Wechsler abbreviated scales of intelligence*. San Antonio: Psychological Corporation.

Weiskrantz, L. (1966). Experimental studies of amnesia, In *Amnesia*, (Eds.). C. Whitty & O. Zangwill, pp 1–31. Butterworth: London.

Werner, E., Dawson, G., Osterling, J., & Dinno, N. (2000). Brief Report: Recognition of autism spectrum disorder before one year of age: A retrospective study based on home video tapes. *Journal of Autism & Developmental Disorders, 30*, 157–162.

Wheeler, M. A., Stuss, D. T., & Tulving, E. (1997). Toward a theory of episodic memory: The frontal lobes and autonoetic consciousness. *Psychological Bulletin, 121*(3).

Whittlesea, B. W., Jacoby, L. L., & Girard, K. (1990). Illusions of immediate memory: Evidence of an attributional basis for feelings of familiarity and perceptual quality. *Journal of Memory and Language, 29*(6).

Williams, D., & Happé, F. (2009). Pre-conceptual aspects of self-awareness in autism spectrum disorder: The case of action-monitoring. *Journal of Autism and Developmental Disorders, 39,* 251–259.

Williams, D.L., Goldstein, G., & Minshew, N.J., (2005a). Impaired memory for faces and social scenes in autism: Clinical implications of memory dysfunction. *Archives of Clinical Neuropsychology, 20,* 1-15.

Williams, D.L., Goldstein, G., & Minshew, N.J., (2006a). The profile of memory function in children with autism. *Neuropsychology, 20,* 21-29.

Williams, D.L., Goldstein, G., & Minshew, N.J., (2006b). Neuropsychologic functioning in children with autism: Further evidence for disordered complex information-processing. *Child Neuropsychology, 12,* 279-298.

Wilson, B. A., Cockburn, J., Baddeley, A., & Hiorns, R. (1991). *The Rivermead Behavioural Memory Test: Supplement Two.* Reading, England: Thames Valley Test Co.

Wilson, R., Blades, M., & Pascalis, O. (2007). Familiar face recognition in children with autistic spectrum disorders. *Journal of Autism and Developmental Disorders, 37,* 314-320.

Wing, L. (2001). *The Autistic Spectrum: A Parents' Guide to Understanding and Helping Your Child*, Berkeley, California: Ulysses Press.

Wing, L., & Potter, D. (2002). The epidemiology of autism spectrum disorder's: is the prevalence rising? *Mental Retardation and Developmental Disorders Research Centers, 8* (3), 151-161.

Wixted, J. T. (2007). Dual-process theory and signal-detection theory of recognition memory. *Psychological Review, 114*, 152-176.

Yin, R. K. (2003) *Case study research. Design and methods*, (3rd eds.). London: Sage.

Yonelinas, A. P. (1994). Receiver-operating characteristics in recognition memory: Evidence for a dual-process model. *Journal of Experimental Psychology: Learning, Memory, & Cognition, 20*, 1341–1354.

Yonelinas, A. P. (1999). The contribution of recollection and familiarity to recognition and source-memory judgments: A formal dual-process model and an analysis of receiver operating characteristics. *Journal of Experimental Psychology: Learning, Memory, and Cognition, 25*(6), 1415–1434.

Yonelinas, A. P. (2001a). Consciousness, control, and confidence: The 3 Cs of recognition memory. *Journal of Experimental Psychology: General, 130*(3), 361–379.

Yonelinas, A.P. (2001b). Components of episodic memory: the contribution of recollection and familiarity. *Philosophical Transcripts of the Royal Society of London, Biological Sciences, 356(*1413), 1363–1374.

Yonelinas, A. P. (2002). The nature of recollection and familiarity: A review of 30 years of research. *Journal of Memory and Language, 46,* 441–517.

Yonelinas, A.P., Dobbins, I., Szymanski, M.D., Dhaliwal, H.S., & King, L. (1996). Signal detection, threshold, and dual process models of recognition memory: ROCs and conscious recollection. *Consciousness and Cognition, 5* (4), 418-441

Yonelinas, A.P., Kroll, N.E.A., Dobbins, I.G., Lazzara, M., & Knight, R.T. (1998). Recollection and familiarity deficits in amnesia: Convergence of remember/know, process dissociation, and receiver operating characteristic data. *Neuropsychology*, 12 (3), 323-339.

Yonelinas, A.P., Kroll, N.E.A., Dobbins, I.G., & Soltani, M. (1999). Recognition Memory for Faces: When Familiarity Supports Associative Recognition Judgments. *Psychonomic Bulletin and Review*, 6 (4), 654-661

Yonelinas, A.P., Aly, M., Wang, W.C., & Koen, J.D. (2010). Recollection and familiarity: examining controversial assumptions and new directions. *Hippocampus*, 20 (11), 1178-94.

Zwaigenbaum, L., Bryson, S. E., Rogers, T., Roberts, W., Brian, J., & Szatmari, P. (2005). Behavioral manifestations of autism in the first year of life. *International Journal of Developmental Neuroscience, 23,* 143–152.